D1287260

UNDISPUTED

NOTRE DAME, NATIONAL CHAMPIONS
1966

MARK O. HUBBARD

Cover design by Pauline Neuwirth

Vantage Press and the Vantage Press colophon are registered trademarks of Vantage Press, Inc.

FIRST EDITION
All rights reserved, including the right of reproduction in whole or in part in any form.

Copyright © 2011 by Mark O. Hubbard

Published by Vantage Press, Inc.
419 Park Ave. South,
New York, NY 10016

Manufactured in the United States of America

ISBN: 978-0533-165124

Library of Congress Catalog Card No: 2011913300

0 9 8 7 6 5 4 3 2 1

DEDICATION

To all the guys who ran the steps in the stadium in
February 1966, and then earned for Notre Dame a precious
gift in December—an undisputed National Championship.
It came at a good time and still gives us hope.

CONTENTS

ACKNOWLEDGEMENTS

A writer is a person for whom writing is more difficult than it is
for other people.   —Thomas Mann

How does one get started on a project like writing a book about
Notre Dame Football? It takes some coaxing. Writing a book is hard
work. And there's no real money in it. Doing the required research for
an historical piece like *Undisputed* takes considerable effort, especially if
you are committed to including lots of accurate data. Getting the words
down on paper is at times excruciating. Having your work edited is
humbling. Grinding out the myriad of details for publication is tedious.
Writing a book can be an altogether unpleasant experience, unless …

Unless you are passionate about the subject and have loyal and
capable collaborators helping you get through the process. I was very
fortunate on both counts.

There were a handful of people who believed that a book about the
1966 National Champions would be timely and well-received. By process
of elimination, they also decided that I was the logical person to write it.

There was already a very fine 1992 work done by Notre Dame graduate Mike Celizic titled, *The Biggest Game of Them All*. Mike was a legendary sports writer known as "El Sombrero" for the hats he always
wore. Regrettably, he passed into the Heavenly Alumni Association in
2009—otherwise you would be reading his updated version of the '66
season. You might consider picking up a copy of Mike's original for your
personal library as I did. It is well worth the time and effort.

Sue Shidler at the Hammes Notre Dame Bookstore pushed me
toward the cliff to start this project. She believed that a follow-up to Jim
Dent's *Resurrection* was in order. Early consultations with Brian Boulac,
Joe Doyle, Roger Valdisseri, Joe Bride, and Tom Reynolds convinced me

that there was a fresh, unexplored slant to chronicling the most written-about college football season in history. In the fall of 2010, they pushed me over the cliff and so I got started writing.

There are many great resources at Notre Dame, but two stand out for projects like this. The Sports Information Office headed by John Heisler has resources second to none in college athletics. They also have Carol Copley, a gal with the sunniest personality on campus, always willing to help a hapless author. Equally professional and helpful are the folks at University Archives on the sixth floor of the Hesburgh Library, especially Charles Lamb and Angie Kindig. They preside over all the University records and photographs, which are required if one is to write an authentic book about Notre Dame. I spent hours and hours at each of these two locations. Then I'd steal away to a quiet space provided to me by the Innovation Park at Notre Dame, thanks to my friend David Brenner. It made for an interesting fall semester.

The most rewarding part of this process was contacting the players, coaches, and key personalities that defined the 1966 season. I started at the top with Father Ted Hesburgh who has been a loyal friend since I was a lowly student. In alphabetical order they are:

Ed Adams, Harry Alexander, Marty Allen, Joe Azzaro, Jim Beatty, Rocky Bleier, Brian Boulac, Mary Ann Boulac, Joe Bride, Harry Buch, Jim Canestaro, Melanie Chapleau, Mike Collins, Larry Conjar, Frank Criniti, Joe Doyle, Ron Dushney, Nick Eddy, Tom Feske, Mike Finnerty, Bob Gladieux, George Goeddeke, Kevin Hardy, Terry Hanratty, Curt Heneghan, Emil T. Hofman, John Horney, Donald Hubbard, Ron Jeziorski, Bob Kuechenberg, George Kunz, John Lattner, Jim Leahy, Chuck Lennon, John Lium, John Lujack, Gloria Lynch, Jim Lynch, Mike McCoy, Mike McGill, Frank Maggio, Tim Miller, Coley O'Brien, Ara Parseghian, Katie Parseghian, Kevin Rassas, Nick Rassas, Don Reid, Tom Reynolds, Tom Rhoades, Jeff Seiter, Jim Seymour, Nancy Seymour, Allen Sack, Dick Rosenthal, Roger Valdiserri

This is their story. If I got any part of it wrong or made a mistake in the telling, please blame me alone.

Along the way two copy editors jumped into the fray. Ed Adams, my friend from Cincinnati, was a former newspaperman and loves Notre Dame as much as I. He kept reading the text, over and over, for no other reason than the stories appealed to him. Bridget O'Rourke Hubbard, my beautiful partner in life, took a different view. She wanted to make sure I didn't embarrass myself. Her copywriting skills are excellent and I appreciate the fact that she refrained from rolling her eyes (too much) as I made simple grammatical mistakes.

There was also an invisible hand in all of this. I was that hayseed freshman from Middlefield, Connecticut (see Chapter 14) who received an assignment back from Professor Frank O'Malley in 1967 with the comment, "You know what I think of this." Subconsciously, I believe I've been trying to please Frank with everything I've ever written since. He believed I could do better. And sometimes that's all you need to get started. Thanks, Frank.

Mark O. Hubbard
2011

FOREWORD

JOE DOYLE

When I first started what would become almost a lifetime of writing about Notre Dame Football, the 1949 Irish were completing four seasons of undefeated play. Little did I realize that it would be seventeen years before the next undisputed National Championship flag would again fly over Notre Dame.

The Golden Years of Irish football (1946-49) came about because of talented players, superior coaching, and the great spirit on an all-male campus that long had concentrated on top academic programs and near-perfect graduation rates.

As I look back at 1949 and 1966, I am struck by the similarities of a great backfield, talented offensive and defensive lines, and a group of well-experienced coaches. There were star players, to be sure, but also some who were showing great skills for the first time.

Unlike 1949, the Irish of 1966 were emerging from only two seasons of outstanding play. But in 1965, the team had not scored a touchdown in its last two games. The 1966 Irish remembered it well.

After the spectacular season in 1964 and the solid follow-up in 1965, the prospects for 1966 again were great. There was still a lack of a passing game, but new young quarterbacks and receivers were on the horizon. Parseghian and his top offensive lieutenant Tom Pagna had created a miracle season once before. And surely they could do it again.

When 1966 started, charismatic third-year coach Ara Parseghian had some deficiencies and question marks. But in his two previous seasons he showed that the Irish would respond. If the team needed No. 1 quarterbacks or great receivers, he would find them.

The two upcoming sophomore quarterbacks, Hanratty and O'Brien, emerged with the passing and catching skills of newcomers, Jim Seymour and Curt Heneghan—seeming to solve the other major problem.

From the start of the season, it was obvious that the rookies would come through.

Parseghian and assistant Pagna worked their magic with the newcomers and soon the offense was starting to measure up to the talents of a veteran defensive team that had carried on so well in 1965.

Opening opponent Purdue was becoming a Big Ten power. And with veteran quarterback Bob Griese, a great passing threat. But Irish defensive coaches John Ray and Paul Shoults had reworked the 4-4-3 defense into a fine-tuned frenzy.

The opener was a nationally-televised battle matching the nearby rivals. The audience had to be delighted, especially when matching long-stroking touchdowns squared the early first period at 7-7. Leroy Keyes ran Irish fumble 95 yards to a score, and Irish halfback Nick Eddy ran 96 with the ensuing kickoff to tie the score.

Then it was Hanratty to Seymour time, and after a crisp 26-14 victory, the Irish were off and running. Northwestern managed a touchdown, but Army and North Carolina were shut out.

Yet there was another test—a visit to undefeated Oklahoma in Norman.

The Sooners previously had had rough times against the Irish, but they insisted it would be different in 1966.

The Irish defense, as expected, throttled the Sooners, but a powerful line, led by middle guard Granville Liggins, kept the Irish at bay. Liggins was then injured by a vicious block and left the game. The Irish gained control and despite losing Seymour to an ankle sprain just before halftime, the mighty Sooners fell, 38-0. The rating polls moved the Irish to No. 1.

Navy scored a meaningless touchdown the following week in Philadelphia, but Pittsburgh and Duke were shut out and the Irish awaited Michigan State with an 8-0 record that included five scoreless opponents.

This set the stage for another No. 1 vs. No. 2 battle for the National Championships in a late November game. Twenty years earlier, Notre Dame (No. 2) versus Army (No. 1) had been acclaimed not only as the game of the year but as the clash of the century.

Notre Dame had won the National Title in 1943, but at West Point, Army built such a powerhouse that the Cadets were undefeated in both

1944 and 1945. Included in their victories were a couple smashing wins, 59-0 and 48-0 over the Irish.

The 1946 game created such a media buildup that major newspapers sent reporters to both West Point and Notre Dame. Scalpers had a real field day for the game at Yankee Stadium in New York City,

Instead of a smashing offensive battle, the game was mostly a defensive struggle where neither team could score. One New York headline captured the hype and the game by saying, "Much to Do about Nothing to Nothing!"

In 1966, it was much different: A really great defensive struggle in which Notre Dame gave up an early 10-0 lead, then battled back to a 10-10 tie. Michigan State closed out its season that day with a 9-0-1 record, but Notre Dame had one more game against Rose Bowl-bound Southern California.

During that hard slashing battle, Notre Dame had been hard-pressed, losing quarterback Hanratty and center George Goeddeke within two plays in the first quarter.

Notre Dame had received the ball in the final minutes but was unable to mount a passing attack against the rugged Spartans whose coaches were shouting, "They played for a tie!" to anyone who would listen.

The Irish kept the ball for the final six plays and kept the Spartans away from a game-winning field goal. For days, Michigan State followers complained about the tie, as the final poll showed Notre Dame as No. 1.

Unlike 1949, the 1966 team played in such a memorable late November game that almost every year since there continue to be "anniversary" stories about the game. We have seen 5-year, 10-year, 20-year, and even 40-year pieces about 1966's game of the century. That tie might have been the most-talked about game in history.

In fact, in the 45th year since the game, an unknowing retired priest and friend commented, "1966? Well, that was the game when Ara went for the tie!"

My answer, then and now, has always been: "He was going for the National Championship. The record book will always say he got it!"

PREFACE

First-time visitors might comprehend the essence of Notre Dame in a single home football weekend, if they are paying close attention. But they'd have to arrive on Thursday, sit for a class or a lecture, spend time with students at the Huddle and then visit Band practice. And they'd have to stay until Sunday to attend one of the over-capacity Masses at the Basilica of the Sacred Heart. Of course, sandwiched in between would be Saturday's football game along with all the pearls of tradition that have been strung together to make this family reunion such a unique experience in college sports.

At its core, Notre Dame is like an expansive and ornate tabletop built on four simple but sturdy legs: academic integrity, Catholic teachings, a family of people who believe in uncommon decency, and football. Failure to understand this simple visual metaphor is a failure to understand the place at all. When one leg is either extended or chopped-off at the expense of the other three, the entire table wobbles and the top tips precariously. As beautiful as the top is, it is powerless to support its own weight.

This isn't a trumped-up scenario to sell a few books about Notre Dame Football. It is a well-considered image. There is a simple validity test. Take away any single element— academics, the Catholic Church, the Notre Dame Family, or football—and you are left with a nondescript remainder that just can't be called Notre Dame as we know it. Ask one hundred random people on the street what they know about Notre Dame and the first three impressions will be "college," "Catholic," and "football." Then they'll mention someone they know who's from Notre Dame: Knute Rockne, Frank Leahy, Ara Parseghian, Lou Holtz,

Condoleezza Rice, Regis Philbin, Rudy, Hanna Storm, Digger Phelps, Joe Montana, Fr. Theodore Hesburgh, or even more likely, a colleague at work or a neighbor down the street.

Building one's institutional identity, one's brand, if you will, on a foundation that includes success at a single intercollegiate sport creates a near-impossible conundrum for Notre Dame. This conundrum has historically confounded so many invested in the very heart of the University of Notre Dame. How can football success be promoted in an institution that also promotes advancement in institutional academics and that must address the issues and demands of a global Church community? The Notre Dame table falls "out of kilter" when any one of its legs is even slightly disproportionate, and things start rolling off the top. So a succession of disappointing football seasons is disruptive to the entire table and places in jeopardy all the programs on the top with significant value—until it is rectified. This has been a constant concern at Notre Dame for nearly one hundred years, since football became a significant source of revenue. Fortunately, it has rarely been a crisis.

For many of us, being a part of the Notre Dame Family and its dependency on football tradition is a highly personal experience that soon becomes a lifetime love affair. The valedictorian at a recent commencement observed the following about Notre Dame, "When you are on the outside looking in, you can't understand it. And when you are on the inside looking out, you can't explain it."

To those who are deeply invested in Notre Dame, football is a ritual that affects their lives to the core, no matter where they are. Losses are like acid reflux with the resulting heartburn lasting for days. In contrast, wins on the football field are like the gentle rain that nourishes the communal fields and supports a harvest of camaraderie, respect, good will, and financial generosity. National Championships are the occasional heavy rains that fill our reservoir to overflowing and sustain us through periods of drought, some of which last too long for comfort. Winning football games is the water required to sustain the unique life and spirit at Notre Dame.

To get a laugh at a luncheon held in Los Angeles many years ago before a Southern Cal game, Notre Dame football-great and Heisman Trophy-winner Johnny Lujack once joked: "People think that at Notre Dame we believe winning football games is a matter of life and death . . . They have it wrong, it is more important than that."

All kidding aside, Lujack was speaking a profound truth, one I can relate to. My grandmother, Virginia Thorne, lived with our family from the time I was about seven. Every autumn on Saturday afternoons she would hibernate in her bedroom, close the blinds, and listen to Notre Dame Football on her brown Bakelite table radio—its glow the only light in the room. My grandmother explained that she became committed to Notre Dame Football because the team stood for the immigrants in America, especially the Catholics, trying to overcome difficulties and prejudice. When Notre Dame won, it was a symbol of hope. When Notre Dame won a lot (and this was the pattern beginning with Rockne's teams), it became a beacon for millions of people to believe in. I didn't fully understand it at the time, but listening to Notre Dame Football worked for her on Saturdays as surely as her rosary beads did on Sunday mornings.

Soon thereafter, I began applying to colleges—the first member of my family with the legitimate expectation of actually going and probably finishing. My grandmother insisted that I apply to Notre Dame. She was basking in the glow of the 1966 National Championship and a fellow named Ara Parseghian, whom she believed was either Catholic or would soon convert. So I left rural Connecticut in the fall of 1967 and journeyed west with my parents in our family's Chevrolet Bel Air station wagon to South Bend with two suitcases and a footlocker, along with the confidence that I was going to someplace special and with the hope that I could make a go of it.

While I was a sophomore at Notre Dame, a truly fortuitous, life-changing event happened. I was in Boston on Easter break when I was set up on a blind date by a high school friend. The girl elected to forego studying on a weeknight to meet a total stranger, based exclusively on the fact that I was from Notre Dame. It seemed that her father had been performing a Saturday ritual similar to my grandmother's, and she wanted to tell him that she had at least met somebody from the venerated school. Her last name was O'Rourke, which certainly explained a lot. Her first name was Bridget, which made her irresistible.

The following fall she visited me at Notre Dame for her first time. On the plane from Boston, she was randomly seated among members of Rockne's last team who were going out for a reunion. At the game, Rocky Bleier was introduced on the field by University President Fr. Theodore Hesburgh at halftime—standing with the aid of a cane because his legs had caught the brunt of an exploding grenade.

Rocky Bleier with Fr. Theodore Hesburgh on the field at halftime of the Notre
Dame—USC game held in Notre Dame Stadium in 1969. When the Irish captain
from 1967 was introduced and walked onto the field with the aid of a cane the
entire crowd went silent. By that time the Vietnam War was very much on the
consciousness of a nation. *Source:* University of Notre Dame Archives.

Our Irish captain from two years earlier was the only NFL player to
be drafted and serve in Vietnam. Sixty-thousand fans were totally silent,
and there wasn't a single dry eye. I hoped the girl would like me. I didn't

know then that she would eventually love Notre Dame and me with the same fidelity.

In 1978, the year after Coach Dan Devine's National Championship team, I was working at starting the first College Football Hall of Fame in Cincinnati. Bridget and I were privileged to host Don Miller and Jim Crowley—the last living members of the legendary Four Horsemen—for the four-day grand opening. My mom and dad joined us for all the festivities. We all got to know Don and Jim in a special way. They were transformed into twenty-year-olds, but trapped in eighty-year-old bodies—humbled by their unexpected notoriety, especially after over fifty years. I may be the last ND grad to see Miller and Crowley together. I remember them at the Cincinnati airport, shuffling down the Jetway, supporting each other so they wouldn't trip and fall. Then they both paused, turned, and waved back—to me!—because we were all part of something transcendent, the Notre Dame Family.

And, yes, Bridget's father got to see a number of Notre Dame games. I think he actually enjoyed the Notre Dame Marching Band more than the football. Eventually he had the pleasure of sharing the experience with his only grandchild, Matthew. Another National Championship came in 1988, with Lou Holtz as head coach. But the following season, 1989, was especially difficult for us. Bridget's dad was dying of cancer, and we all understood that. We made a special effort that year to see the Irish. We cherish the pictures of grandfather and grandson, one with barely the strength to walk, his face gaunt and colorless, the other a mischievous, nine-year-old towhead, each clinging to the other and looking into the camera with the same piercing blue eyes. We were hoping for a miracle as we visited the Grotto. But, it was the last season that Terence O'Rourke, subway alumnus, was to cheer on this earth for the Irish.

That little boy grew up on a steady diet of campus visits. Games in the fall. My brother Donald's graduation from the Law School. Summer baseball camps. Matt applied to only one college. Fortunately for all concerned, Notre Dame accepted him. We haven't quite figured out where Doctor Matt Hubbard's science gene came from, but there is no doubt about the band gene. I'm sure his grandfather watched the Marching Band emerge from the stadium tunnel, heard every note he played on the trumpet, and marched every step right beside him.

Here's the point: Notre Dame Football needs to be great so that common people who struggle with poverty, prejudice, adversity, mediocrity, and secularism can still have a beacon of hope. When I follow the string back, I'm surprised at how many of the truly meaningful pieces of my life—my education, my spouse, my family, my friends, and my own sense of hope—actually had their beginnings with the sounds and the glow from that small radio in my grandmother's darkened room. This is a narrative that has been replicated with slight variations by thousands of Notre Dame graduates over many generations.

With this as background, one has to ask: "How does Notre Dame measure success in football?" Winning games is a good place to start. But that must happen inside the legal and ethical boundaries that add meaning and significance to any success on the field. Notre Dame tries hard to do it right.

Being invited to bowl games provides an external measure that at least Notre Dame is still one of the relevant football programs. Sixty-six teams now go to bowl games each year from Division I-A, from a total universe of about 120 teams. So being in the top half of the class is the minimum threshold for success. The next level beyond that is a long leap. There is no conference championship to contend for since Notre Dame is one of the last major independent holdouts.

No, the tradition, self-inflicted, is that Notre Dame should contend for the National Championship. This would be a ridiculous measure at most institutions. But it isn't at Notre Dame, where for most of the twentieth century a high standard was established and met with regularity.

But the challenge is even more difficult than what might initially be comprehended. Great Notre Dame football teams have been in contention for the national title and still weren't recognized as National Champions. The only Irish teams that have been publicly touted as National Champions were of the years 1924, 1929, 1930, 1943, 1946, 1947, 1949, 1966, 1973, 1977, and 1988. But that list fails to recognize some really deserving teams. Is this a matter of subconscious religious prejudice or the blatant envy of success by the pollsters?

Consider the undefeated 1953 squad (9–0–1). The wire services tipped their scales toward Maryland (undefeated and untied) in December, before any bowl games were played. The Terrapins then lost in the Orange Bowl to Oklahoma (a team Notre Dame had defeated). Some of the "lesser" polls later named Notre Dame number one. But that's not what you'll read in the history books. Maryland stands alone. (This slight was partially corrected in the fiftieth anniversary year when the University awarded players from the 1953 squad National Championship rings. But the official University media guides still haven't ventured toward making a permanent correction.)

The challenge at Notre Dame is that to win a National Championship that counts, it must be undisputed. There could be no more fitting title for a book about Coach Ara Parseghian and the remarkable 1966 undefeated Fighting Irish football team.

As a sports fan, or a Notre Dame fan, you won't be disappointed if your motivation for reading this book was to learn about Coach Parseghian and the young men who earned something very precious for Notre Dame. The games will be dissected with relevant details and undoubtedly new insights will emerge. The myriad of interesting personalities will be exposed under a softer light after forty-five years of historical perspective. The Xs and Os will be explained in a colorful fashion that will awaken memories for the players and for those of us who originally saw the action either from the stands or at home in black and white. You'll come to appreciate the internal bonds of a special collection of teammates, a family inside the Notre Dame Family. This is a book about the best tradition of winning football games at the University of Notre Dame.

But if you love Notre Dame, as I do, you'll recognize the subject is more important than that.

UNDISPUTED

NOTRE DAME,
NATIONAL CHAMPIONS
1966

1

THE LAST TRAIN

It was cold, damn cold, the kind of biting cold you'd expect in mid-January in Michigan, not in mid-November. Darkness had nearly devoured the last vestiges of muted daylight on this overcast putty-grey Saturday afternoon when the unscheduled Grand Trunk Special finally began its journey back to South Bend, Indiana.

Trains had long been an integral component of Notre Dame Football from its emergence into national prominence beginning with the 1913 trip to West Point by Jesse Harper's team, which saw the birth of the modern forward pass. Because of its prolific travel schedule, the football team was for a time nicknamed The Ramblers before a permanent conversion was made to the now familiar Fighting Irish.

Head Coach Knute Rockne had masterfully exploited travel in the 1920s to create a storied football program. Those trips by rail had extended from Northern Indiana to New York, to California, and deep into the South—wherever the stadiums and the paydays were large. The tradition of playing top teams from across the nation continued after Notre Dame Stadium was completed in 1930. The success of the Frank Leahy-coached teams in the 1940s and early 50s cemented the legend of Notre Dame Football for a half-century. All of this was accomplished using trains—rolling classrooms and dormitories, in a fashion—to transport the football teams from South Bend's Union Station.

2   That sudden jerk of motion when the linked chain of railroad cars is dragged from a resting position by the anxious engine always seems to take the passengers by surprise. It interrupted the fitful slumber of a few. But most of the passengers were beyond the point of exhaustion and at heightened alert because of their residual adrenaline. Many were nursing wounds, some serious, from a desperately hard-fought football contest. The lurch was a welcome sign to all on board that they were finally heading home.

Every passenger had come to this location on this day with a sense of purpose, a job to do. Each had given every ounce of strength and emotion he had, especially the young padded warriors who had brutally collided on the athletic battlefield. But everyone was spent: coaches, managers, trainers, University officials, cheerleaders, and about 500 student fans. This particular college football game had been touted as the most important one of the 1966 season. Had it lived up to expectations? As the train began rolling toward Indiana, nobody had the answer. How this day would be recorded in history would be for others to decide.

About thirty hours earlier, the 1966 Notre Dame Football Team had arrived with fanfare on a scheduled train at the main station in Lansing, Michigan. This was the state capitol and home to Michigan State University. The Fighting Irish had already played eight games in a season reminiscent of the Leahy Era, when wins were expected and blowouts were common. The first team defense had only given up 7 points. Thus far, the Irish were undefeated and ranked number one by two major polls: the Associated Press (AP) used writers and United Press International (UPI) used coaches. The Spartans were ranked a close number two, and it was generally agreed that their 1966 team was even better than their 1965 team that had shared the National Championship with Alabama. So early on, opportunistic media collaborators had anointed this battle as the "Game of the Century." It wasn't the first time in the century that such hyperbole had been employed to promote a college football game, and it wouldn't be the last. Again, it would be for historians to eventually decide the merits of the claim.

There was mystique surrounding this game, well beyond number one playing number two. Something unexpected and intriguing had captured the imagination of a nation during this 1966 college football season.

Notre Dame Football was back in prominence, now for a third straight year, led by a charismatic young coach, Ara Parseghian. Cover stories about the team had appeared in *Sports Illustrated* and in *Time Magazine*. So a "return to glory" storyline for the season had been developing, with Notre Dame front and center. Now in November, the denouement of that story's ending would emerge in just a few short weeks.

3

At the center of college football's popularity and profitability are the fans, the fanatics. Especially late in the season, college football can ignite the passions of the partisan faithful, perhaps like no other sport played in America. The fires for this particular game had been lit many weeks earlier when it had become practically inevitable that number one would meet number two at Spartan Stadium on November 19. The teams had met in the two previous seasons (both times in South Bend), each winning one game. The winners had gone on to compete for the National Championship in '64 and '65.

The battle lines for this game had extended well beyond the confines of Indiana, Michigan, or the Midwest. Everyone in the United States with an ounce of sports awareness had marked this day on their calendar. It was like a heavyweight-title fight. ABC Sports was going virtually coast-to-coast with game coverage "in color," a new technology for this televsion network in 1966. It didn't matter if you had a favorite team or not. Seemingly everyone had an opinion on the game.

So by five p.m., the all-male Notre Dame traveling contingent composed of players, coaches, priests, and students had vacated the stadium, boarded buses, or walked across a once-crowded parking lot and through a frost-hardened field to the ad hoc railroad siding. There should have been clarity. Either hopeful frenzy or bitter despair. Something precious was in the balance, a dream fulfilled or maybe a dream lost forever. But the battered, weary, and now freezing band of football pilgrims from South Bend couldn't know for sure. Nobody in America knew for sure.

The same could be said for the Spartan contingent as they shuffled to their cars looking for protection from the elements or rushed to Coral Gables or Dagwoods, campus watering holes, to perform post-mortems on the game, play by play. Doubt lingered in the blustery cold, damp evening air. What there was after this intensely hard-fought contest in East Lansing was exhaustion, an over-abundance of exhaustion.

Football is a game that is practically married to exhaustion. It starts on the very first day of practice. It takes maximum effort to be in shape

4

for a grueling season. The edge goes to the players and to the teams who are prepared for fatigue, the ones that can function until the figurative final gun, flirting with exhaustion. Football is also deceivingly mentally demanding. To see it played for the first time, one would have to wonder if the physical punishment leaves any room for rational thought. Football players at all levels embrace the burden and prepare for both physical and mental exhaustion. Fans don't. Those wearing the Irish or the Spartan regalia were over their limits as they fanned out from Spartan Stadium into the chilled darkness. What everyone craved was satisfaction. There would be none of that, not on this day. The reason was simple.

The "Game of the Century" had ended in a 10–10 tie.

The special train for the excursion back to South Bend was efficiently divided by cars: VIPs, then players, then some students and fans. At the head of the train was a private car owned by a Notre Dame alum. As such it was reserved for University officials, significant donors, coaches, and the favored local press. Joe Doyle, sports editor of the *South Bend Tribune*, clearly remembers his ride home in the private car. Coach Ara Parseghian remembers nothing of it. Steak dinners were served from the dining area of the luxurious car. There was a muted celebratory air among those in the know. Could the pollsters flip the rankings of the teams based on the inconclusive evidence of a tie? Probably not. More accurately, they hoped not.

The football gods had been especially fickle that day, and a sense that anything could happen had followed the team off the playing field and from the stadium. The Irish easily could have lost to the Spartans. They would have, 10–7, if the game had ended at the half. One break either way would have made the difference. Notre Dame's star halfback, Nick Eddy, had been sidelined with an injury before kickoff. ND had lost its starting quarterback, Terry Hanratty, in the first quarter with a shoulder separation dispensed by Spartan legend Bubba Smith. Then ND starting center George Goeddeke limped out for good with an ankle injury two plays later. But the Irish battled back from an early 10–0 deficit and could have won the game outright. Michigan State never ventured beyond the Irish forty-five yard line during the second half. About twelve inches on a missed field goal by Notre Dame kicker Joe Azzaro with 4:39 left to play in the swirling wind could have been decisive.

The fair and logical slant that the sports writers and pollsters should be taking was that the number-one-ranked Irish had entered a hostile

stadium, had overcome substantial adversity, and had steadfastly prevailed. But fairness and logic hadn't been the friend of Notre Dame. The
disappointment of the final game of 1964 season had punctuated that.
While the adults in the first car enjoyed a beverage or two in relative
comfort, there wasn't a single person on the train who could claim to be
both healthy and relaxed.

5

In blackness, the Notre Dame special excursion carved its way from
East Lansing to Indiana without fanfare or recognition from the small
towns and the now-harvested fields of corn and soybeans along the way.
Nick Eddy sat next to Assistant Coach Tom Pagna for the entire trip,
discussing the game, play by play. It was therapeutic. Their conversation
eventually migrated to getting ready for the trip to California, where Eddy
would hopefully be ready to play. Quarterback Coley O'Brien, who was
called into action in the first quarter, would have an extended and ani-
mated conversation with Florine and Maurice Brenner from Mapleton,
Iowa, parents visiting their sons at Notre Dame for the weekend. They
would remember this train trip for the rest of their lives. O'Brien has
absolutely no memory of it. His roommate, halfback Frank Criniti,
maintains that O'Brien wasn't really himself for most of the afternoon—
perhaps the result of adjusting to his new diabetes medications.

There were no supporters holding signs of encouragement along the
rail route, in contrast to what had happened just the day before. The
train finally pulled into Union Station at about seven p.m. There was no
contingent of fans to welcome the warriors home. None was expected.

As the adrenaline wore off, everyone made their way back home.
Joe Doyle took a cab to his office at the *Tribune* to make deadline for
expanded coverage in the Sunday morning edition. The players boarded
buses back to campus. Terry Hanratty, George Goeddeke, Bob Gladieux, and Rocky Bleier were immediately taken to St. Joseph Hospital
to have their injuries attended to. Nick Eddy would find consolation and
comfort with his wife Tiny and their new baby daughter Nicole Marie at
their off-campus apartment.

Ara Parseghian returned to his family and their new home on Washington Street, near the Notre Dame campus. The night was still young,
so Katie Parseghian had accepted an invitation to relax with neighborhood friends, the Connaughtons. Later in the evening while they were
out, there would be a phone call at their friends' home and Ara would
be summoned. A rude sportswriter had given the Parseghian children

(Karen (fifteen), Kristan (thirteen), and Mike (ten)) some made-up story about needing to talk to their father, that it was an emergency. When Ara answered the phone, the caller (Ara remembers a Southern accent) immediately wanted him to explain his play calling in the last minutes of the game. Ara would slam the phone down into its cradle and return to the party. The pebble he would carry around in his shoe, probably for the rest of his life, had been delivered. Unfair or not, the game at Michigan State would never be forgotten.

At The Circle, the gateway to the Notre Dame campus, the team buses pulled in without fanfare. The campus was so quiet that it was eerie, especially for a football Saturday. Linebacker John Horney and his roommate, defensive tackle Pete Duranko, carried their bags past Alumni Hall to their dormitory, Dillon Hall. They were virtually alone on the sidewalks under the soft incandescent glow of the lampposts along the way. For the first time they were aware of how profoundly cold it was.

There were no parties to be seen from the sidewalk inside the sparse dorm rooms facing the Main Quad. Except for the occasional desk lights on in rooms where some studying might have been in progress, the campus was dead. It may not have been what John and Pete expected, but it did reflect how they felt. They just wanted to relax, eat, and sleep maybe. Their first team Notre Dame defensive unit had been on the field for all four quarters—a first for the season.

Their first stop was at the central bank of mailboxes to collect their two days of letters and magazines. In their shared mailbox was a letter addressed to Mr. John Horney from the Marquette University School of Medicine. He had been accepted. It would be the thing Horney would remember most about the day, the football game only a blur. This day would change his life.

When November 19, 1966 finally expired, none of the Notre Dame contingent really knew for sure where their football season was headed. Would it be a return to glory—finally a National Championship after seventeen years? Or would it be a replay of 1964, a remarkable season tainted by the aroma of unfairness in the final quarter of the final game? They had come a very long way since closing out the 7–2–1 "transitional" 1965 season. They deserved to be in contention for the national title. The "Hollywood" storyline hadn't been shattered, but it had been abruptly altered. There was still football to be played, one more game, the next week in Los Angeles against the number-ten-ranked Trojans of Southern California. Would the ghosts, or the referees, from 1964 reappear?

As everyone finally succumbed to exhaustion that night, historical threads were being spun that would leave behind an interesting cobweb of data, more than enough to be assembled with renewed perspective forty-five years later. For example: what nobody knew on November 19, 1966 was that this would be the very last time the Notre Dame Football Team would travel by train.

Change was in the wind.

COLLEGE FOOTBALL IS A COACHES' GAME

It is difficult to place proper emphasis, often not enough, on the importance of coaching in college football success. John Underwood, a gifted writer for *Sports Illustrated*, summarized it well in a coaching film script he composed in 1978 for the first College Football Hall of Fame located near Cincinnati.

More than any other, football is a coaches' game. It is a product of the ability of the men who teach it, a tribute to their genius and their dedication. It is a sport shaped in the image of these men—unique, vigorous, oft-times noble individuals who found in coaching not only a meaningful life's work but a means of expression. A purpose and a fulfillment.

They brought their talents to college football, and the returns from this good fortune have one common denominator: no matter where they coached, they won. No matter how long the odds, no matter how great the challenge, they won—and usually their impact was felt throughout their society.

The best of coaches did not inherit winning teams, they made them.

Winning coaches come in all sizes, shapes and personalities. They have only one common trait: the ability to hold a team in the palm of their hands.

There was only one reason that Notre Dame was competing for the National Championship in 1966—Coach Ara Parseghian. There is not an iota of exaggeration behind that claim. Underwood could have been writing his description with only this one man in mind and it would have been equally accurate.

This idea is universally agreed upon by the people who should know best. Former Notre Dame President, Fr. Theodore Hesburgh, is upfront about the difference the new coach made at Notre Dame. As he sat in his thirteenth-floor office located in the library named after him, with a post card view of the Golden Dome, he waved his lit cigar, cutting the plume of smoke, and simply proclaimed, "Ara made all the difference." The players, to a person, say the same thing in their own words. What it amounts to is, "everything changed when Ara arrived . . . everything."

The student body instinctively knew it the moment Parseghian stepped onto the campus. There was a spontaneous pep rally on the steps of Sorin Hall on a cold and blustery evening in February of 1964. His brief comments to the students were straightforward and resonated: "Football games are won by teams that are both physically and mentally alert; we will be at our peak for every game we play." A few days later the applause was thunderous at a varsity basketball game in the old brick Fieldhouse when Ara was introduced between halves. It was love at first sight. This affection eventually led to a widely-distributed photo among the student body, an eight-by-ten black and white doctored in the darkroom to depict Ara walking across St. Mary's Lake—Ara walking on water. Ara Parseghian and Notre Dame were a marriage made in heaven. That love affair continues uninterrupted even today.

Allen L. Sack, a sophomore reserve player in 1964, now a college professor and author, summarized it beautifully in his 2008 book *Counterfeit Amateurs*.

Any misgivings I might have had about Ara Parseghian were quickly dispelled after his first meeting with the team. I had never met a person with Ara's ability to communicate and inspire. It is no exaggeration to say that the players sat spellbound as he laid out his strategy for how we would win the national championship. I have often told people that after that first meeting, Ara could have told us to jump off the top of Notre Dame Stadium, and many players might have seriously considered it. He had a clear vision of where the program was headed and the charisma to make the rest of us believe in it. In the weeks to come, he also demonstrated organizational skills that would have served him well in a military campaign. He left absolutely nothing to chance. Efficiency and time management were the hallmarks of Ara's system.

Essentially the same sentiments were echoed in *All Rise: The Remarkable Journey of Alan Page*, by Bill McGrane.

Ara made a lasting impression on young Page. "I think it was his first meeting with the team," Alan said. "He drew a football field on the blackboard, then told us the game was really pretty simple; it was about position and possession. That was it."

"I had never stopped to think about a plan for football before." Page said. "I just played. Now here was a coach, and he was making so much sense with this simple, basic theory. He turned a light on for me."

Ara was then, and still is, a very focused person. Therefore, it is with respect and some trepidation that one approaches him today to garner his reflections on Notre Dame Football under his administration. He's had so many people try to extract favors and information over the years that he is understandably guarded when a newcomer arrives. So something is needed to start the conversation on the right foot, an icebreaker.

The Bet

The figurative pre-interview betting was heavy. Too bad it was one-sided. Nobody wanted to bet against the coach because everyone knew it would be a losing proposition. It was to be a test of Ara's memory at age eighty-seven. In Notre Dame's sports information collection, there is a black and white photograph of Ara as a high school football player in 1941 at Akron South, in Ohio. Four backs are standing behind six linemen who are kneeling. The uniforms are rather shapeless canvas, the helmets white leather. The hooded practice sweats have minimal ornamentation, just the word "SOUTH" over an inverted triangle on the front. One of the backs is a young Ara Parseghian, easy to identify with handsome good looks and piercing dark eyes. Standing next to him is a solidly-built young African-American player. The question was: Would Ara be able to identify that fellow in the picture after seventy years? He didn't hesitate for a moment in answering, in fact he didn't even glance at the photograph to provide his answer. "That's Conwell Findley, our tailback." It is a question that nobody had ever asked him before. Black football players weren't common on high school teams in 1941, especially in places like Akron, Ohio. "I wonder what happened to him." It was genuine interest. The first window on Ara Parseghian's personality is that he measures character and performance—there's not a prejudiced bone in his body. As he took a nostalgic look at the photo, it was obvious that he both liked and respected Conwell Findley.

Ara played high school football for Akron (Ohio) South. This photo is of the 1941 team from his senior year. Ara is in the back row. Standing next to him is Conwell Findley. An African-American on a high school football team in a town like Akron would have been considered unusual at the time. *Source:* Notre Dame Sports Information Collection

Ara Parseghian is intense—that's the word you keep hearing—especially about subjects that concern and interest him. For many years of his life, in fact most of it, football was at or near the top of his list. From 1964 until 1975, football meant Notre Dame Football. His memories from that period in his life may need to be coaxed a bit, but once prompted they are clear and expansively detailed. It is altogether quite remarkable. The lesson is to never bet against him.

12

The Teacher

Great teachers were at one time great students who themselves had great teachers. Parseghian credits the legendary Paul Brown with many of his successful coaching techniques. Of the greatest coaches from the professional ranks, Paul Brown is in the elite ranks of George Halas, Vince Lombardi, Don Shula and now perhaps Bill Belichek. The enduring lesson that Ara took away from the legendary coach was, "Never leave a game on the practice field on Thursday or Friday." The translation is not to peak early, too soon in advance of the game. In other words, prepare thoroughly, but don't burn the team out in the process. Save the optimal mental and physical performance for Saturday afternoon —when it counts. The winning edge is to make sure that every player is mentally into the game and believes he is better prepared than his opponent. It is a hallmark of Ara's teams. They believed that their coach was the smartest and best-prepared person on the field—so they had the edge going in. With that understanding, it made practicing during the week and execution on game days easier and more effective.

The respect Parseghian has for Paul Brown is deeply ingrained. When Ara was in high school, most games were held on Saturday afternoons. That wasn't the case for Massillon High School, coached by Brown. They had lights and their games were played on Friday nights, as most high school games are today. So high school players from nearby towns like Akron could go to Massillon to watch the games. This was right before the war and the rationing of gasoline. Coach Parseghian still remembers the precision with which Brown's teams played. He even recalls that Massillon played Kent State in a spring game, high school against college varsity, that Massillon won "something like 35–0."

Parseghian had the opportunity to play for Brown in two different settings. Ara graduated from Akron South in 1942, six months after Pearl Harbor. With the start of the war he volunteered and was identified for his leadership. This got him assigned to Great Lakes Naval Training in Chicago, and they had a football team. The Blue Jackets played Notre Dame during the war years, 1942–45, and even beat the number-one-ranked Irish in 1943, their only loss. After Massillon, Brown moved to Ohio State and eventually joined the war effort at Great Lakes.

After the war, Parseghian played football at Miami of Ohio from 1945–47. By that time Paul Brown had advanced to coaching his name-sake, the Cleveland Browns, in the All-American Football Conference, which later folded into the NFL. After an outstanding college career, Parseghian played for the coach again, for the Browns in 1948 and '49. It was a good team that included Otto Graham, Marion Motley, and Edgar "Special Delivery" Jones. A recurring hip injury ended Ara's playing career, but the example of Paul Brown piqued his interest in coaching. With playing no longer an option, coaching football started out as a way to make a living and then became an inspired career choice. The first stop in 1950 was as freshman coach at Miami of Ohio, his alma mater, working for Head Coach Woody Hayes.

Well before he arrived in South Bend, Ara had made the transition from being a student of the coaching craft to becoming an innovator and a teacher himself. He had two personality traits working for him, both obvious from his youth: intensity and leadership. From Brown he learned organization and management and added these to his portfolio. By the time he got his first head coaching opportunity at Miami, he was ready to fill the shoes of Woody Hayes, who departed for Ohio State in 1951. Ara was only twenty-seven. When Ara's next advancement was to the Big Ten Conference and Northwestern in 1956, it wasn't a surprise to anyone close to the game.

What was a surprise was how well the young coach performed to reinvigorate the traditionally moribund football program in Evanston. Northwestern administrators were the most surprised of all and didn't quite know how to process a coach with lofty aspirations delivering wins on the field and looking for support off the field. Ara was unappreciated, especially by Athletic Director Stu Holcomb, and became frustrated.

Parseghian's Wildcats, thinner on depth and talent, beat the Fighting Irish four consecutive times (1959–62, they did not play in 1963), much to the displeasure of the carnivorous Notre Dame alumni in Chicago, of which there were many. Those may have been the luckiest gridiron losses ever at Notre Dame. The Administration at Notre Dame had no delusions about the contribution of football to the psyche and to the coffers of the academic powerhouse that was emerging in South Bend. They were in desperate need of a head coach who could return the school to football glory and could do it in the context of academic excellence. Northwestern was a good place to look. They also had intimate first-hand knowledge of Ara Parseghian's results on the football field. He became the logical choice and was offered the job in December of 1963.

Signals

One of the many innovations that Ara perfected at Notre Dame was sending signals from the sideline to the team on the field. The prevailing NCAA rule at the time was that coaches couldn't communicate plays, especially offensive plays, from the sideline to the players. Today the coach still rails against what he calls "a stupid rule." When he was at Northwestern, he was even penalized once for a violation. As he retells it, one of his players was forced out of bounds in front of his bench. As the player was getting up, Parseghian verbally gave him the next play to take back to the huddle. The official marking the ball dropped his flag (colored red in those days). So college coaches, including Ara, were forced to innovate. Every coach called plays from the sideline, but none did it better than Ara. In fact, until recently, how he did it was one of Ara's most closely-guarded secrets.

Speaking in confidence, he finally relented and cracked the code, explaining the mechanics after so many years. It was amazing to watch. He had to stand upright in his home office to demonstrate it. The walls and shelves around him were cramped with plaques, trophies, books, photos, and assorted memorabilia—1964 Coach of the Year, MacArthur Bowl 1964, National Championships '66 and '73, too many game balls to dust with regularity—all witnesses. As this was being done, both the coach and the viewers were transported back in time forty-five years.

It wasn't a secret that there was a highly sophisticated series of signals, similar to what base coaches and managers use in baseball. But outsiders never claimed to know how it was done. Those in the know were kept to a select few. Most of them had long careers working for Ara, so they were never in a position to take the code to another team. Those few that did move had too much respect for Ara to reveal his secret—although they probably used it themselves without attribution. As for players, only defensive captains and quarterbacks were tutored on the signals.

Here's how it worked. From the coaches' position on the sideline at mid-field, the angles on forward progress are hard to read, especially near the end zones where calling plays matters most. So team managers were assigned to each sideline to follow the progress of the ball down the field and immediately signal to the Notre Dame coaches the precise distance for a first down or a score. Speed was critical. It provided decision time to plan the next play.

The team immediately retreated into its huddle with the "signal receiver" placed so that he could read the signals from the bench. Terry Hanratty remembers kneeling down and looking at the sideline from between the legs of the standing linemen. The other players in the huddle became in effect a human duck blind. The unsuspecting officials quit paying attention once they saw the huddle. Then the quarterback, or the defensive captain, began translating sign language from the bench to the team.

The language was simultaneously simple, elegant, and complex. It was based on subtle natural and normal gestures from Ara: how he held his play card (the side with the line facing out or the side without the line), which hand he used to hold it, and in which quadrant of the clipboard he held it. Was he standing or kneeling? Were his feet together or apart? If ever they thought an opponent might catch on, the signal-calling was temporarily transferred to one of the coordinators using a key. All the gestures were completely natural: there were none of the gyrations one would expect or that would attract attention.

Even the selection of the coach's attire was part of the program. Almost everyone from that era recalls Ara's custom wool sweater, navy blue with the gold "NOTRE DAME" chenille letters applied in an arc. Ara was captured wearing this sweater for his portrait on the cover of *Time Magazine* in 1964. The convenient story at the time was that Katie Parseghian made this custom sweater as a gift to her husband. In fact, it was a well-considered prop so that the signal callers could immediately pick out the coach on the sideline. That and the fact that Ara virtually straddled the fifty-yard line for the entire game. Then Ara used his hand or his clipboard to cover specific letters on the sweater, adding to his code.

Of course, making this all work with precision took incredible coordination. The head coach had to be entirely in control of his body language, lest a confusing or false signal be communicated. This fact goes a long way in explaining two characteristics of Ara on the sideline. He never wore headsets, ever. It would have been too distracting. And he rarely smiled or celebrated on the sideline. The intensity required to process information and plan the next move wouldn't allow it. He was always thinking one play ahead.

Ara was the equivalent of a human football computer constantly processing information, making decisions, and communicating to the team on the field—all in fewer than fifteen seconds. At the time, there were only two physical computers on the Notre Dame campus, and the newest of those manufactured by IBM occupied practically an entire building called the Computing Center. Ara was the first portable computer at Notre Dame on football Saturdays, but nobody really appreciated it at the time.

This communication scheme also required smart and alert captains and quarterbacks. At a school like Notre Dame, this didn't usually pose a problem. But sometimes having acute vision did. In 1966, Ara recalls that defensive captain Jim Lynch would sometimes squint in the direction of the bench during huddles, adding to the anxiety of what Jim might have thought he saw, or alerting an official to drop a flag. During the 1966 season, that never happened. Even today, Terry Hanratty takes special pride and boasts that he never missed an offensive signal in 1966. It is ironic that the most serious miscommunication during the season was on a play brought in from the sideline that resulted in Hanratty's separated shoulder at Michigan State.

The genius of the system was that the play-calling was specific about formation or play sequence but allowed for multiple variations to be determined based on "formation keys" provided by the opposing team and then processed and reinforced by verbal communication at the line of scrimmage. In a sense, every play was an audible as we understand it today, but had simple commands in the count. All the players were expected to memorize the plays and all the options and then know how to execute instinctively. The playbooks were thick and detailed. Some of these treasures survive today in binders over three inches thick. You had to reflect the coach's intensity and intelligence to play at Notre Dame. Communicating clearly was the necessary first step.

The Box

Another innovation Ara brought to the sideline was "the box." This was a small portable black and white television monitor that was connected to a dedicated TV camera on the roof of the press box. Grad Assistant (essentially another assistant coach) Brian Boulac was assigned to strap on a harness and carry this heavy piece of equipment around at Parseghian's side during the games. Boulac was a former lineman, and it took incredible strength and stamina to carry the box for an entire game. As Brian says, "It was worth it. I had the best seat in the house."

Before every play, the cameraman would be instructed on where to focus the camera. The action was in real time, with no video replay capability. Boulac would communicate what he saw to Ara, especially downs and distance. This all went into the coach's data bank, either for immediate use or to be retained for a future play-call when it was important. Video contraptions like the box were outlawed by the Big Ten in 1965. So for away games in 1966 at Northwestern and Michigan State, Notre Dame was without this tool.

Of course, Ara had a full complement of coaches on the sideline, each one trained to collect data that was judiciously communicated to the Head Coach. John Ray ran the defense. Tom Pagna became the thoughtful back-up computer for Ara on offense. He would be processing much of the same information and performed a check on the decisions that were being made. This was especially important in the area of game management, especially as it pertained to time on the clock. Pagna knew what they could do with time remaining or how to milk the clock to keep the ball out of the opponent's hands. On average, there are fourteen offensive possessions for each team in a college game. When play-calling is benchmarked against statistical probabilities, the decisions become easier, or at least theoretically better. Pagna was in charge of monitoring this for Ara and providing just enough data to help Ara's on-board computer to function.

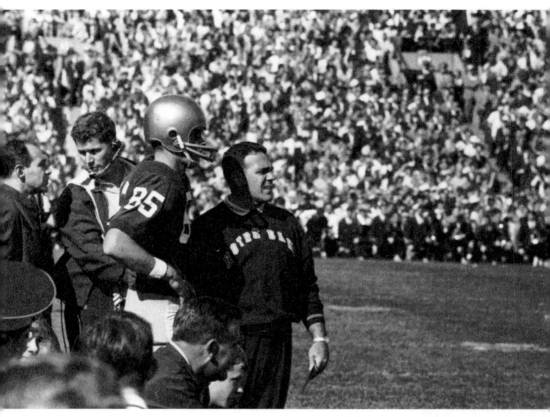

Head Coach Ara Parseghian surveys the field in an early 1966 home game. Also in the frame are (l-r) Assistant Coach Tom Pagna, Graduate Assistant Brian Boulac (with headphones and holding "the box," Jim Seymour (85) and Defensive Coach John Ray (lower right). *Source:* University of Notre Dame Archives

Behind everything, there was a requirement for accurate and immediate information. Speed in data collection was essential. Ara's brain processed information better and faster than any other coach in America. So good was the system that Ara's 1970 team set an NCAA record by averaging ninety-two offensive plays per game over the course of a season. That record may still stand, even in the current era of no-huddle and hurry-up offenses. Instant communication was the secret weapon at Notre Dame that practically nobody understood at the time. But the players did, even though most of them were semi-clueless about how it all happened.

Ara and Joe

Not chronicled during his coaching tenure at Notre Dame was the special relationship between Ara and Joe Doyle, the sportswriter and later the sports editor of the *South Bend Tribune*. Joe is a Notre Dame graduate through and through. He obviously cares for his alma mater very much—so much that his observations and views were not always welcomed on campus or on the football practice field. But they always sprung from a sincere desire to make things better at Notre Dame—especially the football team.

Joe became the gnat that wouldn't go away when meetings between the Administration and Ara began in earnest in December of 1963. Joe seemed to always be at the right place at the right time and in some instances one step ahead of the story. His calls to Parseghian during the negotiations were obviously helpful. From the start, Joe was convinced

Ara Parseghian and Joe Doyle as they appear today in Ara's home office. The coach and the sportswriter became fast friends in 1963 and have remained close since then. *Source:* Collection of Mark Hubbard.

that Ara was the right man for the head coaching position. President Fr. Hesburgh and Executive Vice President Fr. Joyce eventually saw the light. For a time the negotiations broke down. Ara was scheduled for a press conference in South Bend that had to be cancelled. Later it was rescheduled and history was made. This prompted Athletic Director Moose Krause to quip, "[Ara] should be with us a long time; after all, he signed twice."

Ara became the first non-Notre Dame grad to have the job since Jesse Harper was hired as Head Coach in 1913 and also the first non-Catholic if you consider that Knute Rockne converted in 1923 and was a practicing Catholic at the time of his death.

The moment you are named Head Football Coach at Notre Dame, your popularity spikes, but so does your sense of isolation. Ara needed a confidant and a trusted friend to help him negotiate the tricky tides at Notre Dame. An outsider such as himself wouldn't know, without an insider's help, some of the stress points, like historical salaries, the condition of facilities and equipment, or how many scholarships were in play, who could influence scheduling, disciplinary concerns, and the rules for hiring assistants. Essentially, Joe became that insider. The trust developed between him and Ara from the outset continued throughout Parseghian's coaching tenure. It was an odd couple to be sure; the head coach and the sportswriter could well have been antagonists. It happens.

But the two met for coffee almost every day at Milt's Grill in downtown South Bend, at five-thirty a.m. before the coaches' meeting on campus at seven. Joe's private counsel was invaluable to the new coach, especially when it came to understanding local South Bend customs or the Byzantine traditions of the Church. Sometimes it was simply a matter of friendly practical advice. For example, Ara was quite concerned when halfback Nick Eddy wanted to get married during his junior season. Joe thought it might work out just fine. It did. Even today the familiarity between the two is obvious. Joe is always a welcome guest at the Parseghians' home, and you just have the feeling that his favorite coffee mug is sitting in one of the kitchen cabinets. Joe claims their friendship is built on one simple rule: "I never told Ara how to coach and he never told me what to write."

Providential

In 1964, Notre Dame was desperate for a coach who could return to the tradition of winning football games, but do so with a view toward high standards and the more confining rules that were emerging from the NCAA. Ara Parseghian's delivery to Notre Dame was nothing less than providential.

The highly-respected Sports Information Director at Notre Dame, Roger Valdiserri, got to know the coach extremely well as he crafted the team's public information and simultaneously guarded the Notre Dame dogma. His insightful reflection after fifty years, "When you are around Ara you feel like you're at a disadvantage. You might be driving the same make and model car, but through some strange quirk of fate, you figure his came off the assembly line with a bigger engine."

Jim Leahy was a prep team player for Ara in 1966. His Notre Dame Football roots run deep. He's the son of Notre Dame coaching legend Frank Leahy and was later the father of two-time ND football captain Ryan Leahy. He leaves no room for doubt. "My father had tremendous respect for Ara," he says. "We all did."

3

TED, NED, AND ED

In 1952, the Congregation of Holy Cross (CSC) entrusted its jewel, the University of Notre Dame, to Reverend Theodore M. Hesburgh, known with affection as "Father Ted." Fr. Hesburgh, Executive Vice President under Reverend John Cavanaugh, remembers receiving the envelope containing his new assignment at the Congregation's annual gathering where all member priests were informed of their duties under their vows of obedience. Inside that envelope was a small card with a single word, "President." The case could be made that this modest piece of paper is one of the most important documents in Notre Dame history. The term was limited to six years under Congregation rules. That rule was wisely ignored and Father Ted's term was renewed five consecutive times.

Fr. Hesburgh immediately turned to his close friend, Reverend Edmund P. Joyce, also known as "Father Ned," to fill the vacant position of Executive Vice President, essentially the number-two person in charge of managing the University. In addition to his constant counsel as a collaborator, Father Ned was assigned three areas of responsibility: business affairs, athletics, and fund-raising (especially as it related to aggressive plans to expand the physical plant and build the endowment). Thus, Fr.

Joyce became directly responsible for one of the legs of the Notre Dame table and a good portion of the top.

Of course, that job would be too large for one person to handle without help. Fortunately, when it came to athletics there already was a trusted person on board, Edward W. "Moose" Krause, Director of Athletics.

Those three men, Ted, Ned, and Ed, would transform Notre Dame and preserve the integrity of the football program leading up to the 1966 season. It wasn't a smooth ride.

Almost immediately, the Frank Leahy Era was forced into a sudden conclusion following the 1953 football season. A twenty-five-year-old Notre Dame grad, the freshman coach under Leahy, Terry Brennan, was made head coach. It was a decision proposed by Fr. Joyce and approved by Fr. Hesburgh. What were they thinking? When asked if he thought he was too young to be named head coach at the age of twenty-five, Brennan replied, "Oh, I don't know. I'll be twenty-six in a few months." Looking back, the talented but young Brennan never really had a chance to mature under the immediate pressures at Notre Dame. He would have been the perfect candidate had he been a successful head coach at another college and had the skills to understand and navigate the politics of major-college football. But on-the-job training proved costly for him personally and for the University.

There were flashes of brilliance on the field. The 1957 Irish stunned Oklahoma on the road, beating the Sooners 7–0 and breaking their NCAA record forty-seven-game winning streak. Paul Hornung was a Heisman Trophy winner in 1956 (still the only player from a team with a losing record to be so honored). But a 32–18 overall record wasn't good enough to follow the legendary Leahy—at least not in the eyes of a spoiled fan base who had become accustomed to undefeated seasons and National Championships. (It is interesting to note that Brennan's teams finished ranked in the Top Ten in three of the five years he was head coach—which would be considered outstanding by today's standards.)

In fact, Leahy, smarting from his sudden non-celebrity status (he was on the cover of Newsweek only weeks before his "resignation"), actually fueled some of the internal discontent, something not fully understood until decades later. Brennan's five-year term as head coach ended after the 1958 season. Without having to overcome the historical baggage, he may have become a successful long-term head coach at Notre Dame. In 1966, Dick Hackenberg of the *Chicago Sun-Times* said it well. "The tactical terminus of Terry's tenure will forever remain a barnacle on the Notre Dame ship of state."

Many have suggested that the new Notre Dame Administration was actively trying to de-emphasize football. The facts suggest that if there was a strategy at all, it was more subtle. The football leg of the Notre Dame table had grown faster and was disproportionate to the other three legs in 1952. It was time for the new Administration to pay increased attention to academics, to the role of the University in global Church matters, and to vocal alumni who would be called upon to restock the University's post-war coffers. It was a time for growing the other three legs of the table, while holding football steady. Looking back, it is impossible not to be impressed by the wisdom of a strategy that encompassed those goals or the dimensions of its successful execution.

For starters, football scholarships were rationalized. Under Fr. Hesburgh, Notre Dame elected to follow the Big Ten guidelines of a thirty-maximum grants per year and an overall one-hundred-twenty maximum. The Big Ten was the dominant conference at the time. There were no NCAA regulations and other, lesser conferences had much higher limits, some as high as forty-five scholarships per year. Under Leahy, scholarships had been a bit ad hoc and fluid: they were awarded and taken away annually to suit his private needs for the program while the Administration was often kept in the dark.

Under the new University regulations, once you had grant-in-aid, it was in effect even if the player was injured and could no longer perform on the field, or if a player was demoted to the prep team. (This approach was revolutionary at the time and at many big-name football programs, scholarships remain a year-to-year award.) That measure handcuffed Brennan, who inherited legacy commitments that needed to be honored. The effect was that in his first season, only seventeen scholarships were awarded, and Brennan rarely had more than twenty to give to incoming freshmen. But stricter rules were necessary improvements after Leahy's largesse, and those rules put Notre Dame on the vanguard of national policy reforms. Without National Championships, the perception of de-emphasis had some acolytes, especially among the ill-informed press with Notre Dame bias—either good or ill.

After Brennan, the knee-jerk response was to hire a replacement coach from the professional ranks, Joe Kuharich from the Washington Redskins. The thinking was that Kuharich, also a Notre Dame grad, would blunt the criticism that the new coach didn't have prior coaching credentials. But for a number of reasons, far too many to recount, Kuharich was never really able to take advantage of the great opportunity he had at Notre Dame. He left after 1962, going back to professional ball, first as an assistant to NFL Commissioner Pete Rozelle and later with the Philadelphia Eagles as head coach. An interim coach was named for the 1963 season, Hugh Devore, as loyal a Notre Dame man as ever was. It was obvious from the beginning of his tenure that "interim" was the operative word. With an entire year to find a permanent head coach at Notre Dame, interesting possibilities opened up.

At Northwestern, a hot young coach was making a name for himself, marked by four consecutive wins against the Irish. But the career-minded Ara Parseghian knew he had gone about as far as he could at Northwestern. The Northwestern Administration acknowledged this. So in a letter to Fr. Joyce, Ara indicated his interest in the Notre Dame coaching job. Other candidates emerged as well. Today it is unclear who else may have been on the short list, but the often-mentioned name is Dan Devine (who was later to coach the Irish to a National Championship in 1977). After the 1963 season, Father Ted clearly recalls calling the president at Northwestern, Doctor J. Roscoe Miller, and asking for permission to talk to Parseghian. President Miller was impressed by the civility of the call, acknowledged that Parseghian had outgrown Northwestern's program, and provided Fr. Hesburgh with a strong recommendation. Things moved ahead rapidly after that.

Working in secrecy, Father Ned and Father Ted met with Parseghian in a private hotel room in Chicago on a snowy evening in early December. The drive from South Bend over the Indiana Toll Road and the Chicago Sykway was harrowing due to the weather conditions. Father Ted remembers listening intently as Fr. Joyce led the discussion, but asking only one direct question himself, "Will you follow the strict guidelines we've established at Notre Dame?" When Ara answered in the affirmative, Father Ted was satisfied.

Those close to the situation insist that the final decision to offer Ara the job, by the only person holding the power of final veto, was made that night after that answer was provided. But in matters like this, especially at Notre Dame, contractual negotiations don't often follow a straight line. It took a couple more meetings and at least one false start before Parseghian was named the new head coach on December 14, 1963. Joe Doyle speculates that Ara's initial annual salary was about $18,000 (before outside endorsements, speaking fees, and radio-TV shows), or roughly seven times what a Notre Dame student was paying for room, board, and tuition ($2,700). Although penurious by today's standards, this made Parseghian one of the highest-paid employees at

Ted, Ned and Ed, ushered in a new era of Notre Dame Athletics. From left to right, President, Rev. Theodore Hesburgh, Executive Vice-President, Rev. Edmund Joyce and the memorial bronze seated statue and bench honoring Athletic Director, Edward (Moose) Krause. The bench is located just outside the Joyce Athletic and Convocation Center and has a view of the Hesburgh Memorial Library. *Source –* Notre Dame Sports Information Collection

Notre Dame, considering that Fathers Hesburgh and Joyce and most of the top administrators at the time were Holy Cross priests officially drawing no salaries. Through all the negotiations, hovering in the background was the athletic director, Moose Krause, who had to make it all work.

27

Reverend Theodore M. Hesburgh, CSC

The 1967 *Dome*, the Notre Dame yearbook that chronicled the '66 football season, provided the following quote to launch the introductory first section:

> Notre Dame's efflorescence has been one of the most spectacular developments in higher education in the last twenty-five years. I suspect that Notre Dame has done more than any other institution in this period, possibly because there was more to do.
> —Robert Hutchins, Chancellor, University of Chicago

It was an accurate summary and assessment of the changes both past and in motion under Fr. Hesburgh's leadership by the autumn of 1966.

The student yearbook authors went further to expound as follows:

> *One hundred and twenty-five years after its founding in 1842, the University of Notre Dame is the outstanding Catholic institution of higher learning in the United States. Although this is by no means obvious to all, Notre Dame is unquestionably at the forefront of Catholic education, and its president, Father Hesburgh, has been instrumental in gaining for Notre Dame this position.*
>
> *Prior to the appointment of Father Cavanaugh to the presidency in 1948, there was little to indicate the academic prominence that Notre Dame now enjoys.*
>
> *Notre Dame was, quite simply, a financially poor university, and merely keeping the doors open was an all-embracing task.*
>
> *Although far from a scholarly activity, football provided the only reliable source of income in the university's history, thereby indirectly aiding its academic pursuits.*

*Notre Dame, today, despite a slow beginning and continued conserva-
tism, is vastly different from the institution it was ten years ago. It is physically larger, ten times as wealthy, academically respected, and with the new
lay board of trustees, structurally reformed.*

The prevailing joke on campus in 1966 was, "How are God and Fr.
Hesburgh alike? Answer: God is everywhere and Fr. Hesburgh is everywhere but Notre Dame." That joke still gets a chuckle from Father Ted,
now in his ninety-fourth year, because it highlighted an acknowledged
truth. According to records, Hesburgh logged 120,000 miles and visited
fifty nations in calendar 1964 alone, a pattern he was to repeat year after
year. His response at the time was, "The president of a large university
today has to make his university present to the world in all major ques-
tions of the times."

As an educator and priest, no one before or since has had more
simultaneous influence on a university, a nation, or the world outside.
Fr. Hesburgh was the subject of a *Time Magazine* cover story (February
9, 1962). He holds the Guinness record for honorary degrees received at
150, and no one is a close second.

Theodore Hesburgh was raised in Syracuse, New York, and left his
close family to attend the seminary at Notre Dame. He was furthering
his collegiate studies at a seminary in Rome when he was called home
upon the outbreak of the World War II. He graduated from The Catholic University of America in 1945 with a doctorate in sacred theology,
his only academic degree. It may surprise readers to learn that Father
Ted isn't himself a Notre Dame graduate (although one of his honorary
degrees is from the University).

Fr. Hesburgh served with distinction on many presidential commis-
sions, notable among them the Civil Rights Commission (where he was
Chairman), the Atomic Energy Commission, and the Commission on
Immigration Reform. He similarly was called upon by his personal friend
Pope Paul VI to represent the Vatican internationally in areas of science,
especially nuclear energy. Representing the interests of higher education, he was a member of the International Federation of Catholic Universities and the Rockefeller Foundation. Even after retirement he was
a member of the Knight Commission, assisted by Sports Information
Director Roger Valdisseri, which provided guidance to college presidents
on ways to overhaul college athletics. Fr. Hesburgh has been honored

with both of the two highest civilian awards from a grateful nation, the Congressional Gold Medal and the Presidential Medal of Freedom.

Generations of students at Notre Dame knew when Father Ted was on campus. They saw his lights on, burning throughout the night from his second floor corner office in the Administration Building. When the lights weren't on, the University was being carefully monitored by Father Ned Joyce, a role he performed capably and without complaint for thirty-six years.

29

Reverend Edmund P. Joyce, CSC

If Fr. Hesburgh was Notre Dame's Mister Outside, then Fr. Joyce was its Mister Inside. Both were as important to Notre Dame Football as Doc Blanchard and Glenn Davis (the original Mister Outside and Mister Inside, and both Heisman Trophy winners) were to the Army football teams in the '40s. Father Ned held the dual positions of Executive Vice President and Treasurer of the University.

Edmund Joyce was from Spartanburg, South Carolina. He graduated from Notre Dame in 1937 and became a CPA in 1939, before deciding he had a vocation to the priesthood in 1945. He studied at Congregation of Holy Cross seminaries and had a year of graduate studies at Oxford University. He was ordained in 1949.

The financial books at Notre Dame were nothing to cheer about in 1950 when Fr. Joyce was named Assistant Vice President for Business Affairs. So he knew what he was getting into when he accepted Fr. Hesburgh's invitation to join his management team and forge a new era of changes at Notre Dame. He would have been intimately knowledgeable about the cash contribution football was making to the operational budget every year, which was significant at the time. The rumor on campus was that football profits paid the annual heating and electric bills for the entire University, no small matter in cold and snowy South Bend. In reality, the contribution of cash from football may have been even greater than surmised by outsiders. The University's operating budget in 1966 was approximately $31 million. Football contributed between $3-4 million in unrestricted cash. So having athletics (including football) assigned to the purview of Fr. Joyce made perfect sense.

People remember Father Ned as a tall, impeccably-dressed man, an impression difficult to achieve when your entire wardrobe is of a single color—black. He was soft-spoken, conservative, and had an appetite for detail. Those qualities made him the perfect complement to Fr. Hesburgh, and they were the bookends that held the University upright until they retired together in 1987.

With a fresh attitude and emerging wealth from post-war alumni came increased prosperity at Notre Dame. You can visually see it in the building program, starting with O'Shaughnessy Hall in 1951. The march continued with: Fisher, Pangborn, North Dining Hall, Keenan-Stanford, Stepan Center, Hammes Bookstore, Center for Continuing Education, Lobund Center, the Computing Center, the post office, and numerous renovations scattered around campus. The most ambitious projects were Memorial Library (the largest collegiate library structure in the world at the time) in 1964 and the Athletic and Convocation Center, started in the fall of 1966. This building would eventually be named in honor of Reverend Edmund Joyce.

Generations of freshmen and parents in the late '60s will remember Fr. Joyce as the celebrant of the Mass that welcomed new students during freshman orientation. Fr. Hesburgh had a perennial conflict in mid-September. Enter Fr. Joyce. Of course, Father Ned, as Mister Inside, was frequently seen around campus—and therefore not compared to God, even in jest.

Joe Doyle recalls asking Fr. Joyce at the end of his career if he ever lamented not being a priest (in the traditional sense, caring for a flock). He paused for a moment, and then answered, "Yes, I suppose so. When I got here they turned me into a bean counter." There were lots of beans to count. He may have entered Notre Dame as an accountant, a bean counter if you will, but he became so much more. His flock was Notre Dame Athletics.

Edward W. "Moose" Krause

Moose Krause made fast friends with virtually everyone he met. The process was further accelerated if you provided him with a fresh cigar (he liked good ones). This is how everyone pictures Moose today, with his friendly arm over somebody's shoulder and puffing on a cigar. He was the ideal person to execute the athletic plan for the strategists Fathers Hesburgh and Joyce. Essentially he was the brand manager for football.

As anyone who works in the business of athletics will attest, it is a small community based on relationships and trust. Moose Krause understood that and was the designated ambassador of good will. He knew athletics because he was an athlete himself. Ed Krause arrived at Notre Dame from Chicago in 1930 as a freshman to play football for Knute Rockne. Physically, he was the largest person ever to suit-up in a Rockne locker room. After Rockne's accidental death, he stayed to letter in three varsity sports: football, basketball, and track. His most notable accomplishments actually transpired on the basketball court. He is often identified by name as one of the players who forced college basketball to adopt a radical rule change in 1938. Before the change, following each basket or foul shot, there was a jump ball at center court. This slowed the game down and gave an unfair advantage to a team with at least one very tall player. Moose was the poster boy for changing in the rule.

His successor as athletic director, Dick Rosenthal, tells this story:

Moose once won a key basketball game against Butler in the last second of play after being knocked to the floor. The ball bounced into his hands and, while lying flat on his back, he lobbed up the winning basket. As legend has it, the next morning the team left the hotel and boarded a bus for South Bend. While standing near the door of the bus selling his newspapers, a young paperboy shouted "Morning Star." Moose replied "Morning, son."

Moose Krause was inducted into the Basketball Hall of Fame in 1976.

In 1966 football game programs, Moose is credited with being an All-American in both football and basketball. When the College Football Hall of Fame was eager to induct Krause, his friend Joe Doyle was put on the case to establish the "bona fides." A person must have been an All-American to be a Hall of Famer. Try as he could, Joe couldn't find evidence, however remote, that Moose had been so honored. (This same rule applies to Joe Montana who sailed into the Professional Football Hall of Fame, but can never enter the College Hall under current rules).

After short coaching stints at St. Mary's College in Minnesota and Holy Cross in Massachusetts, Ed Krause returned home to Notre Dame in 1942. He became head basketball coach for a time, was assistant athletic director to Leahy in 1948 and became the athletic director in 1949. He was made for the job and the job was made for him.

Of the many roles an assistant director assumes at Notre Dame, two don't usually get written on the job description. The head of athletics has to be the shock absorber for many of the public shots taken at how the University is doing both on and off the field. Some of it is friendly fire. Moose had the personality and the knack to diffuse criticism. Even the most hostile critic couldn't dislike the guy. The second role is that of confessor and motivator to the key coaches. At Notre Dame, that meant football—first, second and third. Ara Parseghian had a particularly close working relationship with Krause, something he readily acknowledges.

Head Coach Ara Parseghian and Athletic Director Moose Krause, at a press conference circa 1965, held at Johnny Lattner's (Notre Dame's Heisman Trophy Winner, 1953) Steakhouse, located at the corner of Madison and Clark in Chicago.

After Notre Dame started going to bowl games again (there had been a hiatus since 1925) in 1969, the Cotton Bowl became a frequent stop for Irish teams. It was during this period in the '70s that Moose started wearing the cowboy hat that many associate with his persona. It fit perfectly. Everything about the guy was Texas-sized.

Moose was well-known and respected throughout the nation in all quarters of the university community, which Rosenthal reflected in his letter to alumni at the time of his friend's passing. Rosenthal wrote, "His unfailing goodness was, indeed, the principal reason for his greatness. He was incapable of malice and never turned away from someone in need. His love affair with his wife and family was the manifestation of a man whose capacity to love was boundless." People who knew him well are quick to mention the dedication he displayed for his wife Elizabeth when she was confined to a nursing home for many years. He was the father of three children: Edward (a Holy Cross priest), Mary, and Phillip.

In December 1992, the open casket containing the body of Edward "Moose" Krause was laid in state inside the Basilica of the Sacred Heart, the main church on the Notre Dame campus. In it were placed two Krause trademarks: his cowboy hat and a cigar. Notre Dame football legend George Connor (tackle, 1946–47, College Football Hall of Fame) noticed the brand of the cigar wasn't up to Moose's usual high standards, so he walked over to the Morris Inn in the cold darkness, purchased the best cigar he could buy, and returned to make the substitution without fanfare. It was a tender gesture from one big Notre Dame man to another.

4

PURGATORY

T he two-year odyssey toward Notre Dame's undisputed 1966 National Championship football season began and ended in the very same (unlikely) spot—the Los Angeles Coliseum. Think of the games against the University of Southern California in 1964 and in 1966 as the historical bookends that define the story of a return to football prominence at Notre Dame.

1964

Parseghian arrived and improved everything about the Notre Dame football program in short order. He discovered that there was an abundance of athletic talent already on the squad—perhaps somewhat to his surprise. The team was loaded with great former high school athletes, most from Catholic schools, guys who always dreamed of playing at Notre Dame.

Recruiting for Notre Dame under his predecessors Kuharich and Devore had been on the fly. Fortunately there was a loyal cadre of "Leahy's Lads" and "Subway Alumni" who acted as bird dogs searching for talent in their home communities. The identity of the incumbent head coach in South Bend wasn't the deciding factor for most of these recruits when they committed to Notre Dame. Somewhere in their lives was an influential person who carried the Notre Dame torch—a parent, a relative, a coach, or a teacher (many of those religious priests, nuns, and brothers).

These young men were disappointed and frustrated when they arrived on campus and found that the football program at Notre Dame wasn't much better organized than the ones at their respective high schools. Truthfully, some of their high school coaches might have done a better job. More alarming was the realization that the equipment used at most high schools was at least as good and often much better than that used at what was thought to be the premier football college program in the nation.

The story is told of Joe Smyth arriving as a freshman in 1963 and being assigned equipment for practice—but his helmet was old and ill fitting. During pass-rushing drills working with "the sled," his helmet kept flopping off. The coach in charge yelled across the line, "Smyth, get your helmet into it." Smyth replied, "Coach when this helmet was new they hadn't even invented the forward pass."

But the talent, enough talent, was already residing in the Notre Dame, Indiana zip code 46556 (the University has its own post office that actually predates the incorporation of South Bend), when Ara moved into his office.

Parseghian immediately raised the standards and the expectations. If there was any complaining about that among the team, it was short lived and forgotten long ago. To the contrary, to a man the team was embarrassed by its records under Kuharich and Devore, who went without a winning season from 1959–63, known at Notre Dame as the Period of Penance. The 1963 campaign was especially dismal at 2–7 (the tenth game at Iowa was cancelled due to the Kennedy assassination, which effectively avoided an eighth defeat).

Individually, many of the players didn't believe they had been given a fair shot at playing on Saturdays. Those that did play didn't think they had been given the tools to develop their talents and compete effectively. The coaching seemed inept, because it was. Frustration permeated the program at the end of 1963. That all ended after Ara's first team meeting.

The new coaching staff had to start over, from the beginning, taking what today in business would be termed a zero-based approach. It was winter and there would be no practice sessions to evaluate the personnel for a few months, so films were used. But many of the players, including some seniors and possible fifth-year candidates, had scant little film footage to evaluate. Spring practice in 1964 became "tryouts," the first real look the coaches had of their team and the first experience the team was to have with the new coaching philosophy put into action.

Ara and his staff believed that some players were miscast for their designated positions and would better fit into their new scheme at a new spot. One important historical footnote assisted the coaches toward convincing players that this approach was in the team's best interest, as well as their own. A permanent rule change was made starting in 1964 so that two platoons (offense and defense) were allowed and the rules around substitutions were relaxed. Single platoon football thus became a permanent thing of the past. The rules are much the same today, so this development is hardly ever mentioned as a factor. At the time it was big.

Playing both ways tended to create situations where a player's weakness was used to offset his strengths in the process of team selection. More open positions, an effective doubling of positions, also meant that more guys would ultimately be able to play in games. The new rules were win-win, and they effectively changed the game of college football forever, as so many rule changes do.

The looming question going into the 1964 season was, Where would the Irish find a quarterback to guide their offense? Stuck on Devore's third team was a quarterback from California who threw semi-side arm style but had a quick release. He was accurate and had very good arm strength. Just as importantly, he had footwork and mobility and . . . he was extraordinarily coachable. Thus John Huarte was promoted to the first team and the rest, as they say, is football history. John picked up the Heisman Trophy in 1964, before he was formally awarded his first varsity monogram "ND" as a senior.

Huarte's primary target became All-American Jack Snow, who finished fifth in Heisman balloting. With the encouragement of the coaching staff, Snow shed some weight and converted from back-up fullback to starting end. The holdover "Elephant Backfield" comprised of Paul Costa (240 pounds), Jim Snowdon (250 pounds), and Pete Duranko (235 pounds) was disbanded and each man was converted to play the line. Costa, Snowdon, and Duranko went on to distinguished college and pro careers thanks to the moves.

According to Huarte, "Ara was very smart in how he handled the players. In my case, he told me just to go out there and play and if I made mistakes they were going to stick with me. He also was very good at using players in the scope of their skill levels. He just was outstanding in developing his offensive scheme to maximize the personnel."

37

The pre-season expectation was "six-and-four in '64." That would indicate a major positive turn in the direction of Notre Dame Football. Much to the surprise of just about everyone following college football in 1964, Notre Dame rolled through its first nine games with only one close encounter. The season began in a driving rain in Madison, Wisconsin, with a 31–7 win over the Badgers on a sloppy field. After that convincing win, the Irish moved into the national rankings for the first time in a very long time, at number nine.

This was followed by a succession of wins and improved national rankings: Purdue 34–15 (number six), Air Force 34–7 (number four), UCLA 24–0 (number two). That's where things stayed through two more wins: Stanford 28–6 and against Navy, with a returning Roger Staubach, the 1963 Heisman Trophy winner, 40–0. This game began the unbeaten run Notre Dame had against the Midshipmen that endured until 2007. When ND escaped with a win over Pittsburgh, 17–15, they moved into the number one ranking for the first time in a decade. There they stayed through successive winning encounters with Michigan State 28–0 and Iowa 28–0.

The final game in 1964 was against traditional rival Southern California at the Coliseum in Los Angeles. Notre Dame went out to a 17–0 halftime lead. In the fourth quarter, a phantom holding call against Bob Meeker on the one-yard line negated an Irish touchdown by Joe Kantor. If the score had counted, the Notre Dame lead would have been 24–13, considered by most observers of the game to be insurmountable.

It wasn't the only questionable call in the contest. Partisan officiating had been considered the norm on recent trips to Los Angeles. There was an invisible fourth-quarter holding call against the Irish on a punt play that resulted in an improved USC field position of thirty-nine yards after the penalty and the repeat kick. Then there was a defensive play that would have backed the Trojans up on an obvious quarterback sack. It was called an incomplete pass because a feeble effort was made to push the ball forward to the ground by Trojan quarterback Craig Fertig. The officiating crew was entirely from the Western Conference. The surviving video is illuminating and seriously calls into question either the officials' competence or their bias—or both. Take your pick.

LIFE Magazine correspondent Joe Bride, an alum who worked for Charlie Callahan in the Notre Dame sports information office as a student, offers this first-hand account:

LIFE wanted to do something special for the game. We convinced Ara that he should let us have special access. On the team bus, in the locker room, close to everyone on the sideline. After a lot of thought he agreed.

We had buttons made. "We like Ara." They were take-offs of the 1952 presidential campaign buttons of Dwight Eisenhower, "We Like Ike." We gave the buttons to priests to wear and to the families of John Huarte and Jack Snow, and took pictures. It was raucous and successful.

Notre Dame owned the first half and the third quarter. Then we scored a touchdown to give us a 24–13 lead, but it was called back by a questionable holding call that no one ever saw when it happened or later on film. Unfortunately there was a history of questionable calls at the Coliseum that benefitted the home team. This was one. SC drove down the field. In the closing seconds Craig Fertig threw a pass to Rod Sherman. SC won 20–17. National Championship gone.

I've still got a picture of me kneeling just beyond the end zone taken from about the twenty-yard line. I look helpless as Sherman catches the pass. I was still in that end zone ten minutes later when Reverend Glen Boarman came up me and said, "Well Joe I knew that you finally had grown up when that touchdown pass was caught. You didn't run on the field and tackle Sherman." Father Boarman was a highly-visible and likeable priest during my time at Notre Dame.

LIFE had a great story. We had Ara telling the team at the half, "Only thirty minutes to go." Quotes and comments that no one else had. We had lots of pictures, particularly of the players, Ara, and the Snow and Huarte families both in joy and sadness. It was a good story. We packaged up the pictures and sent big albums to Ara and the Huarte and Snow Families.

Ara did keep his sense of humor. "We dominated the game for more than three quarters. I like to think our record in 1964 is 9 and 3/4 and 1/4." He didn't have a lot of humor when he talked to me at the hotel after the game. "Bride, that's the last time any blankety-blank reporter and photographer get any special consideration from me. Got it. The last time."

But he didn't hold a grudge. Fifteen months later on a cold and snowy February evening, when I was waiting in Baltimore for Catsy (my wife) and our one-year-old son Cres to emerge from a flight from Louisville, Ara was first off the plane with a big grin on his face. He was carrying Cres.

I saw John Huarte about fifteen years later at a Heisman Trophy reunion at the College Football Hall of Fame. I asked him how his parents were. He said his mother had just passed away after a long illness. After I told him how sorry I was, he said, "You know she kept that album of photos you sent us with her all the time as she got sicker. Thank you. You did something I couldn't. You made that day a winner for her."

The 1964 season is memorable and significant for many reasons. The new coach turned things around quickly and Notre Dame became part of the college football conversation for the first time in years. For this, Ara was recognized by his peers as Coach of the Year, the only time in his career he was so honored. It was well deserved.

The gridiron statistics were mind boggling—twenty-seven team records were broken and another two tied. Notre Dame finished ranked number four, behind Alabama, Arkansas, and Texas. The final rankings were set prior to bowl games at the time. The 10–0–0 Crimson Tide lost to Texas in the Orange Bowl—but Alabama is still in the record books as National Champions. Arkansas beat Nebraska in the Cotton Bowl. Only the National Football Foundation had the courage to name Notre Dame their National Champions with the MacArthur Bowl, taking into account the questionable officiating in California and the fact that the Irish came within 1:33 of retaining their number one ranking. But this is relegated to a footnote today. Notre Dame has never attempted to claim a national title in 1964 among its publicized official list.

That final game in Los Angeles left an indelible mark on everyone associated with Notre Dame at the time—players, coaches, Administration, students, and alumni. In his 2009 book, author Jim Dent uses the title *Resurrection* to capitulate the 1964 season. The book is misnamed. For those familiar with Catholic teaching, the 1964 season's ending made it closer to being cast into Purgatory, with the expectation of salvation, a National Championship, being delayed. That's the background that made the 1966 season so important at Notre Dame. In 1964 the figurative table at the University was significantly stronger, but it was still wobbling slightly.

Religious Counseling

After the 1964 loss at Southern Cal, Fr. Theodore Hesburgh was prompted to write an essay that was published in the student magazine, *Scholastic*. Commenting on a football game is practically unprecedented for a college president, but the erudite priest knew it was appropriate in this case and used it as a teachable moment. It was a thoughtful treatise on the similarities between sports and life, and then between sports and everlasting life. It is something that could only have been written at a place like Notre Dame in 1964. The first paragraph is as follows:

> *It's dark and cold outside. I'm too old to cry and not old enough not to feel hurt . . . We can never be sure of total victory, not even of eternal salvation, until we've won it. Life goes on, the challenge remains and it will be a really dark day and cold place here if we ever lose the desire to be No. 1 in everything we do, or lack grace and style and humanity in doing it.*

In 2010, Father Ted was asked if he thought that Notre Dame was ever unfairly treated on the football field or in the press because of religious prejudice. He paused for a few moments before answering carefully, "As a priest, I'd like to believe that didn't happen." After another significant pause, he felt the need to complete his answer. "But I do think that it was easy to be jealous of our success—and that may have been a factor."

Wheeling

The top of West Virginia, the panhandle, is squeezed between the jaws of a vise by Pennsylvania to the east and Ohio to the west. Both states have massive college football egos. The home-state West Virginia University Mountaineers are way-far south, or so it seems, because the route to Morgantown is circuitous, over hills and through hollows. Both Pittsburgh and Columbus are closer. So in the northern tip of the state, Wheeling maintains some independence when it comes to college football loyalties, one way to maintain its distinct identity.

Distinct it is. In the heart of coal and steel country, there isn't a steel mill or strip mine to be found within city limits. Wheeling exists because of commerce. It sat at the western edge of the National Road and was the hub for early pioneers connecting with the Ohio River that would speed their trips west. Fortunes were made there. More recently, with the legendary call letters WWVA and weekly live shows, the radio show Jamboree was second only to the Grand Ol' Opry and Nashville as a country western music Mecca from the 1920s forward. In this once-bustling river town there are a significant number of disciples of Notre Dame Football, and for them public devotions haven't been forced underground.

So it wasn't at all surprising that Ara Parseghian would be invited to speak to a Wheeling audience early in 1965, or that he'd be warmly received. In fact, the reception was so remarkable that it was vividly recorded in *Notre Dame from Rockne to Parseghian*, the Francis Wallace chronicle that was the eminent Notre Dame must read when it was published just after the 1965 season. Looking back, the author may have regretted not holding out for another year.

The Wheeling airport is located north of town. The landing area is a flattened mountaintop. The terminal is an architectural gem, an art deco Works Progress Administration project constructed for regular airline service that never came. Ara arrived at the Wheeling airport late in the afternoon on a private plane. He was surprised at the welcome. A police escort was assigned to whisk him right into town and to the Elks' lodge. Ara was the keynote speaker for a Multiple Sclerosis fund-raiser, his speaking fee paid by a local grocer, Foodland. The local Notre Dame Club was part of the planning for the event. There was a cocktail reception before the dinner and pictures to be posed for and autographs to be signed after the event. The whole affair was over before nine p.m.

The perennial question for Wheeling always has been, what do you do after nine p.m., celebrity or no celebrity? A local couple, Pat and Harry Buch, spontaneously offered their home to Notre Dame insiders for a post-event reception and cup of coffee. Ara accepted the invitation to join this small gathering. Where else was he going to go on a weeknight in Wheeling? The Buchs lived at 32 Edgelawn Avenue in a modest three-bedroom home. The word got out that Ara was coming over and eventually over one hundred people were stuffed into the crowded first floor. The coffee percolator was tested to its limits. There was only a single bathroom, upstairs next to the bedrooms where the Buch's infant son Joe and daughter Mary Beth slept soundly throughout the party.

Ara was called upon to say a few words to the adoring Notre Dame crowd. Harry distinctly remembers what followed. Standing in front of the smallish fireplace, shirtsleeves rolled up and necktie loosened, Ara started a stream-of-conscious narrative that drew everyone into his inner thoughts about the 1964 season, the Southern Cal game, the officiating, and where the Irish were headed. This lasted a full thirty minutes, and when he was finished there was no need for Q and A. Ara departed for Oglebay Lodge for a night's sleep and was gone early the next morning, off to another speaking date in Flint, Michigan.

When the evening was over, Harry Buch says he knew two things for certain. First, he had to buy a bigger house. Second, as soon as he could afford to do so, he had to buy Notre Dame season tickets. (Eventually, he did both.)

What happened that night in Wheeling may not have been totally unique. But to those in attendance, the message was clear. In the mind of Coach Ara Parseghian, the National Championship was no longer an idea, no longer a possibility, no longer a goal. It had become an obsession.

5

SUCCESS BREEDS
SUCCESS

The impact of the surprising near-National Championship year of 1964 was immeasurable both to the University and to the football program. Without it, the present-day character and fortunes of Notre Dame would be hard to imagine. They would be significantly diminished from what has emerged, and what is now largely taken for granted.

The yoke of de-emphasizing football was finally removed from the backs of Father Ted and Father Ned. After 1964, it was never seriously referenced again. The collective psyches of the Notre Dame community were repaired, from the faculty and staff to the lowliest janitor. Even the "academic-types" were on board. Pride in the football team was once again in fashion. The brand was back. The immediate tangible evidence was a spike in sales for licensed Notre Dame merchandise through the Hammes Bookstore, one of the first college bookstores to have its own mail-order catalog.

Perhaps the most important leap in stature came in the improved applicant pool for freshman admissions. Notre Dame had long been perceived as the best-known Catholic college in America, but other quality schools (especially those in attractive urban settings) were rapidly gaining ground as viable alternative choices for smart Catholic guys during the Period of Penance. The 1964 football season reversed the trend and stretched that gap anew. If a smart fellow from anywhere in America wanted to attend a Catholic college, Notre Dame was once again at the head of his list.

This factor had a long-lasting positive effect on the University. The overall quality of admitted students, always quite good, got even better. With the baby boom bulge and the addition of co-education in 1973, the applicant pool more than doubled in size while the number of positions stayed practically fixed. The effect was that almost overnight, the average SAT scores jumped to a level shared by the self-conscious "academic" schools. This has been sustained ever since. Co-education alone didn't make Notre Dame improve rapidly. It was the combination of high demand along with co-education that catapulted the rankings. The haughty academic elites on the Notre Dame campus were proven wrong. Notre Dame didn't have to endure a sub-standard football program like an Ivy League college to compete for top students. It wasn't an either-or equation that pit academics against athletics. Credit the 1964 Notre Dame Football Team for turning the tide.

Restocking

The increased visibility of Notre Dame Football also had a significant role in improving the long-term prospects of the team. In 1964, if you were a star football player at a Catholic high school, Notre Dame was, once again, automatically part of the conversation. Very few Catholic colleges even had football as a varsity sport. Maintaining a football program was expensive, and they almost always lost money. Some colleges that did have programs were financially stressed and eventually disbanded serious football or relegated the sport to club status (Xavier, Georgetown, Fordham). Others elected to ratchet-back to lower NCAA divisions, with fewer scholarships (Holy Cross, Villanova). Boston College prevailed, just barely, and today is the only other Division I football program among Catholic colleges.

Under Ara, recruiting became much more disciplined. Each assistant coach was assigned a geographic region to cover. Using available information, they started to seek out players, especially ones who could fill some of the known position voids. A network of Notre Dame die-hards and former players was enlisted to identify and encourage candidates. It was all perfectly legal at the time. The source of most of the talent continued to be Catholic high schools, largely in the Midwest, but not exclusively. The goal was to get a prime candidate to campus, especially on a football Saturday. The assistant coaches developed the prospect list. Ara Parseghian was the designated as the closer. He rarely missed his target when he wanted a boy to come to Notre Dame.

Parseghian described his recruiting this way in 1965: "We view over 1,000 high school films each year in order to end up with a working list of about seventy boys, which usually dwindles down to thiry–thirty-five youngsters who are vitally interested in Notre Dame and who are academically acceptable."

It is a little-mentioned fact that Ara did not travel to recruit players in their home communities, in their kitchens, so to speak. It only happened once in the entire tenure of the coach (to substitute for an assistant who was called away), and while that player did attend Notre Dame, he transferred after his freshman year. Campus visits were the thing. The combination of the picturesque campus in the fall, the academic opportunities, the invisible spirit that winning football games provided and the handsome and charismatic head coach made Notre Dame irresistible for good players. That and the fact that in the 1960s, the only viable alternatives for playing serious football were the larger and often impersonal state universities. Yes, the other schools also had the attraction of being co-ed. But Notre Dame students and student athletes alike tended to know what they were getting into under the Golden Dome. This included its all-male culture, and therefore, they fit in almost immediately when they arrived on campus.

The Final Scholarship

There is some controversy about who was the last player to earn a scholarship in 1965 and become a part of the wave of sophomore talent needed to compete in 1966. The stories of the final contenders are illuminating and capture a more innocent time in college athletics.

Bob Kuechenberg came from a football town and a football family. Hobart High School in Indiana is located in the shadow of Gary and is, in Bob's words, "a powerhouse little town with a great football tradition." From anyone else, a deep love for one's high school football heritage would read as an attempt to over-glamorize one's youth. But Kuechenberg has been to the football summits: he was in on National Championship team at Notre Dame under Ara Parseghian, and then was a key player in the only undefeated season (17–0) in professional football playing for the Miami Dolphins and Coach Don Shula in 1972. He rates his experiences playing with the Hobart High Brickies as equal to any he's ever had over many seasons of football. Who's to argue with him?

Bob's brother Rudy was four grades ahead of him and was playing as a senior at Indiana University when "Kooch" was finishing high school. Rudy, who was only 195 pounds as a college senior, started as defensive end and tight end when guys went both ways. He was a great player on a bad team, but as such he got invited to play in the North-South All-Star Game in Miami at the Orange Bowl.

Rudy had the game of his life. He literally knocked-out Roger Staubach, the junior Heisman Trophy winner. With less than two minutes to play, he intercepted a pass and ran it back for a touchdown, dragging three players into the end zone. That was the winning score. For heroics like this he was named the Most Valuable Player for the game. To receive the MVP trophy in the press box, he had to take an elevator up from the locker-room level. The elevator stopped at an intermediate floor and Ara Parseghian walked on. Rudy recognized the Notre Dame head coach immediately.

Talk about the classic elevator pitch. Rudy says, "Coach, I know you probably don't have any scholarships left. But I have a kid brother who lives about an hour from Notre Dame. He's not big and he's not fast. But he's all heart. His name is Bob, same last name as me."

Later that month, Bob received a letter inviting him to visit Notre Dame. He went and then sealed the deal his brother Rudy had pitched in an elevator. Big brother went on to play for the Chicago Bears.

Another person with a possible claim to the last spot is Frank Criniti from Charleston, West Virginia. He was never really on Notre Dame's radar screen through the recruiting process, but he hoped to use his football success as a ticket to an affordable college education. To Frank and his Italian-American family, dreaming about Notre Dame remained just that, a dream. His Charleston Catholic High School buddy Tim Monty was getting a serious look from many name colleges, including the Irish. But not Frank. In the minds of many, Frank was a bit undersized to play in a big-time football program. But you had to be impressed with his determination. As one of his teammates later commented, "That little bastard could hit."

A funny thing can happen when film is viewed by a college coaching staff. Another player, one other than the primary recruit, sometimes catches someone's attention. So it was with Frank. On Letter of Intent Day, Notre Dame unexpectedly had one open slot. The coaches remembered Criniti from the films, and so he got his invitation to Notre Dame that day, over the phone. The Charleston Catholic boys, Monty and Criniti, both got scholarships.

Curt Heneghan provides an incredible story of his own. He wasn't able to play his junior year at Lake Washington High School in Kirkland, Washington. But he had a pretty fair senior season as a wide receiver. At one point, his high school coach asked if he ever considered going to Notre Dame. Curt's father had attended Notre Dame, so it was a place well known to the family. But after that initial conversation, Curt heard nothing more about the school and forgot all about it. In August his bags were packed and he was just two days from enrolling at Washington State University when the phone rang. The message was short, and oh so sweet. "We've had a scholarship open up unexpectedly at Notre Dame. It's yours if you can be here in two days." It was an easy decision. To this day, Curt doesn't really know what went on behind the scenes. He never even filled out an admissions application to Notre Dame.

The complete list of the forty-nine freshman team players in 1965, by position (offense and defense are combined as the tradition was), reads as follows:

Ends (seven): Curt Heneghan, Tom Reynolds, Jim Seymour, Bill Skoglund, Brian Stenger, Jim Winegardner, Bob Zubek

Tackles (six): Gordon Beeker, George Kunz, Mike Malone, Eric Norri, Pat Scharage, Ed Tuck

Guards (seven): Ron Bell, Ray Fischer, Roger Fox, Joe Freebery, John Jordan, Bob Kuechenberg, Tom McKinley

Centers (five): Mike Bars, Richard Harwitz, John Lavin, Jim Leary, Tim Monty

Quarterbacks (defensive backs) (nine): Bob Belden, Mike Brands, Mike Franger, Terry Hanratty, Thomas Lux, Bill Mahoney, Coley O'Brien, Dan O'Connor, Joe Sheeketski

Halfbacks (defensive backs) (twelve): Frank Crinti, Frank Czarnecki, Ron Dushney, Bob Gladieux, Mike Holtzapfel, Chuck Landolfi, Den Liss, Tom Quinn, Tom Slettvet, Paul Snow, Joe Walker, Dave Yonto

Fullbacks (linebackers) (three): Bill Bartholomew, Chick Lauck, Ed Vuillemin

In the end, who was awarded the last scholarship among the 1966 sophomores became a moot point. One player from the list above was still to earn that final scholarship on the practice field.

The Walk-On

Coach Bob Smith of Portage High School (just outside Gary, Indiana) had been nurturing families through football for a dozen years, so when he needed support, there was an overwhelming outpouring of sympathy, and scores of his former players stepped up. The coach's young son Jeff was being laid to rest after suffering a heart attack following his first day at junior high. This was the kid who had hung around practices and on the sidelines practically since he was in diapers. This was the kid that many of the guys had befriended and took under their wings, sort of as a little brother. They couldn't believe this had happened. The pallbearers represented various years of Coach Smith's teams. The youngest was Tom Reynolds, having just graduated from high school that June.

At the reception following the funeral, the guys were sitting around their coach's back yard pounding down beers, getting reacquainted, and telling stories about their antics on the football field. Then someone asked Tom what he was planning to do. The young man had been a two-sport star in high school. He related his decision to attend Valparaiso University to play basketball for Coach Gene Bartow, along with a little Division III football. Then he mentioned, offhandedly, that he'd also been accepted at Notre Dame.

That's when it happened. Between slugs of beer the older guys weighed in. They all agreed; there weren't many of their teammates who had the smarts to get accepted at Notre Dame. So it was determined that that was where he should go. Absolutely. Positively. No doubt. They changed Tom's mind right then and there. He should go to Notre Dame as a tribute to the coach. There was only one problem: Tom's father hated Notre Dame—he hated Notre Dame with a passion.

Two weeks later, Tom was at freshman orientation at Notre Dame. It is only about an hour's drive from Portage to South Bend, so his departure bordered on being almost routine at home. But this hard-nosed 172-pound kid from the land of belching smokestacks had something to prove, and he wasn't about to be deterred. He still wanted to play some more football to honor his coach and he wasn't thinking intramurals.

Every day for three weeks he went to the equipment manager, the crusty (John) Mac McAllister, before the Notre Dame team practiced and pleaded for a uniform. McAllister was a holdover from the Rockne Era (literally) and was legendary for calling all the players piss ants. Part of the lore of Notre Dame Football was that anyone could try out and they could stay until they were cut, or cut themselves. In reality it didn't work quite that way. First you had to be issued equipment. For that to happen under Ara, one of the coaches had to endorse a player's participation as a matter of safety. Persistence paid off. Tom eventually was issued his practice uniform. In so doing, he became the piss ant of the moment. Then he had to make it on the field against the thirty scholarship players on the Freshman Team and about a dozen other walk-ons who had been equally persistent, convincing, or delusional.

Every day Tom dutifully went to practice and got smacked around as defensive back as the freshmen prepared the varsity for their next game. These guys were older, wiser, and bigger. Tom tried to "dish it out as good as [he] got," head to head. When provoked he could be meaner than a mother fire ant. That got him noticed.

Like all his freshmen teammates, Tom spent Saturdays watching the real games from the student section of Notre Dame Stadium. Freshman football action was limited to the practice field in 1965 because there were no freshman games. The frosh were going against the talented remainder of the team that came just 1:33 short of winning the National Championship in 1964, and would finish 1965 ranked eighth by UPI.

49

Before the final home game of the season against Michigan State, Tom remembers meeting his father and Coach Smith at the pep rally in the old Fieldhouse. That single event turned his father's attitude around for good. He became a Notre Dame fan on the spot. It was Coach Bob Smith who drove John Reynolds over from his trucking business in Portage on a Friday night to surprise Tom and to see the game on Saturday. This done because Coach Smith knew there was unfinished emotional work to be done and he just never gave up on nurturing his boys and their families through football.

A football scholarship unexpectedly became available at the end of the 1965–66 school year. Over the winter, Tom's dad, John Reynolds died suddenly in a private airplane accident. He did not live long enough to see his son Tom earn that final scholarship to play football for the 1966 Fighting Irish, but he would have understood it was a big deal, as Coach Smith did. Father and son, Coach Bob Smith had changed both of their lives forever. That's what great coaches do.

6

TRENCH WARFARE

The 1965 Notre Dame Football season is often described today as transitional. The implication is that in historical perspective, the Irish were in motion, coming from somewhere and going to somewhere. We know the context. It was from a near-National Championship in 1964, after a decade of near obscurity, to an undisputed National Championship in 1966. From heartbreak at the Los Angeles Coliseum to elation at the Los Angeles Coliseum.

But football seasons are comprised of a series of consecutive days, including conditioning, meetings, practices, scrimmages, and games. For the players and coaches in 1965, they never had the luxury of knowing they were in transition, moving forward. It was a struggle every single day.

Because of the drama of 1964 and of 1966, the quality of the 1965 Notre Dame Football team is often overlooked. It was a great team, the bridge between two remarkable teams. It started out as the pre-season number-one team, a ranking it held for exactly one game. Through the course of the season the team climbed back from number nine to number four. It ultimately finished ranked number eight. By any measure, then or now, this was pretty darned good. But at Notre Dame, the 1965 season isn't remembered with the clarity or the fondness of either '64 or '66 because it has been awkwardly stuck between exceptional and extraordinary.

A Change in Plans

If Ara Parseghian and his coaches had known at the time what we know today, they may have enjoyed more family time and slept better 1965. The reality was that their jobs became much harder as they walked off the turf in Los Angeles in 1964. For one, the expectations were now higher across the board among the Notre Dame Family. Six and four wouldn't be considered progress ever again in South Bend. There would be no sneaking up on opponents who may have underestimated the Irish in 1964.

For another, they were graduating a surprisingly good group of seniors that played over their heads, especially on offense. It isn't trivial to replace a Heisman Trophy quarterback and an All-American receiver who finished fifth in the same balloting. That, in a nutshell became the most daunting challenge. The freshmen who were moving up to eligibility were talented, more talented than could have been expected in a cobbled-together recruiting effort in early 1964. But barring surprises, à la Huarte and Snow, the available talent wouldn't fill the gaping holes on offense. That was pretty well acknowledged, at least privately among the coaching staff, as the calendar year turned into 1965.

The emphasis in early 1965 was to restock the talent woodpile. It was an extraordinarily successful effort, one that should have given the coaches courage as they prepared the team for the 1965 campaign. But this potential bonanza was a year away from maturation and eligibility. With the considerable talent still remaining, the strategy for winning had to be more specifically targeted. The defense, largely intact, would have to be even stingier with yardage and touchdowns, and it would have to constantly wrestle for every inch of field position. The offense would have to be run oriented with an untried quarterback. But the credentials of running backs Bill Wolski, Nick Eddy, and Larry Conjar were well established, along with the credentials of a promising sophomore, Bob Bleier (the name Rocky would be applied later in his career at Notre Dame). Defensive and offensive line play would be the critical battleground for success. It would be trench warfare. That was the focus of spring practice in 1965.

Writing for the *Scholastic* after the 1965 season, student Tom Bettag would reflect, "Perhaps the single most important factor in the season was the graduation of John Huarte and Jack Snow in June. But how could anyone know that at the beginning of the season? Ara had bemoaned his troubles at the "skilled positions." But who could have known after the varsity beat the Old-Timers 72–0?"

Enthusiasm Runneth Over

In September the season started with sky-high expectations. Even if the coaches had concerns, the students and the pollsters were blindly enthusiastic. The Irish were good enough to almost win the National Championship in 1964, and with better officiating or a time-clock faster by 1:33 in Los Angeles, they would have. So Notre Dame was installed as pre-season favorites. Undoubtedly, this decision to feature the Irish on magazine covers across the nation was also good for circulation. Like 'em or hate 'em, Notre Dame Football is always good copy.

Going into the new season, the students were pumped. In fact, the enthusiasm had "runneth over." An unfortunate and ill-advised tradition was renewed prior to the first game, an away contest at the University of California at Berkley. A banner, more accurately a bed sheet attached with a rope, was hung from the venerated Golden Dome at the feet of Our Lady (Notre Dame)—reading "kill cal." This didn't happen very often and in the minds of most it shouldn't ever happen. Reaching that height to hang a banner takes some serious lock-picking and the climbing of a tightly-enclosed set of rickety stairs sandwiched between the exterior dome structure and the plaster ceiling visible underneath from the rotunda of the Administration Building. It would be the first indication that spirit at Notre Dame had perhaps gone too far and degenerated into thoughtlessness.

The insensitivity to religious symbolism aside, the possible damage to the expensive eighteen-karat gold leaf on the Dome was unconscionable. But there the banner was, and although it didn't stay in place very long, the photographs have survived as evidence. If someone reading this is swelling with pride, please keep it to yourself.

Tame by comparison but just as interesting is a photo appearing in the *South Bend Tribune*. This one was taken at the South Bend airport

Before the first game against Cal in 1965 students hung a banner on the Golden Dome. It didn't last long. But it did capture the excessive student enthusiasm that erupted after a near-National Championship in 1964. *Source:* University of   Notre Dame Archives

as the players were climbing the portable stairs, boarding the plane for the season opener at California. For historical perspective, in 1965 this American Airlines charter was a four-prop job—not a jet. In the photo, a twenty-foot banner is being held by Coach Parseghian and local civic officials: "GOOD LUCK IRISH, SOUTH BEND MISHAWAKA CHAMBER OF COMMERCE." South Bend realized where its bread was buttered after the Studebaker automobile plant closing in 1963.

Game One – vs. University of California

Away, September 18, Won 48–6

Dick Hackenberg, *Chicago Sun-Times*:

> *Notre Dame's Fighting Irish carried with pride and considerable distinc-*
> *tion the glory of their 9–1, 1964 resurgence to an amazing 48–6 triumph*
> *over the University of California here Saturday.*
>> *"Carried" is the word. A crowd of 53,000 shirtsleeved fans, basking*
> *in the brilliant sunshine, watched aghast as Ara Parseghian's relent-*
> *less machine ground out 381 yards on the ground and 68 on only seven*
> *passes for an astounding total of 449.*
>> *Nick Eddy alone scampered ninety-nine yards, Bill Wolski seventy-*
> *seven, and Larry Conjar sixty-seven. Each tallied one touchdown and*
> *quarterback Bill Zloch, superbly mixing his plays, scored two. Nick*
> *Rassas streaked sixty-five yards to still another with a punt return and,*
> *in the closing minutes, second-string halfback Dan Harshman got the*
> *seventh. Ken Ivan kicked a twenty-eight-yard field goal and three extra*
> *points.*

The Cal game was a convincing win and it raised the stakes for the next game, at West Lafayette against Purdue. The scoring in the Cal game progressed as follows: Ken Ivan field goal, Bill Zloch three-yard keeper, Larry Conjar one-yard plunge, Nick Rassas sixty-five-yard punt return, Nick Eddy twenty-four-yard pass from Zloch, Bill Wolski six-yard run, Dan Harshman another one-yard plunge. The offensive statistics mirrored the score and were overwhelmingly one-sided.

The defense was led by senior Nick Rassas. The first Notre Dame drive of eighty yards resulted in a field goal. On the next Cal possession Rassas gathered in the first of his two interceptions and ran the ball down to the Golden Bears' twelve-yard line. This led to the first ND touchdown. On the next series Cal was forced to punt. Rassas ran this one back sixty-five yards for a touchdown. He wasn't finished. He had another interception and ran back another punt forty-one yards. Ara was impressed. "I never saw Nick Rassas play any better. He was terrific."

Ara's recorded post-game quotes were uncharacteristically technical and revealing.

We're not that good and they're not that bad. It's difficult to judge your true strength in a game like this. We had good field position all afternoon.

We wanted to establish our inside running strength, because we guessed they'd try to stack a defense against us. When we got them out of that 4–5 lineup, we could open up a little more. But we had all the breaks.

Bill [Zloch] gave us a good performance. He called good plays, ran the team well, and his running helps. We didn't throw much but we didn't plan to. We did open them up with some key passes.

He thought the defense needed work, this on a day when only a single touchdown (with a missed PAT, point after touchdown) was scored, Ara said, "You have to realize though that we don't have much experience on that defensive team. Alan Page is playing on the opposite side this year, Pete Duranko has never played tackle, and Mike Wadsworth and Harry Long are both coming back from knee operations. And of the linebackers, Jim Lynch is the only one with experience." They would come around.

Cal coach Ray Willsey was terse. "They had the ball for eighty-eight offensive plays and after a while that begins to tell on your defense."

One historical note, the game was broadcast regionally by NBC-TV. The announcing team was Lindsey Nelson and former Irish head coach Terry Brennan. This would be the last year that NBC would broadcast regular season college games until 1990, when it signed an exclusive contract with Notre Dame to broadcast all home games.

Game Two – vs. Purdue

Away, September 25, Lost 21–25

Dan Jenkins, "Boilermakers Shatter an Ambitious Dream," *Sports Illustrated*:

Purdue University is the Big Ten's contribution to ethnic jokes. It is a pile of engineering textbooks, asphalt, and dull-red buildings on the plain of West Lafayette, Ind., and through the years its football players have been referred to as Rail Splitters, Pumpkin Shuckers, Cedar Choppers, Blacksmiths, Hayseeds, Cornfield Sailors and—curtain please—Boilermakers. For a moment consider the term Boilermakers, a derisive name Purdue liked and adopted officially. Does a Boilermaker sound like the kind of guy you would want your sister to date? Does he sound like fun? He's got to drive a beat-up '57 Buick, come from a family of 14 in Gary and spend most of his time breathing rivet dust. Yeah, yeah, he'll study for you and maybe he'll become an astronaut—big deal—but he couldn't do the jerk if he loaded up on Dexies, he couldn't find Chez Paul in Chicago with a compass and he'd stumble on a carpet. Naw, man. To have any class you've got to come from a cooled-out school like Michigan or Wisconsin or Northwestern. Purdue? Man, Purdue is like Iowa. After all, how many Boilermakers do you know who can chew gum and walk at the same time?

Well, as of last Saturday, there was at least one. His name is Bob Griese and he may be a farm-type boy from Evansville, and he might have made the terrible social mistake of going to Purdue, but in playing No. 1-ranked Notre Dame he was outlined against the pale blue September sky so dramatically that 61,921 people suffered hysterical seizures, and there was one in a group of frantic, shocked sportswriters who became so deadline-destitute that he labeled Griese the Lone Horseman "riding into the Valley of Death." Griese had that kind of day. He brought out the Apocalypse in you.

Back in 1965 without sports-talk radio, cable TV, and *SportsCenter*, magazines were the media where facts and commentary were woven together by design into clever, often sarcastic fare that would spawn controversy and become the talk around watercoolers and coffee machines at work. As a writer, Jenkins could jab at someone or something with the best of them, especially when there was no incentive to economize on words. In long-form pieces, days were spent writing in advance and much of an article was virtually complete before a sporting event.. Truth could be irrelevant, especially if it was uninteresting. Like him or hate him, Jenkins wasn't going to be ignored. To illuminate the point, contrast his lead above with one from a respected newspaper man, a writer with time pressure to tell a story that would comport with the facts that thousands of fans had witnessed for themselves.

Joe Doyle, *South Bend Tribune*:

Fantastic Bob Griese, throwing the ball as if he invented the forward pass, picked Notre Dame's defenses to pieces and Purdue knocked the never quit Irish out of the nation's top ranking Saturday afternoon.

A record breaking Purdue crowd watched the magnificent battle of Griese's passes against the power-running of the Irish and agreed it had to be an all time classic.

While Jenkins was reveling in his own cleverness, Joe got right to the point. The Notre Dame-Purdue game in 1965 was one heck of a game. In the end, the incredible play by junior quarterback Bob Griese was the difference. He was nineteen of twenty-two passing for 283 yards and three touchdowns. He ran nine times for forty-five yards. He punted three times. He set four Purdue records. Most importantly, he led the Boilermakers back from a late deficit with less than four minutes on the clock.

With heroics like that, what was forgotten was how close a game it really was. The in-state rivalry was played in West Lafayette before the largest crowd ever to watch a football game in Indiana. There were 726 total yards of offense, including thirty-seven plays of over ten yards. The lead changed five times. Notre Dame came back from behind and thought it was going to win after a field goal that literally bounced over the crossbar. Four plays later Purdue scored and prevailed. Still with 3:11 on the clock, the Irish attempted a comeback. Irish quarterback Bill Zloch missed sophomore Dan Harshman on their final offensive play. He was wide open. It was a bitter disappointment for the Irish, and dropped them from number one to number nine in the polls.

There were bright spots. Bill Wolski had 127 yards on thirteen carries. But the weakness in the Irish offense had become exposed. They only attempted nine passes in the entire game. Only one pass was attempted in the first half. Of the remaining eight passes, four were attempted in the final failed drive.

At the time, linebacker Jim Lynch commented, "We played a bad game. We let them win by our mistakes." Today he simply reflects, "Bob Griese had a heck of game." His other lingering memory is that defensive lineman Kevin Hardy was injured and lost for the season. "That hurt."

Ara was respectfully gracious in defeat. "I don't have to see the statistics sheets to tell you what happened. That was the most fantastic passing performance I've ever seen. Why that's hard to do even in practice let alone in a game. Can you imagine a passer hitting nineteen out of twenty-two?"

His disappointment was only mildly tempered by what he was observing on his own practice fields. As he reflects on it today, "We [coaches] were frustrated. We were watching the freshmen at practice and these kids were flinging the ball all over the field." The opening game of 1966 was scheduled against Purdue at home.

Game Three — vs. Northwestern

Home, October 2, Won 38–7

Joe Doyle, *South Bend Tribune*:

> *Defense!*
> *That was the name of the game all week on Notre Dame's Cartier Field practice grounds. And it was the big difference Saturday when the Irish broke open a tense low scoring duel to beat Northwestern, 38–7.*
>
> *Eight times in the second half the visiting Wildcats put the ball into play. And five times the Irish took it away either to score or set the offense in motion.*
>
> *Improved tackle play by the Irish and a better performance by the linebackers undoubtedly helped the cause. Dick Arrington, moved over from the offensive unit, was a stout performer at tackle along with Pete Duranko, who played his greatest game for the Irish.*
>
> *But Alan Page, Harry Long, and new contenders like Tom Rhoads and Allen Sack at ends also helped contain the "Cats."*

One-and-one and no longer number one, the Irish returned home to play their first home game of the season against Northwestern. This was the first meeting between Ara and his former team, now coached by his closest friend Alex Agase. The game was surprisingly close, closer than the final score. The first tally of the game came in the first quarter when Wildcat defensive back Phil Clarke picked off a Zloch pass and returned it fifty yards for a score. Nick Eddy left the game in the same quarter with a mild concussion. An ailing Bill Wolski scored for the Irish in the second quarter, but the extra point was missed. Northwestern went into the locker room at halftime ahead 7–6.

In the third quarter, Nick Rassas fumbled a punt that was recovered on the Notre Dame twenty. But Rassas quickly redeemed himself by stepping in front of a Dave Milam pass intended for halfback Woody Campbell. He ran the ball back ninety yards for a touchdown. Alex Agase later commented, "He had so many blockers, I thought he got some of them off the bench."

Notre Dame scored 24 points in the fourth quarter. Rassas intercepted a pass for a touchdown. Rocky Bleier and Paul May each had running touchdowns. Wolski had a two-point conversion and Ken Ivan had three kicks for PAT conversions.

Northwestern's Agase summed it up, "When you make a mistake against Notre Dame it shows up on the scoreboard."

Buried in the box score, the Notre Dame defense held the Wildcats to minus two yards rushing. Trench warfare.

Game Four – vs. Army

Away, October 9, Won 17–0

Bob Stewart, *New York Herald Tribune*:

> "Cheer, cheer for old Notre Dame," sung with exultation and tipsy exuberance, echoed hollowly and faintly in the curving, dank tunnel beneath Shea Stadium. Alumni of the Golden Dome and the IRT-7th Ave. were reliving those glory days when the Irish had come to New York to whip Army. Now, after 19 years the Zlochs, Wolskis, Conjars, and Sheridans had returned again to dominate the Long Gray Line.
>
> Outside, the Subway Alumni were proving that conditioning and breeding can carry through two decades. They moved with the creeping good humor in a solid mass of humanity through the turnstiles. For them, nothing had changed. Notre Dame had won as usual and they still had to stand in the subway.

That night's football game at the new Shea Stadium was the renewal of a storied rivalry that had been played in four previous New York locations: West Point, Ebbets Field, the Polo Grounds, and Yankee

Stadium. In the summer of 1965, Shea was remembered for being the first venue of the Beatles tour, thus ushering in the new concept of stadium concerts.

Army played well in the first half, having the edge in time of possession. Replacing Zloch, ND sophomore quarterback Tom Schoen completed three passes in a late drive in the second quarter, the final connection to tight end Don Gmitter for a touchdown. It was the first Notre Dame touchdown in New York since 1943.

The score was close going into the locker room, but thereafter the contest wasn't. Notre Dame would score 10 more points on a five-yard Eddy run and a twenty-three-yard Ken Ivan field goal. Before that kick, Larry Conjar carried the ball ten times in a twelve play drive, eight times in succession. Today he recalls, "I was exhausted."

Army Coach Paul Dietzel's take after the game: "They just whipped us. They're beautifully coached. They're explosive. They hit and hit. And they keep coming on and on and on."

The Cadets had marched down the field after the opening kickoff to the Irish twenty-six. That would be as close to the goal line as they would get. Defensive captain Jim Lynch and sophomore linebacker Mike McGill led the stalwart defense. Tom Rhoads had an interception, Rassas had another. Army never crossed the fifty-yard line in the second half.

Before returning home, the next day the team visited the New York World's Fair, exactly one week before it closed permanently.

Bye-week, October 16

Junior halfback Nick Eddy married his high school sweetheart Audrey Jean—known to everyone as Tiny. The wedding was held on campus in the Lady Chapel of Sacred Heart Church. Tiny's parents weren't able to make the long trip from California, so one of Nick's teammates from the 1965 squad, defensive tackle Mike "The Bear" Webster from Vancouver, BC, was enlisted to walk the bride down the aisle. Nick's best man was guard Peter Thronton from Portland, Maine. The entire 1965 team was invited.

The wedding reception was held a few blocks off campus at the private residence of James Murray, '66, on Michigan Avenue. If coaches were in attendance, they must have had the good sense to waive the "no alcohol during the season" rule. By the start of the 1966 football season, the Eddy's were proud parents of a baby daughter, Nicole Marie. The baby was delivered free of charge by team physician Dr. Nicholas Johns. Nick loves to say, "That little girl had lots of godfathers."

Game Five – vs. USC

Home, October 23, Won 28–7

Jim Murray, *Los Angeles Times*:

> *Outlined against the blue-grey October sky, Notre Dame kicked the bejabers out of USC on a leaky Saturday afternoon. The Fighting Croats did it again. The Eleven Horsemen rode again. And again.*
>
> *The Trojans spent the day on their haircuts. Notre Dame spent it in the end zone.*
>
> *For the benefit of the Trojans, the football Saturday was a Spalding J2V oblong in shape, seamed in the corners and usually found in the arms of a Notre Dame halfback.*
>
> *USC made several mistakes at the outset, not the least of which was scheduling the game in the first place. They should have seen if Yale was available. "There is no question the mind, the emotions, the spirit, play a very important part in this game of football," announced Parseghian at the end of the game. But I notice he teaches blocking all the same. And keeps his scouts going down in the Pennsylvania coal mines with a canary and a letter of intent.*

This was the first home game of consequence as far as the students were concerned. It was time to "wake up the echoes" and remember 1964. There were rallies on campus every single night leading up to the game, migrating from dorm to dorm.

According to student Tom Bettag, "Most of all, you had confidence in the coach, Ara Parseghian. It was good to have him, his strategy, his psychology, and enthusiasm on your side. And there were the individual team members whom you had come to know for their dedication and determination. And you found yourself believing strongly in the magical powers of the 'Notre Dame spirit' that you had seen manifested so fully through the week leading up to the Southern California game."

If revenge is sweet, October 23 was a good day in South Bend. Southern Cal had a fine running back, Mike Garrett. He was averaging 170 yards rushing per game. He would be held to forty-three yards by a determined defensive unit. On offense, this day is one Larry Conjar will always remember. He scored all four touchdowns—with heaps of help from the offensive line. His total of 116 yards would be 42 more than the USC offense made all afternoon. All the starting Notre Dame backs had more yardage than Garrett—Eddy (sixty-five), Wolski (sixty-four), and as Ara correctly recalled forty-five years later, quarterback Bill Zloch (fifty).

In comments after winning the Heisman Trophy, Mike Garrett was classy. "Notre Dame football players are, in my opinion, great examples of what football can be," he said. "They have strength. They have drive . . . At the final gun, as in the opening minutes, they are just one great unit of desire to play football with the will to win."

As of 1965, USC had won only three games in the Midwest (two were played at Soldier Field in Chicago) in a series going back to 1926, and had not won at Notre Dame Stadium since 1939. After the game, about half the Notre Dame student body poured out onto the damp playing field to celebrate the emotional importance of the victory on national television. Unfortunately, it was a year too late.

Game Six — vs. Navy
Home, October 30, Won 29–3

Chip Magnus, *Chicago Sun-Times*:

> *Football games are always a little tougher away from home. For Notre Dame's visitors, they're nightmares. Navy, a 29–3 loser to the Irish Saturday, doesn't suffer by comparison with the other victims of the South Bend slaughterhouse.*
>
> *In the eight games here since Ara Parseghian took over as head coach, the Irish haven't come close to losing. They've outscored the visitors 243–45.*

Parseghian's legion has patented its own way of winning. The Irish start their games slowly, wait for the other guy to make the mistake, and then pound the ball down his throat again and again.

For almost a half, this game was more of a wrestling match than a football game, with zero points scored. Very late in the second quarter Navy tried going for it on fourth and short with the ball spotted on the ND forty-five-yard line. They failed. On the next play, Bill Zloch threw a screen pass to Nick Eddy and he was properly escorted into the end zone. Explaining the forth down call, Navy coach Bill Elias later said, "We felt we could run out the clock. We may also have been influenced by Notre Dame's pitiful efforts to that time."

Statistically the game ended at the half with one play. But in the second half Notre Dame added 22 more points—a one-yard run by Zloch, a Conjar crash through the line, and a sixty-six-yard Rassas punt return—all for touchdowns with extra points added by Ivan and Wolski.

The defense was rock solid yet again. Tackling leaders were Pete Duranko and John Horney with eleven apiece, with Jim Lynch having ten. But the book on Notre Dame was that they were one-dimensional on offense. For the entire game, Navy kept nine men up, all eleven within five yards, and then dared Notre Dame to pass. It worked, but only for one-half of the football game.

Game Seven — vs. Pitt

Away, November 6, Won 69–13

Roy McHugh, *Pittsburgh Press*:

Pitt's football team made believers out of even the most skeptical at Pitt Stadium yesterday. The Panthers lost convincingly to Notre Dame 69–13.

Could Pitt be that bad? Yes. At the half the score was 35–6, and the scoring was almost exactly a mirror image between the two halves of the game.

Bill Wolski scored five touchdowns, which tied a Notre Dame record, gaining fifty-four yards in the process. And he was only the third leading rusher behind Eddy and Conjar, both with eighty-eight yards. Other Notre Dame players to score: Gmitter, Bleier, Conway, and May, while Ivan had nine conversions.

Game Eight – North Carolina

Home, November 13, Won 17–0

Bill Gleason, *Chicago American*:

> *With one minute gone in the fourth period, the boisterous Tar Heels of North Carolina were trampling greasy footsteps all over college football's "game of the year."*
>
> *Mighty Notre Dame, which had scored 69 against Pittsburgh, had scored exactly none against the Tar Heels, who were not at all impressed by the historical import of the Fighting Irish date with top-ranked Michigan State next Saturday afternoon.*

More trench warfare. The Irish offense moved the ball, but couldn't score. After three periods the score was 0-0.

Ken Ivan kicked a thirty-eight-yard field goal with 13:09 remaining. Nick Eddy carried the team offense after that. He had a sixty-six-yard touchdown run. Moments later, McGill intercepted a Danny Talbott pass and was downed at the North Carolina forty-one. Seven plays later Eddy ran for a three-yard score. He rushed for a total of 163 yards on that day, 66 more than all Carolina backs combined.

On this cool and blustery day, the ND defense kept its side of the game scoreless. Duranko led with fourteen tackles. There were three turnovers, interceptions by Mike McGill and Tom Longo, and a John Horney fumble recovery.

A student body tradition of recent vintage was broken. Coach Parseghian and Athletic Director Moose Krause asked students not to jump onto the grass playing field at halftime, as they'd done before to create a tunnel welcoming the players back from the locker room. The students' shoes were damaging the playing surface. They stayed put.

When the polls were announced, the 7–1 Irish were ranked fourth behind Michigan State, Arkansas, and Nebraska, all three at 9–0. Purdue had dropped to number ten with a 6–2–1 record. It was a long shot, but the Irish still could have contended for the National Championship. Beating Michigan State would be required.

Warning Shot

Traditionally, Notre Dame has prided itself on the hospitality it extends to teams, fans, and visitors to the campus and stadium on game days. It is easier to be friendly when the football team is winning. The Period of Penance prior to Ara's arrival had strained off-the-field sportsmanship. In 1964, after previously losing to Michigan State University eight consecutive times, "Hate State" week was christened. Notre Dame won the game 34–7, but regrettable student behavior escalated nonetheless and marred the victory. There was an attack on the Michigan State Band as it marched across campus after the game. One student was knocked unconscious, instruments were damaged, and expensive band caps were swiped.

For Notre Dame President Reverend Theodore Hesburgh, this was absolutely intolerable. So the week before the 1965 Michigan State game, again in South Bend, he delivered a letter to every member of the Notre Dame community. While he didn't specifically reference the band incident, the language and the message were clear and direct.

Spirit is more than noise. It should not be confused with rowdiness, buffoonery, or inhospitality to opponents.

Those responsible here—students, faculty and administration—are increasingly unwilling to continue on this course, even if it means eliminating what can be a very good and wholesome activity.

It [football] is, after all, only a game, and this place is first and foremost a university.

The threat to abandon football was a hollow one. The university needed the influx of revenue. In fact, it depended on it. The veiled threat to severely punish anyone who would put *that* in jeopardy was quite real.

Game Nine – Michigan State

Home, November 20, Lost 3–12   67

Red Smith, *New York Herald Tribune*:

> If Patterson and Clay hit as hard as Michigan State and Notre Dame,
> then we'll see another Dempsey–Firpo fight in Las Vegas Monday night.
> This year's football game of the century was strictly as advertised, a mon-
> umental defensive struggle between the finest of college teams fired up
> like the boilers of the Robert E. Lee.
>
> The wild gang tackling and the ferocious pursuit would have raised
> goose bumps if the contest had been a scoreless tie, but it was made
> doubly exciting by the fact that the weaker team was in front until the
> 39th minute of play.
>
> All Notre Dame stars were of the defensive unit—Horney, Pete
> Duranko, Dick Arrington, Tom Regner, Mike McGill, Tom Longo, and
> Jim Lynch.

Historically, this was the second most important game ever played between Michigan State and Notre Dame. Number-one-ranked MSU was already a Big Ten champion and Rose Bowl bound. What a game.

Going into the contest, incredibly, Notre Dame was tied for first in the nation in scoring. This, for a team with only one offensive dimension that had found ways to win, often after halftime. The Spartan defense held the Irish to minus rushing yards. That was the story of the game. The passing game was held to twenty-four yards on two completions.

But the Notre Dame defense kept the game close and provided three critical turnovers in Michigan State territory that created opportunities to score: a recovered fumble on the nineteen, an intercepted pass on the twenty-five, and another fumble recovery on the eighteen. In the end, all that could be mustered was a Ken Ivan thirty-two-yard field goal. That was good enough to keep the Irish ahead through the first half, 3–0. But on this day it would take more than three points to win, and the Irish were thwarted at every attempt. While the Spartans had a meager ninety-one yards on the ground and twenty-one yards passing in the second half, it was enough for 12 points on two touchdowns.

The following letter was sent to the Notre Dame student body, dated

November 26, 1965:

Gentlemen:

Let me sincerely congratulate the students on their superb behavior at the Michigan State–Notre Dame Game.

I have been connected with games between Michigan State and Notre Dame from 1948 through 1952 as Head Football Coach and as Director of Athletics from 1954 on and the relationship with Notre Dame University has been tremendous, in fact, Director Krause and I have scheduled games for Michigan State–Notre Dame through 1974. I do hope that we will be able to carry on this fine relationship for many, many years to come.

Again congratulations—what a game.

Cordially,
"Biggie" Munn, Athletic Director
Michigan State University

This game was Ara's first loss in Notre Dame Stadium. The table was set for the 1966 "Game of the Century" at Spartan Stadium.

Game Ten – Miami

Away, November 27, Tie 0–0

Edwin Pope, *Miami Herald*:

Only the steady thunder of Miami's student section and the staccato cannonading of Touchdown Tommy kept the area around Notre Dame's bench from resembling a funeral scene Saturday night after the 0–0 tie with the Hurricanes.

Ken Ivan, who missed two short to medium-distance field goals, did not even wait until the end to express himself. He simply put his head between his hands and wept without shame.

When players are asked about this game today, they simply groan. Notre Dame was out of gas. The environment at the Orange Bowl in Miami was memorable because it was so wretched. The trench warfare reached the sidelines. All the players on the bench were instructed to wear their helmets throughout the game to protect themselves from debris tossed from the stands. It was hot and humid. The roster was so depleted that George Goddeke was called into action only two weeks after having his appendix removed. He was still bandaged and stitched up.

Give the Irish defense credit. Under terrible conditions, they held the Hurricanes to zero points. But Miami had seen the films, knew how to defend against Notre Dame, and had the players to execute the plan. No points were scored against them either. Ara lamented: "When your passing attack isn't really strong, people catch up with you. But they stormed. They stacked up on us. Half the time we were running against virtually a nine-man line."

Tom Bettag wrote in *Scholastic*:

> *0-0. A tough way to end the season. The team just couldn't move the ball. You see game films. Miami had stacked the line badly, totally disregarding any pass threat. They waited at the line letting the backs commit themselves. No wonder it was impossible to rush. A pass might have done the trick, but there was no one to pass. Miami knew it. They did not have what it takes to win, but neither do you.*
>
> *As one old fan commented as he slowly made his way out of the Orange Bowl: "I'm glad the season is over. It's been a hard one to see through. I'm just happy Parseghian was running the team and making the decisions. With him I'm sure we couldn't have done any more than we did."*

Mixed Emotions

By the time Ara was seated in the chartered aircraft back from Miami to South Bend, he was probably already plotting his strategy for 1966. The team on the plane with him was long on character and short on passing offense. One can only imagine what he might have been thinking if he closed his eyes. The long, hard season was finally over. It ended with a thud, no touchdowns and no wins in the final two games. But the team would hold on to a national Top Ten ranking.

Most of the guys in the trenches would be coming back for another year, but there might have been some slight alterations there. Heck, Notre Dame had over 1,000 offensive plays—thanks to the defense. Hardy should return healthy. That would help . . . a lot. The defensive backfield would be graduating: Tom Longo, Tony Carey, and Nick Rassas—collectively with thirteen interceptions. It would be a challenge to replace them, especially Rassas. He would be a lock for All-American.

Then on offense, 118 pass attempts, only 53 completions and 10 interceptions! The tireless Bill Zloch was graduating. Ara already knew he had quarterback talent waiting in the wings, along with passers and some pretty good guys to catch the ball, especially Heneghan and Seymour. He'd miss Bill Wolski in the backfield (who finished eleventh in Heisman balloting). But the idea of starting 1966 with Eddy, Conjar, and an experienced Bleier was more than comforting. Overall the backfield guys averaged nearly four yards per carry. But lots of credit should go to the offensive line. Graduating Dick Arrington would earn his All-American status; for much of the season the guy played both ways, for goodness sakes (the last ND player to do so). Otherwise the unit would be back, and stronger. With that quick assessment, Ara may have had time for a short nap. He deserved it.

Changing of the Guard

In December, Charlie Callahan, the man who literally defined the sports information office at Notre Dame, resigned to take the position of Publicity Director for the Miami Dolphins. He had been on the job for over twenty years and had orchestrated five Heisman Trophy PR campaigns—for Johnny Lujack, Leon Hart, Johnny Lattner, Paul Hornung, and John Huarte. But Miami weather was better, the money was very good, and pro football was starting to really come of age and dominate the media. Ara commented, "In my time at Notre Dame, Charlie Callahan has been a good friend and a tremendous help to me, the assistant coaches, and the players. He has our gratitude. We will miss him."

The new guy in that office would be Roger Valdiserri, a Notre Dame man who had been a student secretary for Frank Leahy and his staff. He would be assigned to compile the stats for the 1966 season, a task that he and his staff would perform with distinction for the next thirty-four years. Valdiserri would retire as Associate Athletic Director in 1995. Thus Ara would acquire another life-long friend. Roger couldn't have started his new job at a more auspicious time.

7

GOOD CLEAN FOOTBALL

The Bunker

It was about the most unassuming location on campus, but from 1964 to 1967, it was one of the most important. It was where the football leg of the Notre Dame table was solidified. We're not talking about Notre Dame Stadium. In fact, this location was about as physically removed from the stadium or the Cartier Field practice areas as it could be and still be on Notre Dame property.

It was once the quaint custom to have personalized signs marking every reserved parking place on the Notre Dame campus. These were hand lettered at the Notre Dame sign shop, yellow-painted letters over black boards and placed on stakes in front of the designated spaces. Parents delivering their young men back to campus would have been confused when taking the exterior access road behind Rockne Memorial and spotting the parking signs for Parseghian and all the other assistant coaches. The only more remote location was a "temporary" structure known as the ROTC Building across the street, a hold-over from the Navy program in the 1940s (remarkably it is still standing and in use in 2011). Also across the street were the Notre Dame (Burke) Golf Course and open fields that extended to Route 31, with Saint Mary's College across the road beyond.

Inside Rockne Memorial, on the ground floor as one entered from the South Quad, was the football office. This is where the strategies and plans for Ara's teams were formulated. It is also where recruits would have been brought to meet with the head coach. It was the equivalent of Churchill's underground bunker in London during World War II, today referred to as the "War Rooms."

As you enter "The Rock," on the first floor to the right of the foyer is a large, high-ceiling room that was originally designed for formal physical education classes (this academic major was dropped in 1963, to the pleasure of Fr. Hesburgh). The football office had been itinerant over the years. Moved first from the Administration Building (where Rockne had a single office) to cramped quarters among two floors at the south end of Breen-Phillips Hall where the entire Athletic Department was housed, starting in the 1930s. Frank Leahy worked out of the Breen-Phillips offices, and during football season was known to sleep in the Notre Dame firehouse rather than make the tedious roundtrip to his family home in Long Beach, Michigan. Terry Brennan's office was originally there as well; the sign for it now decorates a popular South Bend restaurant. When the space opened up in Rockne Memorial, football operations were moved over. (In 1968 the football office was moved again to the new Athletic and Convocation Center. Now Notre Dame Football has its own palatial building, the Guglielmino Family Athletics Center, "The Gug.")

Within the confines of this former classroom-gym, there was a combination outer office and reception area. Coach Parseghian's secretary, Barb Nicholas, was the gatekeeper. This area provided access to a single private office reserved for the head coach, and an open bull pen. Ara's office was in the corner facing the South Quad and Lyons Hall.

The remainder of the space was essentially open with desks partitioned by file cabinets that defined the assistant coaches' areas. Toward the rear was another room for film and meetings, termed the conference room (which had a large table and was where the grad assistant was put). It was a crowded and noisy boiler room with desks, file cabinets, bookshelves, telephones, film-viewing machines, tack boards and blackboards. Except for the clutter, it was almost military in its configuration and lack of creature comforts. For ten men on a mission, it was the perfect setup.

Head Coach Ara Parseghian in his Rockne Memorial office with assistant coach Joe Yonto. *Source*: Notre Dame Sports Information Collection

But these were good-sized men, physically, and the office space was quite crowded. The personalities and egos of the coaching staff were even bigger than their physical statures. Living together could have been disastrous, but it worked well for two reasons. First, with Ara in command, the focus was constantly on tangible team goals—no office politics were tolerated. Second, when there was steam to let off, it was no trouble to find a swimming pool, handball courts, weight rooms, basketball courts, or a place to hit some golf balls. The fact that this enclave was so far removed from both the Administration Building and the Athletic Department in Breen-Phillips Hall also created a welcomed buffer.

It was from this bare-boned (it's difficult to resist using the word Spartan) outpost that football at Notre Dame was transformed and elevated to meet the expectations of high standards both on and off the field. It's a campus location that today deserves an historical marker.

The Fraternity

Under NCAA guidelines, football programs could employ a maximum of eight assistant coaches and one graduate assistant. Ara got to handpick each of his assistants. There were no required holdovers from previous Notre Dame teams, one of the conditions that was undoubtedly negotiated before Parseghian accepted the job.

Ara treated all his coaches as equals, but two were more equal than the others. John Ray ran the defense and Ara gave him enormous latitude in doing do. Tom Pagna was Ara's right-hand man on the offensive side and he also relieved Ara of the burden of attending to cumbersome internal administrative details—the paperwork.

Recruiting was rationalized. The map of the United States was carved up so that each assistant had an area of recruiting responsibility and was expected to mine his area. It was a new concept at a time when only a couple of universities could claim to be truly "national."

Defensive Coaches

John Ray commanded the defensive unit and handled the linebackers. After the 1966 season he was named Assistant Head Football Coach. This was well deserved and hardly a surprise.

Ray was reportedly on his way to Wake Forest as the head coach when Ara called him in 1964. He had been the head coach at John Carroll University in Cleveland where he had amassed a 29–6 record. He was already known as a defensive guru when Ara called with the offer to become an assistant at Notre Dame.

Moving from a head coaching position and ignoring a promotion to run a larger program as head coach for the opportunity to be an assistant coach wouldn't have made sense to many guys. But Ara knew who he wanted, and as years of recruits were to testify, when Ara wanted something, he could be very convincing.

John Ray may not have needed all that much convincing. First, he was a South Bend native. Second, before the war, he was the first team center on the 1944 Notre Dame squad. So returning to Notre Dame was a homecoming. Ara got his man.

He also got a determined man who could eloquently express the new tougher, meaner, attitude of Ara's team without worrying about political correctness. It wasn't uncommon to hear Ray say, "I want that man hit. And I want him buried. Tear off his head if he tries to run with that ball. But remember, I want good clean football." The message couldn't be any clearer. The now-familiar "Play Like a Champion Today" sign that Lou Holtz added to the locker room was a kinder, gentler version of Ray's motto.

Paul Shoults was charged with developing the defensive secondary. He started coaching with Ara in 1952 and followed him from Miami to Northwestern and ultimately to Notre Dame in 1964. Shoults was a star player at Miami from 1945–48, and was named captain and most valuable player in his senior year. He shared backfield duties with Parseghian on the 1946 and 1947 squads.

Shoults was faced with rebuilding the secondary in 1966 after the departure of Nick Rassas, Tom Longo, and Tony Carey—as good a group as ever played at Notre Dame. The new defensive backfield of Tom Schoen, Jim Smithberger, and Tom O'Leary more than stepped up. In 1966 they were ranked second nationally in pass interceptions (twenty-six) and first in yards on interception returns (497).

Joe Yonto was destined to become a Notre Dame legend as a defensive line coach. People forget that it was Ara who gave him his first college job in 1964. Joe played football for the Irish under Frank Leahy, as a fullback in 1945 and as a guard in 1946. He was injured as a senior and served as an assistant freshman coach. Prior to his return to South Bend, he spent sixteen years as a successful high school coach. His last assignment was at Notre Dame High School in Niles, Illinois were he had a 42–18–5 record and won three consecutive Chicago Suburban Catholic League titles.

Hiring this successful high school coach was something that Ara never regretted. Although Yonto was short in stature, that's not how the parade of All-Americans and preppers he coached at Notre Dame remember him. He was admired for his attention to blocking fundamentals, his enormous passion for the game, and the personal interest he took in each of his players.

Offensive Coaches

Tom Pagna was officially listed as the offensive backfield coach. In reality he was more than that. He was Ara's executive assistant, alter ego on offense, and all-around right-hand man. The two worked hand and glove. Tom was technically proficient in every aspect of coaching football. He combined that arcane knowledge with the personality and temperament of a Catholic parish pastor—picture a young Spencer Tracy as a no-nonsense priest with a soft heart . . . and a whistle around his neck.

Tom was an outstanding football player in his own right at Miami University. He was a "little All-American" and was the first Miami player to gain over 1,000 yards in a season. Tom played professionally for the Packers and the Browns before his career was cut short by injuries. Just like Parseghian, he turned to coaching. Under Ara he was the freshman coach at Miami in 1959 and moved with his mentor and friend to Northwestern and ultimately to Notre Dame.

Among his many talents, Pagna was a gifted writer and communicator. For years, on Fridays before games, "The Phantom," wrote an inspirational message that was deposited in the locker of every player. These missives broke the ensuing game down to essential elements and added more than enough red meat to get the troops fired up. Nobody quite knew for sure who was writing this stuff, although Pagna was the suspected author for many years (the signature "T.P." being a logical clue). It is fortunate that most of these have survived over the years and were compiled into a single volume, *The Phantom Letters: Motivation at Notre Dame in the Parseghian Era.*

When Ara stepped down as Notre Dames' head coach, the position was immediately filled by Dan Devine through a family connection with Fr. Joyce. Many insiders were disappointed that Pagna wasn't named interim head coach, with the possibility of Ara returning after a year's respite. The history of promoting assistant coaches to the head job at Notre Dame has never been one of success. The only person to make the leap was Knute Rockne at a time when college football was a much less sophisticated sport. Not wanting to make another "Terry Brennan mistake," the Administration could hardly be indicted for looking for an established head coach. In retrospect, Tom Pagna would have been a great college head coach, but fate never gave him the opportunity to prove it.

George Sefcik coached the offensive receivers in 1966. He was an all-around athlete at Notre Dame when he was a student there, earning five monograms. He played both offense and defense as a halfback, receiver, and punt returner from 1959-1962. He also starred in baseball where he led the team with a .367 batting average in his senior year. After graduation Sefcik worked under Joe Yonto at Notre Dame High School in suburban Chicago. In 1964 he became Ara's first graduate assistant and then moved up to assistant coach after earning his master's degree at Notre Dame.

Jerry Wampfler had the difficult task of rebuilding the offensive line going into the 1966 season. It was his first season on Ara's staff, replacing Doc Urich. His record tells the story. The 1966 line blocked and pass-protected for 3,925 yards of total offense, nearly a 400-yard-per-game average. Jerry played tackle at Miami under Parseghian where he blocked for Tom Pagna. After graduation from the Cradle of Coaches, he was a successful high school coach until Bo Schembechler called him back to his alma mater as offensive coordinator, where he toiled for three years. Jerry always had a particularly close relationship with his former coach and jumped at the Notre Dame assistant position when Ara called.

Freshman Coaches

Wally Moore was also in his first year of college coaching in 1966 as a freshman coach, but he didn't have to move very far to do it. Moore was the head coach at St. Joseph's High School in South Bend, located right across the road, Route 31, from Notre Dame with an unobstructed view of the Golden Dome. As a high school coach Moore was named Indiana Coach of the Year and National High School Football Coach by the Rockne Club of America. Wally successfully made the transition to the college game. In 1966 the Notre Dame freshman team was undefeated, with wins against Pittsburgh (29–0) and Michigan State (30–27).

John Murphy, as Assistant Freshman Coach, was the sole holdover from the Notre Dame coaching staff in 1963, at Ara's election. John earned a monogram at ND at end and was a member of the 1935, '36 and '37 teams. Murphy was a South Bend native who had coaching stints in New York, at Chicago's Holy Trinity High, and as an assistant at Auburn University before returning to John Adams High School in South Bend. He joined the Notre Dame staff in 1959.

Brian Boulac was the graduate assistant for the 1966 season, which effectively translated into being the ninth assistant coach. It was a position that would determine the direction of his professional life. On practice days he helped where necessary, usually with the freshman team. On game days he carried the infamous box (television monitor) at Ara's side. It was a unique vantage point to watch the miracle season unfold and learn from a master.

After 1966, and with his master's degree in hand, Ara added Brian to the permanent coaching staff in 1967. He assumed the duties of a recruiting co-coordinator at Notre Dame and along the way helped define that emerging role in college football. He would remain at Notre Dame as a coach for nearly forty years. He is one of only a handful of individuals who can claim to own four Notre Dame National Championship rings, under Parseghian (1966, 1973), Dan Devine (1977) and Lou Holtz (1988).

Undoubtedly, Brian could have been an outstanding college head coach in his own right. But that would have meant leaving Notre Dame, and that was something he could never emotionally do. He should have no regrets. Brian is beloved by generations of Notre Dame players—from prep team players to the biggest names who went on to professional stardom.

Behind the Scenes

"In the world of hurt and pain and bruise that is sometimes football, it is the medicative personality and talents of Notre Dame's head trainer Gene Paszkiet which serve as the difference between participation and idleness." That's how Paszkiet was introduced in the *1967 Notre Dame Football Guide*, following the 1966 season. He received equal billing with all the assistant coaches, and deservedly so. Keeping the players on the field was an instrumental component of success for the '66 National Champions.

Gene was a South Bend native and Notre Dame graduate in 1951. He was part of Hugh Burn's training staff as a student. He became head trainer in 1952 under Frank Leahy when Burns left for the Detroit Lions. The task of caring for the Irish football team would have been overwhelming for a single person. Part of Paszkiet's success was built on the cadre of student trainers that he personally trained and then managed. One of those, Tom Feske recalls that part of his job was visiting the players after-hours in their dorm rooms to provide muscle massage or physical therapy to get them back on the playing field. Because the stadium had only a small training room with just two whirlpools, the dorm visits became a necessary innovation as Notre Dame emerged from its threadbare period, pre-Ara.

Three team doctors rounded out the medical staff: Dr. Nicholas Johns, Dr. George Colip, and Dr. George Green—all practicing physicians in South Bend. Over the course of an entire football season there wasn't a single Irish player who didn't get some attention by the Notre Dame training and medical staff. Sometimes it is easy to forget how brutally physical football is at its core. Doctors know.

So did John Ray, and he never let the team forget that.

Summer 1966

By the end of spring practice, Ara and his coaches were finally able to exhale. They were feeling pretty good about the personnel they had assembled and the prospects for the coming 1966 campaign. The bunker became the epicenter for the strategic planning that would be required to outwit opponents and advance the football program beyond the 7–2–1 record and the number eight ranking of 1965. If only everyone returned from summer break in good health and in good shape, the coaching staff knew they'd be ready.

But there was to be a change in plans. On a summer's evening in Kirkland, Washington, receiver Curt Heneghan was playing what he describes as "grab-ass football" with some of his buddiess. Running full speed with spikes up the field, he planted his right foot, but it didn't release cleanly. Right away he knew it was a serious knee injury and sought local medical attention. The next day he was on a plane to South Bend for examination by the Notre Dame orthopedic doctors. They advised against surgery and opted for rehab. That effectively rendered him dubious for the 1966 season. He would have corrective surgery after the season ended and play as a junior and a senior. But the knee was never the same.

Some have speculated about a rivalry between Heneghan and Seymour. There may have been a bit of that but, it was confined to the practice field. Both players were constantly trying to move up on the depth chart, but not at the expense of the other. Ara coveted having both on the field at the same time. During their final two years at Notre Dame, Curt and Jim were roommates in 205 Walsh Hall (it's not uncommon for players to remember their exact room numbers after so many years).

With two great sophomore receivers, Heneghan and Seymour, the coaches weren't contemplating one over the other. Their plan was a shift in the backfield, from three backs to two, while adding a flanker. With the injury to Heneghan, those plans had to be abandoned. The most surprised player returning in August was Rocky Bleier. He figured to be odd-man-out in the new configuration (sitting either Eddy or Conjar was unthinkable). He was reinstated back into the three-back set and went on to contribute in ways he never would have imagined as he worked out privately over the summer in Appleton, Wisconsin.

Uncle Mike

Frank Criniti returned to Charleston, West Virginia, for summer break pretty pumped up. His family was justifiably over the moon about his success and excited about the coming 1966 season. None more than Frank's Uncle Mike.

Frank is from a proud Italian family. Like so many of the students at Notre Dame from ethnic families in the 1960s, he was weaned on a diet of Irish football, first delivered by a national radio network on Saturdays and later by the occasional televised game. For a family like the Crinitis, just having a boy at Notre Dame was a big deal and cause for minor celebrity in the neighborhood. Actually having a family member on the Notre Dame football team was, well, more than most families could dream about.

Frank endured his freshman year of battering by the 1965 varsity without injury. Ironically, one reason may have been that he was the smallest member of the team at five-foot-seven-inches, and a generously-listed weight of 165 (but probably 10 pounds lighter). Frank had the advantages of quick feet and a nimble mind and thus became the back the larger lineman hated to practice against because he was hard to find and then harder to trap because of his dancing skills. Frank's big challenge was blocking out of the backfield and then living to tell about it. Alan Page was on one side and Pete Duranko on the other—two of the greatest defensive linemen in Notre Dame history, All-Americans, both future pros. His size and stature didn't quite measure up for head-on collisions, something akin to a Ford Pinto hitting a fully-loaded Peterbilt, both going full speed. But with glancing blows and deception, he was able to survive spring practice and be listed number three in the depth chart behind Rocky Bleier and Dave Haley.

At a family gathering over the summer, Frank's Uncle Mike wanted to know all about the Irish team and the prospects for the coming season. He needed fodder for lunch breaks when conversations invariably turned toward sports. Frank loved telling his uncle all the stories and predicted that the Irish would be much improved. The reasoning was sound, a veteran defense combined with an offense that would have more of a passing attack. Uncle Mike took it all in and then took it to heart.

What Frank didn't know was that good ol' Uncle Mike had a standing bet with one of his coworkers regarding Irish football. For ease, the rules were simple. A point spread was determined for the entire season. Uncle Mike would have Notre Dame and his buddy would have the opponent of the week. This had been going on for years, and up until 1964, Uncle Mike had been suffering with the Irish in a special way—through his wallet. But going into the 1966 season, he would have inside information, really inside information. Things were looking up. The Irish were going to be improved. His nephew promised. Frankie wouldn't lie to his uncle.

So it came as a surprise to Frank when he learned later that summer that Uncle Mike had made his usual friendly bet and spotted the Irish 30 points for every single game over the season. When he tells this story forty-five years later, Frank still buries his shaking head into his hands. "What was he thinking? Spotting every team on the schedule 30 points. Who in their right mind does this?"

Asked to summarize the remarkable 1966 season, Frank Criniti uses this one simple family story as the benchmark. Uncle Mike won his standing bet six out of ten times and it easily could have been eight (except for narrow misses with Northwestern and Navy). "That's how good our team was."

But we are getting ahead the story—about the coach, the team, the season, and the "Game of the Century" that was destined to captivate the nation.

8

"YOU'VE JOINED THE TEAM!!"

Not long ago, Red Smith recalled a college football hero who was "brave, fast as light, and violent as a crime of passion, but not pretentiously intellectual. 'In fact,' his coach said, 'if his IQ were any lower, he'd be a plant.'"

—*Look* Magazine, September 20, 1966

One of the cruelest stereotypes is that college athletes, especially football players, aren't smart. The actual data fails to support the stereotype. But sometimes incidental observations, especially raucous off-field social behaviors, contribute to the misconception. One only has to understand the demands of an athlete in a major college football program to conclude that the intellectual challenges are substantial. Football is like taking another academic course in the classroom, which is then followed by real-world daily quizzes and weekly tests. The grading is much tougher than classroom subjects, often resulting in physical pain and injury. The least of it is embarrassment in front of thousands of fans and perhaps a TV audience in the millions.

You are never more aware of this until you have studied an actual college playbook. As you might expect, the playbooks devised by Ara

Parseghian and his staff were extensive, detailed, and innovative—all well ahead of their time. So for many years (almost a half century), the few of these documents that have escaped confiscation at the end of a season have been guarded like military secrets. Coach Parseghian conceded to the rare opportunity for the 1966 Notre Dame playbook to be studied—just to look at it, not to own. To the layman, the secrets remain largely secure, because it would take a strategic genius of the caliber of Ara to absorb the whole thing and then to execute it. But the document continues to be worthy of high security clearance because, in the hands of the right mind(s), perhaps with some minor adjustments, it could be effectively adopted and effectively used today.

The first page of the playbook is so eloquent that it is presented below in its entirety.

You've Joined The Team!!

1966 will ask a lot of Notre Dame team members. It will ask you to play with a "full heart", to never have a "breaking point", to go for "60 minutes". It will further ask that your dress, your manner, your appearance, your behavior, be that of young men nobly privileged to represent Notre Dame.

Physically you will tire. Mentally you will feel great pressure and studying will be tough. Emotionally you will become highly sensitive—frayed—upset and confused. You will be idolized by all youngsters, looked down upon by pseudo scholars, praised by parents, torn by the wants and pressures of outside groups, guided & discussed by coaches—but most important you will have been a part of a group of men that will give you an equal return.

With your commitment and that of all other team members, we will be an inseparable—strong—united force—ready to fight only the good fight—winning if we can, losing only when destiny says we must. Bring on the opponents! Notre Dame is ready! If "no army is as powerful as an idea whose time has come" it is time we all commit to the acceptance of the "team idea"—this is the commitment that we can never have cause to regret—further, we will only prosper from the great force that unity ignites!—It can make our 1966 season—a brilliant page in the book of your life.

– The Notre Dame Coaching Staff

The playbook is divided into twenty-five sections, chapters of sorts, each with a separate colored tab. All of this is thoughtfully inserted into a fat three-ringed binder. It is a comprehensive piece of work.

No detail is too large or too small. For example, is it really necessary to include the 1966 football schedule? Never mind, it's there. As is the daily schedule for pre-season practices, in half-hour blocks, from six thirty a.m. "Wake Up" to ten thirty p.m. "Lights Out." There's a map of the Cartier Field practice areas (Fields 1-5), just so getting lost at practice isn't an option.

The administrative rules are instructive. "Section I, Player's Book Responsibility" lays it out right up front: "The Book will be returned at conclusion of season (before USC game)." This is followed by, "Caution not to lose (can hurt entire team if wrong person has access)."

Training regulations are no-nonsense. "No smoking or drinking (that's a twelve month proposition)." "All bars are off limits." "We will police." Then the most interesting paragraph that reinforces page one says, "Your complete cooperation is expected, and insubordination will not be tolerated. High morale is essential to team success. You will have gripes, but you must set them aside in the interest of loyalty to team and coaching staff. The team is bigger than any individual connected with it. This game is not compulsory, but those who play must abide by regulations. No days off."

The "Training Hints" are equally detailed and direct. For example, "Watch your blisters (important)," or, "We will not tolerate stealing of equipment or practical joking with equipment. Your body protection is too valuable to be a toy." The approach is very adult for actions and consequences. "Discipline action for being late to practice and training room (five laps)...Continual lateness will cost you your uniform."

Personal hygiene is addressed. After each practice, "Expose feet to sun and air – elevate and bathe with warm saltwater solution." It would be interesting to know how religiously that was practiced. Finding sunny days in South Bend in the fall can be challenging. The "Dormitory Regulations" have this interesting admonition: "Please keep card-playing at an absolute minimum (or it will be abolished)." Surprisingly, there is no clarity about what "an absolute minimum" should be. But the unwritten subtext throughout is, "This is Notre Dame, so don't screw up."

The daily practices are broken down and orchestrated with the precision not unlike a symphony orchestra preparing for the *1812 Overture*.

Each action—jogging, calisthenics, stretching, sprints—is listed and put into the sequence of a thoughtful design. It wouldn't be an exaggeration to believe that the players could instinctively walk through a complete practice forty-five years after the fact without many prompts. That was probably the point—less thinking and more time for actually practicing.

The drills by position were well known and purposeful, some with names colorful to recall. You'd expect offensive backs to have ball-exchange drills, blocking drills and an anti-fumble drill. But what were "distraction drills"? Is that the place in the schedule where the Saint Mary's girls walked through the practice fields?

The O line spent lots of time on the sleds. The "1/2 line drill on sacks over guard, tackle and end" prepared for what are now called blitzes. You didn't see or hear that term back in 1966. The defensive line had a "shed drill," a "spin drill," and a "peek-a-boo drill." One can only imagine Alan Page playing "peek-a-boo." The outcome would be that an opposing player would be the one who got drilled. The defensive backs had the best-named drills: tip, angle tip, flag, combat, wave, and squeeze.

Offensive critical situations are exposed and addressed. They are the same at every level from peewee to pro, but they are thoroughly addressed nonetheless for clarity, as follows:

> **Kick Off:** *You must watch the ball kicked off the tee.*
> **Punt:** *Block until sound of the ball.*
> **Beat Clock:** *Be sure you get out of bounds.*
> **Safety:** *Offense can never be tackled in own end zone.*
> **Fumble:** *A fumble is the greatest sin an offensive player can commit—be aware of the ball and our trust in you—proper carry, etc.*

Heisman Trophy-winner Johnny Lattner (1953) could probably write a book on that last one. Frank Leahy famously called Lattner's fumbles against Purdue "mortal sins" and made Lattner constantly carry a ball with him on campus for a week.

Reading the playbook in sequence is surprisingly seductive. It's like Einstein explaining the Theory of Relativity, but this time, for the first time, it starts to make sense. The real gem in the book is written directly by Ara and comes as close to the heart of his coaching philosophy as a single sheet of paper can capture. Again, it is presented in its entirety:

THE INTERVAL THAT CAUSES GREATNESS
Three things comprise the "GREAT INTERVAL"

EFFORT + EXECUTION + ENDURANCE = INTERVAL

The longest play in football—a long kick off return is approximately 12 seconds in length.

The shortest is a no gain direct line drive. Its duration about 2.5 seconds in length.

The average play is near to 4 seconds.

When we say INTERVAL, we are talking about that time period from the ball snap that ignites us, to 4 seconds later. Nothing else really matters in a game.

On average, offense runs 80 or so plays. Defense runs nearly the same.

We are talking about 4 = [sic] 80 or 320 seconds, or about 5 minutes.

When we say INTERVAL, we are asking if you will give of EFFORT, EXECUTION, AND ENDURANCE for Notre Dame—just 5 minutes worth a game. A 4 second interval by every player on every play will make us a GREAT TEAM!!

Listen and watch for the word throughout practice.
WE WILL BECOME WHAT WE DO!
DO THE INTERVAL!

ARA PARSEGHIAN

So far in this chapter, only a single tab out of twenty-five in the book has been discussed. The remaining twenty-four tabs are filled with excruciating details and all the diagrams you could imagine, using geometric shapes, Xs, Os, boxes, arrows, lines, dotted lines, numbers—about what you'd expect. But the detail is impressive, actually overwhelming, when seen in its entirety in a single binder.

The stances by position are explained with specifics by situation. No one could possibly memorize this content. It has to be absorbed and then become habitual. The detail is intricate. For example, base split is two feet between players. Position by position is as follows:

Center: Feet parallel and shoulder-width, knees turned out.

Guards, Tackles, and Ends: Feet armpit-width, straight upfield— stagger—heel, toe—weight on balls of feet.

Halfbacks: Feet—inside leg back shoulder-width. Inside hand down, Stagger—heel, toe.

Fullbacks: Feet parallel (right or left hand down), don't tip off play by weight shift.

Tailback: Feet parallel, hands on knees.

Every position has five of more directives just about stance. So far the ball hasn't even been snapped.

There are step-by-step techniques for thirteen different types of blocks. For example, the "Downfield Block":

Hit out with count.
Cutoff release when necessary.
Get close to opponent, step on his toes.
Throw high—through and beyond opponent.
Roll with opponent. Get up and throw again.
Don't spend yourself too early.
Get close enough to make contact.

There are forty-two different defensive alignments to recognize, each with its own code name. For example:

To apply our Blocking System, one must understand the terms used for communication purposes. Our blocking strategy is based on the following:

The play call
Defensive alignment
Ratio of blockers to defenders
Tendencies of the defense
Tendencies of the individual defender
We arrive at various blocking combinations through the use of:
Base rule—for a particular play
Master calls – intra-line communication used to control full line of ½

line (example—Reach—Seal—6)
Individual calls—intra line. Communication between two individuals
(example—S–X–R)
Individual calls may be used within a master call.

This is tedious stuff. And this is all information under the second tab of the book. It takes a high degree of intelligence first to understand the specifics and then to recognize and apply rules as a team in real time with game pressure. This is not *Football for Dummies.*

On the offense there are thirty-nine different run plays, all with variations. There are thirty-two different pass plays, again with variations. Then there are special team plays, such as punts with at least ten different variations. All of them are fully diagrammed.

The defense is equally complex. An effective defensive philosophy is explained.

DEFENSIVE OBJECTIVES

The major objective of defensive football is to keep your opponent from scoring. Every member of the defensive team should keep this fact upper-most in his mind at all times. To repeat, the first and only mission of the defense is to prevent a score. Strong as it may seem, defensive players often lose sight of this vital fact.

TEN BASIC "MUSTS" IF OUR DEFENSE IS TO BE SOUND:

Do not allow the long pass for an easy TD.
Do not allow the long run for an easy TD.
Do not allow the offense to score inside our five yard line by running.
Do not allow a kick off return for a TD.
Cut down on kick off return, so as to allow no more than 5 yards per kick.
The defense must intercept 3 out of every 14 passes attempted.
The defense must average 20 yards per interception.
During the season we must return 3 interceptions for TD's.
The defense must make our opponent fumble a least 3 times a game.
We must recover at least 2 fumbles of our opponents every game.

DEFENSIVE THEORY

The theory of defensive football is based on three objectives.

Prevent your opponent from scoring
Gain possession of the football
Score ourselves

The "Defensive Suggestions" list is filled with helpful nuggets that every player should embrace, such as:

—Gang tackle, Gang tackle, Gang tackle.
—Love body contact. Be a competitor.
—Keep your feet moving.
—Rush the passer with hands high.
—Be hitters, not catchers.

There are twenty of these helpful reminders. The most interesting is number seventeen: "Any player lying on the ground watching the play and not attempting to give a second effort will get a better seat next week—ON THE BENCH."

After multiple pages of schemes and diagrams there is a page for "Terms We Should Know." The list is designed to summarize and simplify the complexity that comes before it.

Strong Side—*Strong side of off. formation.*
Weak Side—*Weak side of off. formation.*
Fan or Sprint—*No run action threat inside.*
Run Action—*Has threat of run inside.*
Red—*No switch in man coverage (HB & S).*
Green—*Switch if necessary in man coverage (HB & S).*
Field Balance—*Lateral position on the ball.*
Field Position—*Vertical position on the ball.*

The closer the ball gets to our goal line, the tighter we play, Man or zone.
Don't defend the end zone. Defend the goal line.
Use the side lines as an extra man.

Talk to one another on coverage & routes.
Know the down & distance.
Play the ball tough. The offense wins all ties.
You must read your keys.
Camouflage or hide the defense.

The entire playbook is over 300 pages and includes over 1,500 diagrams. If studying this book as a technical textbook were a required course for the general college population, there would be very few As and a significant failure rate. Being a football player at a major college program is intellectually demanding, more so than most academics could ever admit. Playing at Notre Dame for Ara Parseghian was that much harder.

The Student Athlete

It was the goal of University President Fr. Hesburgh and Executive Vice President Fr. Joyce to combine excellence on the football field with excellence in the classroom through direct University engagement. This vision was put into motion when they asked Mike DeCicco, a professor of engineering, to take on the roll of advisor to the student athletes at Notre Dame in 1964.

Professor DeCicco was himself also the coach of the highly-successful Irish fencing team and was already an advocate for his athletes. As he recalls the chain of events today, he was called to a meeting with Fr. Hesburgh where he was asked to take on this new role. The role wasn't just new to Notre Dame, it was new to college athletics. DeCicco heard the university president out and then asked for some time to think about it. He went home and discussed it with his wife. Her reaction was very straightforward. "When the boss asks you to do something, you do it." That's how he got started.

Unfortunately, there was no established playbook for the new role. Oftentimes it required tough love. But DeCicco always started with the student's best interests, became an advocate for the athletes at Notre Dame, and made their college experiences easier and more rewarding. They have never forgotten that.

As a result of the groundbreaking efforts of Fathers Hesburgh and Joyce, combined with the seemingly limitless energy of a gregarious Mike DeCicco, the NCAA took notice. In 1966, a national committee was established on the topic of athletic advising. The goal was to add sanity to college athletics. Today, virtually all universities with national prominence have this important resource for their student athletes. It all started at Notre Dame.

Ara Parseghian wasn't the only person at Notre Dame with a playbook. Father Ted and Father Ned had an invisible one of their own. The two playbooks merged together effectively and with legendary results.

9

THE REAL DEAL

Steps

The 1966 Notre Dame Football season had an inauspicious beginning on a bitterly cold Monday morning in February. All the mornings in February in South Bend are so cold that you can imagine seeing your breath before you even exhale. At that time, first semester exams at Notre Dame were scheduled in late January. With the beginning of a new academic semester came a new routine.

Football Captain Jim Lynch called for daily workouts early in the morning so that the team could stay in shape. The workouts were held under the stadium grandstands, the only enclosed facility on campus that could accommodate over one hundred athletes rotating among a progression of fitness stations around the perimeter. The entire interior concrete concourse doubled as an indoor track. There was no heat. Sweatpants and hooded sweatshirts were the universal attire, and some of them may have been occasionally washed. After the workouts, the guys would retreat to their individual dorms for showers. It wasn't technically legal to use the locker room located in the stadium. But it didn't matter anyway, because the stadium water had been drained to avoid frozen pipes.

By everyone's admission, the toughest station was the climbing ropes hanging from the underside of the concrete structure. They were used to develop upper-body and arm strength. Pete Duranko, by acclamation the strongest man on the team, was able to rapidly climb the ropes without ever having his legs engaged in the rope in a locking configuration—his technique was all grip and upper body strength. Watching Pete, all 240 pounds of him, scramble up the rope always created a spectacle and reminded the remaining mere mortals how far their personal strength training was from the ultimate goal. Duranko could also climb the steps of the Administration Building upside down on his hands. Because his feet never actually touched a single step, this act of circus gymnastics paid quirky homage to the time-honored Notre Dame tradition of not walking normally up the exterior stairs until graduation.

Sophomore Kevin Rassas was in awe of Duranko, like everyone else.

I remember when I asked Pete before one of our spring training workouts how he had developed such strength and agility. I said his whole body seemed as hard as wood. He laughed and said "I climb trees! It takes all of your muscles, requires balance and agility because you get into so many different positions." I told him that he must have been kidding. He said he was serious. We were outside of the stadium waiting for the conditioning session to start. I turned to someone else and when I turned around Pete was gone. I looked up and sure enough there was Pete smiling proudly from the top of a tree and laughing. "See!!" Needless to say he looked like King Kong up there.

The daily stadium workouts were strictly "voluntary" in keeping with NCAA rules. From time to time, assistant coaches could be spied in the press box—undoubtedly there to inspect the meticulous maintenance of the field turf that was covered by a tarp and many inches of snow in February. From this perch, they could also observe the final group exercise every day, the "running of the steps." Led by the captain, followed by the juniors moving up, the team would form a single line and run up one set of steps, cross over to the next set at the top row and then go down. Upon reaching the bottom, with another cross over, the process was repeated—over and over. Before the renovation, the old Stadium had sixty rows and sixty steps. The team wasn't in good enough shape to do the entire stadium in this fashion on the first workout day in

February. By spring practice in April, however, the entire stadium circuit had been mastered by everyone.

These workouts were universally despised, but respect for Lynch carried the day. And the team of seniors moving up knew what it was like to smell a National Championship. They were well aware that they had only one more chance to grasp one. In February and March, the team prayed for overnight snow that would temporarily postpone the final test of endurance. The steps were always held last, before breakfast, for good reason. There was already enough puking.

Spring Game

With the advent of spring practices in '66, the coaching staff was reinvigorated. Finally they could add a passing dimension to the Irish offense. With two promising quarterbacks, Hanratty and O'Brien, and two promising receivers, Seymour and Heneghan, the offensive playbook was expanded dramatically.

The defense was solid up front after Pete Duranko moved from linebacker to defensive tackle. But there were holes to fill in the defensive backfield. Backup quarterback Tom Schoen was asked to try playing DB. This caused a temporary ruckus. Tom's father Norm, like so many dads in America, had always dreamed of his son playing quarterback at Notre Dame. Threats were made that Tom might transfer away from Notre Dame to play quarterback elsewhere. That prompted some straight-talk from the coaches. John Ray laid it out directly for the senior Mr. Schoen. Tom wasn't going to play QB at ND, but he had the potential to become an All-American at defensive back. Cool heads eventually prevailed. Tom stayed at Notre Dame, had a remarkable junior season, and did go on to become an All-American in 1967 as a senior.

The format of the spring game was much different in 1966. Today it is an intra-squad scrimmage where players actually vie for positions on the depth chart and hard-hitting is semi-encouraged. The 1966 spring game didn't mean much, except that it signaled the end of spring practices and raised scholarship money for the local Notre Dame club in St. Joseph County.

In 1966 the game was between a team of old-timers and the varsity, with scrubs added to the old-timers to fill out the roster. This tradition hearkened back to the days of Knute Rockne, when the graduating seniors and former players alike relished one more opportunity to play football on campus. The pro leagues were in their infancy and very few Notre Dame grads selected professional football as an immediate career path in the 1920s. But by 1966, old-timers willing to play against the Notre Dame varsity were a vanishing breed. Pro players, and seniors with a shot at the pros, were reluctant to risk injury in an exhibition game. The last game nominally in this format was held in the spring of 1967, but the format had, de facto, already been changed. That last game was broadcast live on ABC's *Wide World of Sports*. But the old-timers, former players like Johnny Lattner, merely roamed the sidelines and did media interviews.

If there was a score kept for the 1966 spring game, it has disappeared into obscurity. Opposing teams' scouts in the stands got to see very little of what Ara really had planned for the season to follow. There wasn't much passing on display.

But there was courage that spring. Ron Jeziorski remembers that.

One other almost-unknown story relative to the type of spirit we had among our team members involves Tim Wengierski. During spring practice of our junior year prior to the '66 Championship season, Tim caught a kickoff in a scrimmage, ran it back so many yards, and was hit in such a way that he sustained a fractured vertebrate. Thank God Timmy's back healed . . . and for the next season. But, after he sustained the injury, Coach Ara called him into his office and told him that because of the severity of the injury, Tim did not have to show up, play, or participate on the field. It was clear, with the people in front of him at halfback, that Tim would spend his senior year on the bench and in a prep role. Timmy absolutely refused. He insisted on being in the mix of practice and a regular player on the team. It's a story few know about, even among our own players.

Summer Games

The prevailing NCAA rule was that football practices could commence twenty-one days before the first scheduled game. The custom at the time was for colleges to begin play in mid-September, approximately at the same time as college classes began at most institutions. Of course, while the same rule applies today, schools are now more likely to schedule games late in August. Certainly all major schools have an official game by Labor Day weekend. The schedules have expanded from ten to eleven or twelve games at every college. The television appetite for college football is voracious. That hunger was in its infancy in 1966, the first year that a network (ABC) had a contract with the NCAA for the entire regular season.

While Notre Dame had an active summer academic semester back in 1966, the predominant summer student profile was that of a priest, nun, or religious brother seeking an advanced degree with emphasis on theology or philosophy. Athletes were not encouraged to take summer courses or to stay on campus for more "unofficial workouts." So the rank and file of the Notre Dame football squad returned home to work in steel mills, factories, farms, and family businesses. Some players had softer jobs and many caught up with old friends and occasionally drank a beer or two—something they would never have admitted to the head coach at the time. A few even smoked cigarettes—again more commonplace at the time before the Surgeon General provided clinical evidence to the dangers and mandated warnings on every pack.

The penalty for coming back to campus out of shape for the first workout on August 31, 1966 was severe. The first order of business on the first day was having pictures taken, Picture Day, open to the ever-curious media.

After that, everything was private and at one hundred percent full speed. Only a few members of the team had to pay the price for relaxing too much, but those that did have never forgotten it. Many returned in the best shapes of their lives. Pete Duranko was stronger, if that was possible. Alan Page was quicker, if that was possible. And Jim Lynch was even more focused—which most people believed was impossible. Free spirit George Goeddeke admits to returning totally out of shape. He commented offhandedly, "I ran around the block once in June, once in July, and once in August. I'm ready." A week later he was back to his normal, tenacious self—without gasping for air and hoping for a premature death after every drill.

Jeff Seiter from Xenia, Ohio, arrived on campus early for the 1966 football camp in an attempt to make the freshman team as a walk-on. He had been a pretty good offensive guard from a tough central Ohio league, so he had been officially encouraged to arrive early and give it

NATIONAL CHAMPIONS

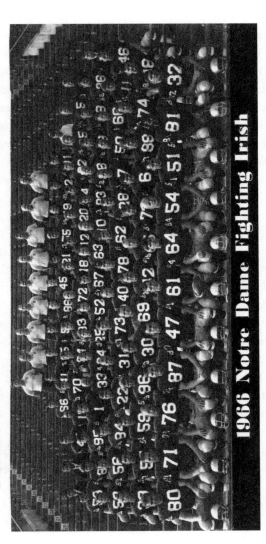

1966 Notre Dame Fighting Irish

First Row (left to right): Don Gmitter, Paul Seiler, Tom Regner, Tom Rhoads, Nick Eddy, Captain Jim Lynch, Peter Duranko, George Goeddeke, John Horney, Alan Page, Larry Conjar. *Second Row* (left to right): Bob Hagerty, Tim Gorman, Dick Swatland, Leo Collins, Jim Kelly, Joe Marisco, Angelo Schiralli, Ron Jeziorski, Harry Alexander, Hugh O'Malley, Allen Sack, Kevin Hardy, Dave Zurowski. *Third Row* (left to right): Gerald Kelly, Dave Martin, Mike Heaton, Dave Haley, Paul May, Rudy Konieczny, Tom O'leary, Mike Kuzmicz, Steve Quinn, Bob Bleier, Tom Schoen, John Pergine, Mike McGill, Jim Ryan, Tim Wengierski. *Fourth Row* (left to right): John Lium, Alan VanHuffel, Lou Fournier, Kevin Rasas, Mike Burgener, Dan Harshman, Jim Smithberger, Chuck Grable, Dan Dickman, Joe Freebery, Mike Earley, Bob Zubek, Roger Fox, Tom Quinn, Mike Bars, Bill Bartholomew, Jack Sullivan, Manager. *Fifth Row* (left to right): Al Kramer, Head Manager, Kevin Moran, Manager, Mike Holtzapfel, Chuck Landolfi, Fred Schnurr, Bill Skoglund, Chuck Lauck, Eric Nori, Tom Slettvet, Tom Reynolds, Bob Gladieux, Mike Franger, Paul Snow, Ed Vuillemin, Bob Kuechewberg, Coley O'Brien. *Sixth Row* (left to right): Pat Schrage, John Lavin, Jim Seymour, Terry Hanratty, Curt Heneghan, Jim Leahy,Frank Criniti, Tim Monty, Tom McKinley, George Kunz, Brian Stenger, Gene Paszkiet, Trainer. *Back Row* (left to right): Coaches Brian Boulac, George Sefcik, Jerry Wampfler, Tom Pagna, Head Coach Ara Parseghian, Paul Shoults, John Ray, Joe Yonto, Walley Moore *Source:* Notre Dame Sports Information a shot. The hitting was bone crushing from the very first day. Imagine lining up against Rhoads, Hardy, Duranko, and Page right out of high school. But Jeff held his own . . . until the fifth day. A separated shoulder provided him with an unexpected trip to the emergency room at nearby St. Joseph Hospital. He remembers sitting in the waiting room with a lanky sophomore from Michigan named Seymour. The two boys only a year apart, one's football career at Notre Dame was effectively over (Jeff was done with the team, but he had to hang around another week with his arm in a sling until freshman orientation), while another's was poised to explode into national stardom. The folks at St. Joseph Hospital saw a regular parade of Notre Dame football injuries. There was no coddling of players once they strapped on a gold helmet.

Play Favorites

Ara Parseghian approached practices with military precision. With Ara's focused leadership, the other coaches and the players were able to approach their practice objectives with absolute clarity. Ara played favorites. Everybody understood this. The favorites that Ara played were the guys who gave everything they had, the guys who proved they were better than the next guy on the depth chart. There was a constant sense of competition combined with an uncommon sense of fairness not found in many football programs, then or now. The guys that earned it played on Saturdays. It was that simple. It didn't matter if you were a highly-recruited scholarship guy or a determined walk-on. Ara played *his favorites.*

To reinforce the point, Ara and the coaching staff reviewed the progress of every single player every day in morning sessions before practice. Call it overkill if you like, but the discipline of keeping this routine kept everyone alert and made for an even playing field. It was a business lesson that many players successfully carried with them beyond the confines of football. Brian Boulac recalls a session like this, after '66, when he was an assistant coach. Try as they could, the coaches just couldn't find the right spot on the field for one seemingly talented player. Finally in frustration Ara asked, "Why can't we find a place to play this guy?" Tom Pagna's memorable response was, "Because the kid has a pimple for a heart."

This element of Ara's coaching style, measuring a player's heart, combined with tireless preparation, became the cornerstones of his success, especially in 1966. The best players, be they green sophomores or hardened fifth-year players, were on the field. They had all been tested in practice by some of the best football players they would ever face. The genius wasn't in the plays or the schemes (which were also quite innovative for the time), it was in the motivation of each player to survive, succeed, and contribute to the team. Ara understood that the only true motivation is self-motivation. He was a master at creating an atmosphere of incentives that challenged every player to reach his full potential.

When a player arrived every day at practice, it was obvious where he was on the depth chart because it was posted on the bulletin board for all to see, along with a schedule of where each player was expected to be and what was being drilled. It was as simple and fair as it could be.

One way to move up on the chart was to be flexible to play a new position if the coaches saw something they wanted to develop or if they needed to fill a void. Players understood that as well. Many embraced the chance to advance and finally get dressed or play on Saturday. Allen Sack arrived as a freshman quarterback recruit in 1963, one of six. At one point he was told by an assistant coach that he would never even dress for a Saturday game—and that was that, sorry. But he eventually bulked-up and played his way to success as a defensive lineman. As the fifth defensive lineman on the 1966 squad, Sack was drafted by an NFL team in the spring of 1967.

The House that Rock Built

Notre Dame Stadium was state of the art for college football stadiums in 1930 when it was constructed to Knute Rockne's specifications. Perhaps out of respect for Rock, or more likely because there wasn't an extra nickel in the University budget, the football facilities hadn't been upgraded in thirty-six years. The ghost of Rockne himself could have walked in and recognized every stick of furniture.

As a former student manager, Mike Finnerty remembers it.

Much has been said and claimed about the administration under the Golden Dome's attempts to de-emphasize football, but when it came to football facilities at that time, there was really little or no emphasis. The facilities that supported that 1966 team were meager, at best. The team operated out of the circa 1930 stadium locker room, no a/c, and lots of plumbing problems. All the toilets in the locker room were out of commission during the first week of the '66 season while the stadium was excavated for emergency repairs.

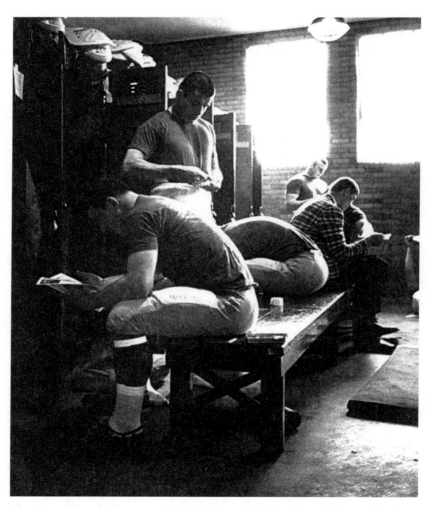

The Notre Dame locker room had stayed essentially unchanged from 1930 when Notre Dame Stadium was constructed. Knute Rockne would have felt right at home – except the players were physically larger and the equipment had improved. *Source:* Notre Dame Sports Information Collection

The game of football had changed from the late 1920s in fundamental ways. Even the football itself was leaner and had pointed ends, all designed to make throwing it much easier than throwing the balloons of the early '20s. All the players' equipment was more sophisticated too, especially the helmets, which were composite plastic with mandatory face guards. But the equipment manager was still right out of central casting for a 1930s movie. According to Finnerty, "If a football player had a uniform or equipment problem, he would have to head across campus to the equipment room in the ancient Fieldhouse and deal with Notre Dame's legendary cantankerous equipment manager Mac [McAllister]."

The players were much bigger, gargantuan by the standards of Rockne's days. And there were more of them to accommodate. Therefore both the home and the visitors' locker rooms were used on practice days during the week. According to Finnerty, "On Thursdays before home games players were required to pack up their uniforms and gear and move it all to their dorm rooms. On Fridays they would have to dress in their dorm rooms and walk across campus to get to practice." Some freshmen were actually relegated to dressing in the same antique facilities in the old Fieldhouse used by the Four Horsemen, and then they had to walk across campus every day in full pads to practice. This is what Ara inherited and what persisted until the fall of 1968, when the practice locker room for everyone was moved into the new Athletic and Convocation Center. After that, the Notre Dame Stadium locker rooms were used exclusively for game days.

Monday, Monday

During the season, Mondays were the most interesting days on the practice field, especially if you were a player attempting to work your way up the depth chart. The starters from the previous Saturday's game were given a light workout with minimal contact. The goals for them were to heal minor injuries and regain strength. Everyone else was inserted into live scrimmages to determine who wanted to earn, or keep, a spot on the roster for the following Saturday. These scrimmages were coined "Toilet Bowls" because everyone on the shit squad wanted to get in.

There is hardly a player from this generation who doesn't have a Monday story to tell. As one player expressed it, "It was the real deal."

You knew you were playing against the best in the nation and you had to give one hundred percent just to hold your position. There were no soft hits or easy yards during Toilet Bowls.

Larry Conjar was just one Toilet Bowl success story. He still remembers sitting on the top row of Notre Dame Stadium late on a Sunday after a home game in his sophomore year. He had just run the steps before he planned on heading in for a shower. "I looked over the field and just asked myself, What are you doing here? If you aren't going to go out and prove you belong in the games, what are you doing here? Right then I committed to give it my maximum effort on Monday."

The coaches remember this well. Larry was asked to carry on four consecutive running plays. Each time he delivered a punishing blow. It got noticed and prompted Coach Tom Pagna to say, "It's about time." Larry moved up that day and went on to have one of the most impressive careers at fullback position in Notre Dame history. His comment today is, "Yeah, Monday was the real deal alright."

Rituals

Part of the culture of football is the liturgy of rituals that teams invoke to either get stoked up or alternatively to break the tension of anxiety over an upcoming game. Ara believed in such rituals as much as any other coach for a simple reason. They seemed to work. At least in 1966 that was the case. As generations of more jaded high school athletes with NFL stars in their eyes were recruited in later years, not so much.

The high priest of rituals in 1966 was Coach Tom Pagna. Unknown to the team, it was Pagna who composed and delivered the weekly messages from "The Phantom." It was Pagna who oversaw posting messages on the Clobber Board—usually stuff from the next opposing team's local newspaper with an inflammatory statement highlighted. If Pagna couldn't find something juicy, then he made something up. These letters and postings were the fire and brimstone that offset Ara's consistently-focused and businesslike demeanor.

Another of the little rituals concocted by Pagna occurred at the end of practice on Thursdays before games. Recall that Ara remembered learning from Paul Brown not to leave your best game on the field during practice on Friday (save it for game day). To ease the mounting tension of constantly playing teams for which "Notre Dame was the biggest game of the year," a tension-cutting device was employed on Thursdays, right after practice. Sections of the team were assigned to compose poems or limericks about their positions (say, the offensive line) in the context of the impending contest. Time and creativity were expended in advance of the exercise—to be the best, be the crudest, or just to get the biggest laugh. The rewards were meaningless—maybe first shot at hot water in the showers, or being first in line at training table. None of these creative works seem to have survived. As Jim Seymour stated, "You wouldn't be able to print them anyway." But the players all remember the ritual.

Paradox

When you think about it, playing major college football is a paradox. The participants play long and hard (in practices) to play just seconds or minutes in the actual games. There are only about fifteen minutes of real action in a typical college game, split fairly evenly between the offense and the defense. So starters, even if they remain on the field constantly, expend a maximum of seven or eight minutes of intense exertion. Some really talented players, especially at a place like Notre Dame, never get to play at all. Some who religiously endure six days of practice never even dress for a single game. They become fans on Saturdays.

The paying fans on Saturdays never get to see or feel the real football that is played for hours and hours leading up to the game. The paradox is that they see a condensed highlight reel. It pits the best select few from one team against the best of another. But that doesn't really tell the story of the team— at least not at a place like Notre Dame. When the '66 Notre Dame team practice, it played against the best in the nation— itself. Coach John Murphy, who did the scouting of opposing teams on the schedule, was quoted as saying that the second teams at Notre Dame would have won at least seven games on the schedule.

For everyone who was ever assigned a practice uniform, pads, and a gold helmet, and then endured one of Ara Parseghian's practices, practice was "the real deal." They played football at Notre Dame and it was as real as it could be. Don't just ask the stars. Ask guys who had to hang on to make it, like Tim Wengierski. Then ask the guys who tried but didn't, like Jeff Seiter

Offensive Pep Squad, front row, from left to right: Mike Heaton, Kevin Rasas, Ed Tuck, Tim Gorman, Angelo Schiralli, John Lium, Jim Leahy, Gerry Wisne, and Jim Winegardner. Back row: Bob Belden, Mike Hotzapfel, Joe Marisco, Mike Earley, Ron Dushney, Bob Hagerty, Chuck Landolfi, Tom Slettvet, Mike Franger, Dave Haley, and Assistant Coach John Murphy. *Source:* University of Notre Dame Archives

Defensive Prep Squad, front row, from left to right: Lou Fournier, Bob Zubek, Vic Paternostro, Mike Malone, Bill Bartholomew, Ron Jeziorski and Tom Reynolds. Back row: Assistant Coach Brian Boulac, Tim Wengierski, Dan O'Connor, Bill Skogland, Dennis Kiliany, Chuck Lauck, Leo Collins, Dan Dickman, Jim Kelly, and Pete Lamantia. *Source:* University of Notre Dame Archives

10

ONLY THREE RULES

Freshmen arriving for orientation in September 1966 were clueless as to the events swirling around them, as freshmen always are. They were about to be swept into one of the most memorable and historic football seasons ever seen at Notre Dame. For a few months the dream-like season would mask the harsher realities that they would eventually encounter.

The Times They Are A-Changin'

There was institutional reorganization within the University itself that would become transformational over the next forty-five years. Having been forever under the direct control of the Congregation of Holy Cross, Notre Dame would be legally reorganized under a lay Board of Trustees for the first time in 1966. That major change had no practical effect on the students, and so it went largely unnoticed. But the long-term effects would be profound as the endowment exploded. Women would be admitted for the first time and laymen would eventually occupy the top administrative positions (except the president's position, which has to be occupied by a Holy Cross priest).

There was the fermenting counterculture revolution at college campuses from coast to coast, a generation of pre-war parents versus a generation of post-war children, fueled by a soon-to-be unpopular war in Vietnam. Very few Notre Dame students were engaged in anti-war protests in 1966.

But the war would dominate the news for the remainder of their college experiences. Many of the students had family or friends who would be injured or killed. The death toll would surpass 5,000 in 1966 and eventually consume ten times that amount of American youth. The night of the first draft lottery, December 1, 1969, was something unforgettable at Notre Dame, if you were there.

There were race riots again in Watts (Los Angeles) in March of 1966, after bloody summer riots in 1965 that left thirty-four dead, one thousand injured, four thousand arrested, and over $175 million of property damage. Malcolm X had been shot to death at a Harlem (New York) rally in '65. There were, however, so few Black students at Notre Dame (under sixty total) that the national undercurrent of racial unrest largely bypassed the campus. The movement had very few meaningful advocates or outlets for expression, and there was little dialogue about it on campus, regrettably. The irony was that Father Ted was central to changes in governmental policies and visibly prominent on the Civil Rights Commission. To the outside world, Notre Dame appeared engaged.

As the students on campus in 1966 matured, the assassinations of Robert F. Kennedy and Martin Luther King Jr. in 1968 would shock them. Just as shocking, Neil Armstrong and Buzz Aldrin would become the first humans to walk on the surface of the moon while some students, who were at Notre Dame in '66, were still in college on July 20, 1969. One can still argue that this is the most amazing technical accomplishment of the twentieth century. The space program made engineering a popular major at ND.

It would be a time when growing up wouldn't be optional. However, there was a brief calm before the proverbial storm. There was the 1966 football season.

RIGHT: Anti-war protests at Notre Dame were infrequent and small in 1966. Eventually the movement would grow and affect Notre Dame, as it did every college campus in America. *Source*: University of Notre Dame Archives

In the Bubble

Freshmen entering from a decade on either side of 1966 wouldn't recognize the Notre Dame student experience that existed in that year. Nineteen sixty-six was radically different from 1956. And 1976 would be radically different from 1966. All of the campus institutions, like the country itself, were in flux. Progress was being made. But it wasn't necessarily a clean and smooth process. Indeed, it was often messy, quite messy.

In 1966, Notre Dame was still an all-male institution with about 6,000 undergraduate students, about 2,000 living off campus. It wasn't exactly the Catholic West Point that students from the 1950s remember. Discipline was still the watchword. Essentially there were three core University rules: 1) Restriction of liquor from campus is a state law, 2) No cars on campus (except for second-semester seniors), and 3) No girls in dormitory rooms on campus. It took a printed manual of over thirty pages to explain these simple rules and the detailed ramifications of violating them.

Fr. Charles McCarragher, the dreaded "Black Mac" of the '50s, was now Vice President of Student Affairs, a promotion in name only from his former role as Prefect of Discipline. Gone were the draconian measures to manage lighting in the dorms at night (lights out at ten p.m.), which ended up being unnecessary and counterproductive. If a student wanted to study harder, why should there be an arbitrary limit to the time and place that that could happen? Looking back, lights out was stupid. It made life especially difficult for varsity athletes who had time commitments in the afternoon, training tables, perhaps team meetings, and then needed to study to maintain grade point averages for eligibility. The practice of football players going to summer school to have lighter class loads in the fall hadn't yet been exploited.

In 1966, freshmen were still required to be in their dorms by eleven p.m. on weeknights, one a.m. on weekends. Bed checks on each floor (physical counts of who was actually in his room) were conducted by resident assistants at ten p.m. sharp. If you weren't there, your name was sent to a list held by the uniformed security guard at the entrance to each dorm. All other doors were locked at curfew. If you hadn't signed in by eleven p.m., you were in trouble. What "trouble" meant was somewhat nebulous and at the discretion of the individual rector (usually a priest) for each dormitory. But if the situation persisted or the violation was flagrant, the violator was sent to an office under the Dome for harsher penalties. That usually started with a call home, and this tended to remedy most situations.

The Vending Machine

Notre Dame football players have always lived among the general student population with no special privileges. In contrast to some other institutions, there are no athletic dormitories, no special classes reserved for athletes, and no looking the other way when an athlete has a disciplinary problem. Quite the contrary, when a Notre Dame athlete causes a problem, it often becomes national news. Right or wrong, the outside world seems to hold Notre Dame to a higher standard, one not expected at the typical state university. So disciplining errant athletes, especially football players, has been both swift and severe. The Administration has always known that this is necessary to preserve the brand.

Nick Eddy had an instructive experience. Eddy was recruited by Joe Kuharich out of Tracy High School in California. He arrived at Notre Dame as a freshman in 1962. Early in his second semester he found himself in a fix. There were vending machines in the basement of Keenan Hall, one of the all-freshmen dorms. Sometimes the machines would jam and confiscate the inserted change. Some of Nick's buddies from the dorm were victimized by one such ravenous cigarette machine. So they enlisted their burley pal to help them extricate their money— turning the machine upside down and damaging it in the process. They were caught in the act. With minimal judicial process, all involved in the incident were immediately suspended for a year, including the promising halfback.

Eddy was devastated. He returned home to his mother and found a job. Now back in his native California, he was also able to spend more and better time with his girlfriend . He was no longer a football idol, but just a working stiff. It was quality time that solidified their relationship.

In the spring of 1964, Nick was eligible to return to Notre Dame, which he did. His impact on the football field was evident in the miraculous

1964 season and he distinguished himself in 1965. Technically he had one year of eligibility left and was taken by the Detroit Lions in the supplementary draft. But there was unfinished business in South Bend. Now married and with a baby daughter, Nick elected to play his final season for the Irish and get his college degree. That's what he promised his mother he'd do when he was sent home as a freshman. That's what he did.

Asked to tell this story years later, Nick was forthcoming. Of course, it was embarrassing to be sent home. But Eddy is quick to add:

I learned a lot from that experience. I learned that one stupid mistake could be costly. I was able to spend time with Jean and that made a big difference in my life. [They are still married forty-six years later.] I was able to redeem myself through hard work. Now I work with young people every day in my job [as a youth counselor] and I'd like them to know my story and I hope they can learn from it.

Imagine the leadership that a low-key fellow like Nick Eddy provided in the 1966 locker room. Everybody knew his story. But that only made everyone respect him more. Nick Eddy had one of the greatest playing careers of any player ever at Notre Dame. He saved his best for the 1966 season. Lucky for him, since that team won the National Championship. Luckier still for Notre Dame. Discipline and a cigarette machine were prominent factors in that success.

Jacket and Tie

In 1966, all students were required to wear jackets and ties to the evening meal at the dining halls (North and South). This throwback tradition would have had more merit if there were a good reason for guys to tidy-up once a day—the best possible reason being to impress girls. Of course that wasn't an issue. Everyone obeyed the rule for a simple reason: growing boys get hungry. But there was distain in the background. Rugby (a club sport) players would mock the system by coming to the dining halls with muddy shorts, cleats, and legs, but they would wear a jacket and a clip-on tie.

What can be said about the dining halls' food? Not much. Allowing unlimited glasses of milk and all the deserts you could eat saved the day. There was a food riot in early 1968 after half the campus got ptomaine poisoning at the North Dining Hall from bad creamed corn during midterm exams. That made national news. Then there was a persistent rumor that saltpeter was surreptitiously added to the mashed potatoes— the old military trick alleged to subdue sex drive. The mashed potatoes never quite tasted the same after hearing that.

An issue that began to gain traction in 1966 was visitation in the dorms by females, or the so-called "parietal hours." It is interesting to note that nearly fifty years later, this is still a hot topic, maybe the hottest topic on campus. Back in 1966, the only place for a visiting woman in a Notre Dame dorm was the reception lounge that was located near the front door. Those lounges were typically poorly lit, outfitted with furniture your grandmother would discard, and supplied with magazines that were at least a year old.

The exception to the rule was the corps of blue-uniformed maids, generally elderly (meaning over forty years old) women that cleaned the dorm rooms every day, making every bed on campus. It can't be accurately determined when this housekeeping service was instituted. It may have been a jobs program for the recently-depressed local community.

The no-women rule was unofficially relaxed on football Saturdays when family members would be allowed to roam the halls a couple of hours before the games, meeting sons and roommates and roommates' families. There weren't many other places for folks to go—no restaurants, pre-game areas, or lounges for on-campus visitors, especially on days of inclement weather. But for the remainder of the year, girlfriends, sisters, mothers, and grandmothers were confined to dreary lounges just inside the main doors to each dorm. No exceptions. The first moves toward a more relaxed visitation policy didn't occur until 1968.

The first time Notre Dame students would see females in class who weren't nuns was the fall of 1966. A program of shared resources was established with Saint Mary's College across the road (Indiana Route 31). Students from each school could register and take classes at the other, especially to enhance the variety of courses within their major. It was a welcomed innovation at the time. The implementation left room for significant improvement. The first year there was one small yellow school bus that transported both men and women between the campuses. One bus stop was outside McCandless Hall at Saint Mary's, the other at the old Fieldhouse at Notre Dame. From there you had to walk to classroom buildings. With only ten minutes between classes, it was impossible to schedule back-to-back classes on two different campuses. That slowed down implementation. But the die was cast and women would henceforth become part of the Notre Dame educational experience.

Not all the alumni thought the shared resources program was a positive move. Dave Condon of the *Chicago Tribune* had this response: "After 123 years of surviving Indians, fire, war, pestilence, depression and Joe Kuharich, Notre Dame has some intent of beginning to live dangerously; they propose to let some junior and senior coeds from St.

In 1966 a program, named Co-exchange, was started between Notre Dame and Saint Mary's College whereby students could take courses on either campus and use a shuttle bus for transportation. This was the beginning of female students in Notre Dame classrooms which eventually led to coeducation in 1973. *Source:* University of Notre Dame Archives

Mary's College, that matrimonial farm across the highway, attend a few classes. Well, there goes the old neighborhood."

Shortages

The Dome described the Notre Dame student body as follows: "Although academically far superior to its predecessors, and national in representation, the composition has been consistently white, middle class and Catholic." Women would become a welcomed addition to classes. But diversity was scarce. According to the *Dome*, "At the level of minority groups, interest focuses on Negro, Chinese and Spanish-speaking groups."

Culture was also in short supply on the Notre Dame campus. If a student desired to be part of a theatrical production, it probably required a trip to Saint Mary's. The attraction for Notre Dame thespians and non-thespians alike had more to do with meeting girls. There was a single singing ensemble on campus, the Glee Club. One positive cultural note from 1966 was that the Glee Club made a trip to California in September for a taped appearance on the Andy Williams television show. That show ran on November 6, and included other guests: Jimmy Dean, Jonathan Winters, and Miss America.

Testosterone

There was a full menu of activities you'd expect at an all-male institution. Notre Dame was one of the few colleges in the nation that offered ROTC from all three of the service branches: Army, Navy, and Air Force. That tradition continues. Freshmen could elect to take either Physical Education or ROTC as electives. About half the students chose ROTC because scholarships were available to upperclassmen and PE classes were too early in the morning. Cadets were required to wear uniforms to class. The ROTC branches held to the tradition of junior cadets saluting senior cadets on campus. It made for lots of gratuitous saluting on the sidewalks to and from classes.

Notre Dame has always been one of only a couple of schools to have intramural tackle football with full equipment—where the hand-me-downs from the varsity were recycled as they became obsolete. Nineteen residence halls each had their own team. In 1966, there were over 800 guys engaged in this activity. Most teams were stacked with all-city, all-conference, and all-state players that weren't quite big enough or fast enough to play on the real team. The games were played on Sundays with high school referees. It was serious stuff.

Student Amenities

Living on campus meant residing in one of the nineteen residence halls. They were all overcrowded. Singles became forced doubles, doubles became forced triples. Everyone got the same monastic furniture: a bed (bunk), one locker for all clothing, a small desk, and a desk chair. You could repaint your room if you liked, but you had to use official O'Brien paint (manufactured in South Bend) from a limited palette of colors that could only be procured at the ND facilities building. Decorating consisted of a limited range of options. Carpet remnants were added to cover the tiled floors. Those students with available transportation could purchase a sofa at the Salvation Army or the St. Vincent de Paul Society. Some sofas were stored over the summer and handed down as bequests. The "art" on the walls was limited to posters. By far, the favorites were of Jane Fonda (from *Barbarella*) and Raquel Welch in an animal hide.

The contents of typical lockers were likewise organized for efficiency. One suit jacket (for the dining halls), at least one tie, at least two weeks' worth of socks and underwear, a couple of dress shirts, two pairs of gym shorts, athletic socks, sneakers (preferably Chuck Taylor All Stars), a sweatshirt and sweatpants, a spring jacket, a winter coat, one pair of jeans, one pair of dress shoes (Bass Weejuns were pretty standard), one pair of sloppy-weather shoes, and lots of khaki pants. Much more than that and a student's locker would be stuffed.

Laundry was sent down a common chute at each dorm on its designated day. You had to have two laundry bags to make it work, one for the clean laundry and one for the dirty laundry. The Notre Dame laundry service was quite efficient. Everyone was required to have laundry tags marked with the owner's name and pre-assigned number.

The clean clothes all came back neatly folded and wrapped in brown paper with a string. It was better than home.

Student Center

When a student wasn't in his room, at the library, or eating in the dining hall, there was only one other place you had to look to find him—LaFortune Student Center. Here you'd find some game rooms, a juke box, lounges, student activities, and government offices. Girls' high schools from Chicago actually ran excursions to Notre Dame on Sunday afternoons, and mixers were held in the Rathskeller (basement) of the Student Center. Here freshmen actually had an opportunity to meet a female. Some guys even dated these visitors and took trips to Chicago after a single meeting.

For students, the actual center of campus wasn't the Administration Building (Golden Dome), it was a snack bar cleverly named the Huddle. If you missed a meal or wanted to taste a real hamburger, the Huddle was your place. They served soft drinks from the fountain. One popular concoction was a Cherry Coke, a regular Coca-Cola with cherry syrup generously pumped in. It became a favorite because of how it was ordered from the soda jerk (typically a student with a part-time job). "One Coke, then pop the cherry." There was little danger of offending a female within earshot. The crude joke never got old.

Outlets

In the fall of '66, the student newspaper *The Voice* ran out of gas and stopped publication. It was replaced in mid-November by *The Observer*, which continues today. The unfortunate fallout from this is that there are precious few accounts or photographs from 1966 football games or weekends in Notre Dame's archives. What few exist are from the weekly student magazine, *Scholastic*. There was one radio station, WSND-AM. It was transmitted on carrier current—basically over the water pipes to dormitories. Many prominent broadcasters and journalists got valuable experience from the studios located in the tower of O'Shaughnessy Hall.

The station could not be heard anywhere off campus or at any distance away from pipes.

Students then, as they do now, gravitated toward music to kill time. Every room seemed to have a portable stereo with a turntable and two speakers attached to it with flimsy cords that could be detached and moved to one side or the other. Walking down the halls of dormitories, you'd likely hear anything from Frank Sinatra to Jefferson Airplane. The following eclectic mix includes number one songs from 1966: "I'm a Believer" by The Monkees, "Summer in the City" by The Lovin' Spoonful, "Wild Thing" by The Troggs, "Hanky Panky" by Tommy James and the Shondells, "You Can't Hurry Love" by The Supremes, "(You're My) Soul and Heart's Inspiration" by The Righteous Brothers, "Monday, Monday" by The Mamas & the Papas, "Good Vibrations" by The Beach Boys, "These Boots are Made for Walkin'" by Nancy Sinatra, and "Reach Out, I'll Be There" by The Four Tops.

Rock 'n' roll historians point to the release on August 5, 1966 of the Beatles album *Revolver*. VH1 has it listed as "the best album by the best rock 'n' roll band of all time." No doubt that LP would have been packed by Notre Dame students returning back to campus from home to start classes.

Looking back to that time, there is a human tendency to romanticize good feelings into a collapsed time frame. Folk music benefits from just this kind of thinking. The great names—and there were many, including Peter, Paul, and Mary, Joan Baez, Judy Collins, The Kingston Trio, and Pete Seeger—all paid homage to the genius of one weird, skinny kid with a chiseled countenance framed by explosively wild hair—Bob Dylan. But even he was changing. In July 1965, he appeared at the Newport Folk Festival backed up by a rock 'n' roll band and was nearly booed off the stage by the crowd numbering an estimated 80,000. He was later quoted as saying, "I no longer want to be the spokesman for a generation." Times were a-changin'.

There were only five football weekends. When the outside world wasn't coming to Notre Dame, Notre Dame students had to venture off campus. There were three movie theatres in downtown South Bend, all now closed. In 1966, the major films of the year were: *A Man for All Seasons* (Academy Award Best Picture), *The Russians Are Coming, The Russians Are Coming* (about the invasion of a small island off the coast of

Massachusetts named Nantucket), *Sand Pebbles, Alfie*, and *Who's Afraid of Virginia Woolf?*

In 1965, one of the two blockbuster Hollywood releases was *Dr. Zhivago* (*The Sound of Music* was the other). Walking out of the State Theatre on Michigan Avenue in downtown South Bend in January, it wasn't hard for students to imagine what living in Siberia was really like—only without Geraldine Chaplin or Julie Christie.

11

THE OLD FIELDHOUSE

The lore of student pep rallies in the old Fieldhouse (built 1899) before home games in the '60s provides a spectrum of insights into Notre Dame culture, all pre-coeducation of course. Pep rallies are remembered fondly as volcanic events, the likes of which will never be seen again at the now kinder and gentler Nation of Notre Dame du Lac.

Those who were there in gritty attendance now, with passing years, retain fewer and fewer of the details, and their memories are generously selective as they cling to their youth. It is true, the current versions of the Friday rituals on campus contain very few elements of the forbearers. The pep rallies have been systematically moved from the beloved old Fieldhouse to the soon-to-vanish Stepan Center (entertainer John Davidson famously called the building the world's largest Jiffy Pop on national television) to the Athletic and Convocation Center, with temporary visits to Notre Dame Stadium, the Main Quad, and someplace new called Irish Green. They are still held on Friday evenings at seven p.m., somewhere on campus. Other than that, they have evolved into something no participant in 1966 would likely recognize or find remotely familiar. This might be a good thing.

Then, as now, there was very little happening on campus during

Thursdays before home football games. The team practiced in private, students scurried to and from classes, and the infamous professor Emil T. Hofman's quiz on Friday morning had a majority of the freshmen preoccupied well into the wee hours. The anticipation of home football games among the students was palpable. To some of them, the weekends were family events when parents and siblings arrived. That took some planning. To others, a girl from home might be visiting—maybe even "the girl." That took considerably more planning. To the average student in 1966, neither of these situations was commonplace.

Sixty Thousand, More or Less

Everyone on campus and for miles around knew that 60,000 people, more or less, would arrive for the game on Saturday, and that created the sense of an important regional event. It was likely that one or two games would be televised by ABC, and that gave Notre Dame renewed notoriety. It also provided the city of South Bend with a boost, some national visibility at a time when it was in steep economic decline. The money left in the local economy was really appreciated, especially at the hotels and restaurants that required five sold-out weekends just to survive. The town bonded to the "gown" out of necessity after the Studebaker plant in South Bend closed in the early 1960s. For the most part, that spirit of cooperation has endured ever since.

Visitors trickled in during the day on Friday, but still there really wasn't much to do. Visit the Grotto and read the Doctor Tom Dooley Letter, guaranteed to make mothers cry. Then visit Sacred Heart Church with the gilded Bernini alter and French stained glass windows. Swing by the Administration Building to see the mural on the underside of the Dome and point to Fr. Hesburgh's second-story office. Rub the nose of Knute Rockne's bronze bust at Rockne Memorial and then have lunch at the Pay Cafeteria in the South Dining Hall.

The major attraction was the Hammes Bookstore, located on the Main Quad. It was rumored that prices were raised after closing on Friday at five thirty p.m., so the prudent shopper headed that way to avoid the price increases and the out-the-door lines on overcrowded Saturdays. This emporium was quite unique for a college campus at the time. Only the second floor (of two) was dedicated to books and almost exclusively to textbooks, at that. The ground floor was a carnival of Notre Dame logos—printed, embossed, silkscreened, or engraved on every matter and kind of apparel or gift item popular at the time. An enterprising Holy Cross brother, known as Brother Bookstore, discovered this vein of gold well ahead of other colleges and implemented an aggressive program of property rights and fees that made Notre Dame the envy of the sports world. This, too, has continued.

During the '60s, Saturday morning classes were still very common. The football game wasn't just the centerpiece of the weekend, it was *the* thing. All the ancillary events that have since been packed into the total weekend show hadn't yet been imagined. However, there was one uniquely Notre Dame exception that took place on Friday—the pep rally.

Meat Squad

At about six p.m. on Friday, something quite unusual and distinct from any other college campus morphed into being. This could best be observed from the grassy area just north of the Huddle, south of Cavanaugh Hall and west of the Fieldhouse. There was a paved area outside of what was known as the Band Annex (the same building was once a campus epicenter as the first Huddle before La Fortune became the student center). Today, this location is occupied by picnic tables and trees. After an early dinner, bandsmen arrived from the dining halls and filtered into their practice room under Washington Hall. As they began tuning up, an alternative band of barbarians was collecting outside.

They were known as the Meat Squad. How members were recruited for this rag-tag group was a mystery. Looking at them it wasn't hard to imagine that the process could have been self-selection. The University admissions committee should have questioned some of their decisions. The only things Squad members had in common were sneakers and gym shorts. Oh, and one more thing. Somehow, somewhere, they had already consumed way too much of the golden medical elixir from the pharmaceutical companies in Milwaukee and St. Louis. It turned them into chest-bumping, out-of-control crazies.

Each person had a signature look. Body paint was the order of the day. Without a doubt, the maids that dutifully cleaned the dorms could have identified them immediately. Their trail of debris was hardly a tidy one. Headgear was the topper, quite literally. Remember, this was well before The Village People of "YMCA" musical fame. But those musicians could have been in the crowd taking notes. One fellow had Viking horns and a hair shirt. Another would have a military helmet and fatigues. Somebody from Texas would have an oversized cowboy hat. Variations of construction headgear with Virgin Mary dashboard ornaments mounted on top were popular—all spray-painted gold of course. This was a drunken collection of campus ruffians that relished a specific task. They were self-assigned to protect the Marching Band as they coursed through the campus on their way to the pep rally. The Band never requested this honor guard.

By six thirty, the Marching Band would form outside Washington Hall. The Band at Notre Dame has always been a big deal. Notre Dame claims to have the first university band in America and that it was the first to perform during a football halftime. No other institution has disputed the claim. In 1966, the Band numbered about 125 musicians. While this was representative in size, it didn't nearly have the numbers of the larger visiting institutions, many of them co-ed, that were traditionally on the football schedule. But the Band had a unique roll in the evolution of Notre Dame Football and was a spirited group of fit male musicians with attitude. The drum major would blow his whistle one long count, followed by three short ones, and the Band would begin to roll.

The logistical theory for this tradition from a long-past era was that it called the students out of their dorms and into a makeshift parade. So the Band marched deeply into the South Quad, past Badin, Howard, Morrissey, Lyons, Pangborn, and Fisher before curling back past Dillon and Alumni toward the North Quad. Some students religiously followed the Band out of tradition. Nobody got in its way. Being associated with the Meat Squad was disincentive enough. The Irish Guard, officially part of the Band, would march out front to protect the dental work of band members with horns from anyone, including stumbling members of the Meat Squad, who tried to impede the determined marchers. They moved quite swiftly.

After circling the North Quad, the parade eventually made its way into the Fieldhouse. The Band announced their presence to the assembled crowd by playing the "Notre Dame Victory March" (the greatest of all university fight songs). The first few steps into the building were hazards due to the slight embankment of the dirt track that clung to the outside walls of the structure near the double-wide side utility door. But for the Band, and for everyone inside the poorly-lit, now-dusty haze, that was the least of the dangers.

Six Thousand, More or Less

Students concerned with prime locations had filtered into the building well ahead of the Band. Daring parents and adult fans did as well, but they tended to retreat to the farthest reaches of the place, at the edge of or onto the basketball floor at the eastern end of the building. The maximum capacity of the building strained at about 6,000, although today that estimate is nostalgically exaggerated by a factor of at least three. Students were dressed with about the same formality as the Meat Squad, sans head gear. There was no need for any other garment, even on the coldest day. The inside of the Fieldhouse quickly became a warming oven and the aromas weren't pleasant, like putting dirty sneakers into a clothes dryer.

By the time the Band arrived, the adventuresome students, some as self-medicated as the Meat Squad, had become well-practiced in the art of building human pyramids. The goal was to build a pyramid high enough so that a single person could climb onto the tie-rods that crossed over the space, holding the iron structural arches together. This required three layers before the last loon was deployed. Eventually the human structures collapsed onto the tightly-packed crowd below, a danger for all nearby. Pep rallies weren't for the proper Saint Mary's girls from across the road. Guys with visiting girlfriends would hoist them onto their shoulders. The lucky few—the guys, not the girls.

If you weren't watching out for a tumbling mass of sweaty drunken humanity, there was always the prospect of a roll of toilet paper hitting you in the head from any direction. For generations, ND students had used toilet paper as makeshift streamers. A steady barrage of partial rolls of TP crisscrossed the huddled masses as the ends were held and the rolls were flung. Draping TP over the girders was part of the fun. It was mayhem at its finest. Seniors eventually lost interest in the littered ritual as they were forced off campus by housing shortages. If there were a TV camera crew in town, they would huddle by the side door attempting to capture as much of the frenzy as they dared without entering. They would have become appealing targets if they had ventured farther.

Cheerleaders warmed up the crowd with simple but familiar cheers like: "Go o o o Irish, beat boilers!" This would be followed by unofficial cheers from the crowd, like: "Rip 'em up, tear 'em up, give 'em hell, Irish." Officially, the rally began from the balcony on the west end as a suited student government official introduced the team. The players, all in jackets and ties, carefully made their way up the rickety stairs at the front (west side) of the building to sit in the tiny, tiered, second-story balcony. It took a number of rounds of the "Victory March" for them to all be in place. If the balcony had ever collapsed, the fortunes of Notre Dame, the

The pep rally before the Michigan State game, held on Thursday evening, was one of the most memorable in Notre Dame history. This is a view from the balcony of the Fieldhouse as students create a human pyramid. *Source* – University of Notre Dame Archives

financial ones for sure, would have been in serious peril. Ara attended these events more often than not in the early years. The reverberating sound of the crowd combined with the Band was deafening, worse than a rock concert.

Players were introduced to say a few words, interspersed with the Band playing the unique repertoire of Notre Dame songs such as "Hike, Notre Dame," "When Irish Backs Go Marching By" and "Down the Line." Sometimes there were special guests. Actor Pat O'Brien reprising his famous "Win One for the Gipper" speech from the movie *Knute Rockne All-American* was a fan favorite. After this speech and the following tumultuous applause, someone would start the chant "Don't go Knute. Don't go Knute. Don't go Knute," a sacrilegious reference to Rockne's final airplane trip that resulted in his death in March of 1931.

If Ara were there, he'd roust the crowd one last time. The alma mater, "Notre Dame Our Mother," would signal that the event was about over. The players filed down the stairs to the repetitive strains of the "Notre Dame Victory March" and out to school buses that took them across the lake to Moreau Seminary for an overnight stay away from campus. A few children camped out at the base of the stairs collecting autographs, but it was only a few. There were no adult autograph hounds yet to spoil this quaint part of the ritual.

Families and guests departed for the parking lots, headed toward their reservations at local restaurants and bars: Eddie's, Villa Capri, the Loft, Frankie's, Giuseppe's, and Rocco's. There were official mixers on campus for those who had female friends. Not many guys did. In fact, mathematically, six out of seven guys didn't, including virtually all of the freshmen. Some pep rally casualties landed in the infirmary, but most of the students had no place to go except back to their dorms. There, hot showers were in high demand. While you patiently waited for your turn, there was ample medicinal relief from cans, bottles, and kegs, all out of sight of the hall rectors, of course.

It didn't take long before the freshmen were rudely introduced to a new challenge. After a pep rally, there was no toilet paper to be had anywhere on campus. It was all draped over the girders or scattered on the dirt floor of the now-locked old Fieldhouse.

12

GEMINI

Benchmarks

There are specific dates in Notre Dame Football history that are benchmarks. The dates may be significant because of the opponent or the score of a game, but that's not always necessary. Fans and sportswriters tend to view events with this short-term perspective. Historians take a different view. The benchmark dates are defined by one simple rule: after the particular date, there is a fundamental change in the course of history from which there is no reversal.

For example, there would be universal agreement that college football changed forever after the 1913 Army–Notre Dame game (November 1), which effectively legitimized the forward pass as an offensive weapon. There was no turning back the clock after the Gus Dorais to Knute Rockne combination was heralded in the New York papers. It was a combination that allowed Notre Dame to beat the Cadets 35–13. Much the same can be said about the 1924 season, the first "National Championship" when Rockne's Four Horsemen won in the Rose Bowl (January 1, 1925) against Stanford with standout Ernie Nevers, 27–10. The national attention, based largely on having star players crafted into media personalities during the '20s, advanced the spectator appeal of college football and then encouraged a wave of college stadium projects to capture enormous paydays. This has continued, uninterrupted. The phenomenon was to turn the likes of Babe Ruth, Red Grange, Bobby Jones, and Jack Dempsey into household names. This happened almost exclusively in newsprint (radio wasn't even used commercially until 1927).

The 1936 Notre Dame game at Ohio State merits consideration as a benchmark because it went right down to the final play in Columbus, a pass from Bill Shakespeare to Wayne Milner, for the Irish win at 18–13. This was a radio event, probably the first landmark one for Notre Dame Football. Likewise, the 1946 0–0 tie with Army should be added to the list of benchmarks, if simply because of the long-standing rivalry (it was number one (Army) versus number two (ND)) and the array of Heisman Award winners in uniform (four) that day.

December 3, 1949 may be the absolute pinnacle of Notre Dame Football, the day the Irish beat Southern Methodist and finished four consecutive seasons undefeated under Frank Leahy. It's hard to imagine that feat ever being repeated. When Notre Dame knocked off Oklahoma in 1957 at 7–0 (November 16), it ended the longest winning streak in NCAA history at forty-seven consecutive games, and this was significant enough to keep the pilot light lit for Notre Dame Football tradition during the Period of Penance. Oddly, the win against the best in the nation may have accelerated the demise of Head Coach Terry Brennan— why couldn't the team perform like that every week? The arrival of Ara Parseghian on campus in 1964 (exact day unknown) put hot, blue flames in the Notre Dame burners.

In 1966, there were two authentic benchmark dates. One is easy to guess. The other was the first game of the season, September 24, at home versus Purdue. This game marked the beginning of the first season of exclusive NCAA-controlled football coverage on a television network (ABC), the brainchild of broadcast innovator Roone Arledge. College football was about to become a Saturday staple on TV, and there has been no looking back. The network was giddy over the prospect of having a national audience for a game that showcased college football's most storied program.

The season opener against Purdue also marked the first game of the first season when *all* Notre Dame home games were sold out. In fact, they were pre-sold out. This high-water mark was a huge fiscal accomplishment after thirty-six years. At the initial home game at Notre Dame Stadium in 1930, only about 15,000 seats were actually sold. During the Depression, South Bend businesses were flogged with regularity to purchase season tickets to help the team and the local economy. Otherwise visiting teams wouldn't come to South Bend and the entire aura of Notre Dame Football would have become pedestrian. But until 1966, there were actually very few sold-out games on campus. Since 1966, every home game has been sold out and this revenue stream has been as predictable as rain in a South Bend September.

While September 24, 1966 may not jump off the page as a benchmark event in Notre Dame Football history, Fr. Joyce would have certainly agreed with the designation. With $112,000 of television revenue paid to the University and a sold-out crowd at $6 per ticket (before parking, concessions, programs, and bookstore sales), this was the single largest revenue day in Notre Dame history (and would be for another year to come). The date meets the benchmark criteria. There was a fundamental change from which there has been no reversal. Mark the day in history, September 24, 1966. *This is the day that Notre Dame Football became the undisputed most valuable economic franchise in collegiate sports.*

Lastly, there was the importance of the game itself as a barometer, the predictor of the football climate to come. Was success in 1964 temporary, or was the Era of Ara for real? The loss to Purdue in 1965 was a defeat very few had seen coming, and it was a rude interruption to the hoped-for story of Notre Dame Football redemption. In 1964, the team really believed it was beaten by the officials in Los Angeles. In 1965, the team knew its first defeat was at the hands of a superior opponent in West Lafayette, no matter how close the score was. With no touchdowns and no wins in the final two games of 1965, the faithful were wondering where things were headed.

Purdue will tax us. They can run and pass. They are dogged pursuers on defense. They have pride, etc, but because we feel and know through pride of being here that we can never play flat! We must play with high emotion. The will to win is in all people. Those with the most will always wind up winning! This is national TV . . . The opener. We owe Purdue something sure, but to ourselves and Notre Dame and the nation that follows us we owe much more.

—The Phantom

Breakfast

After a quiet Friday evening at Moreau Seminary watching John Wayne movies, the Notre Dame football team moved back onto campus and their highly-structured game day schedule. There was Mass at Sacred Heart Church, celebrated by team chaplain Father James Riehle. After that was the private pre-game meal at the North Dining Hall, well after breakfast had been served to the regular students, and well before the normal lunch meal. After breakfast was a team meeting before everyone headed to the stadium to dress and warm up.

It had been announced that three sophomores would start the game: Terry Hanratty at quarterback, Jim Seymour at receiver, and George Kunz at offensive tackle. In the dining hall, the upperclassmen were keeping an eye on these three players, hoping that pre-game jitters wouldn't set in. In the case of one of the boys, they needn't have worried.

The story of Terry Hanratty eating steak for breakfast that morning has been well circulated. Even many years later, Terry still enjoys retelling it. Steak wasn't a normal dietary staple of the Hanratty household when Terry was growing up, not with four kids. Nor was it a menu item for the normal student at Notre Dame dining halls when Terry was a freshman. He can only remember having had steak once before in his life, at a lunch with Ara in a Pittsburgh hotel dining room when he was being recruited. So he was surprised to see steak, heaps of it, served at the pre-game meal. He wasn't about to be shortchanged. So he went back for three helpings. His upperclassmen teammates watched in amazement. Obviously, the kid wasn't concerned about feeling bloated in the heat of the action on the field only hours later. The upperclassmen took note. Terry "Rat" Hanratty was a cool customer.

Fireworks

If you were one of the fortunate 59,075 ticket holders to the sold-out Notre Dame Stadium and arrived late for the Purdue game on September 24, you didn't miss much. It was halfway through the first quarter before the fireworks began. Then you saw quite a show, especially if you were an Irish fan. You got your money's worth.

The pre-game stories tended to focus on the quarterbacks. Purdue had a great one, All-American Bob Griese playing in his senior year. He was the man for Purdue coach Jack Mollenkoph, Griese's face adorning the *1966 Purdue Media Guide*. Notre Dame was well aware of his abilities. It was Griese who guided the Boilermakers to a late score in 1965 to beat Notre Dame 25–21 (one of only two losses). That day he set an ND record for opposing quarterbacks, going nineteen of twenty-two, which stood until 1981.

For a different reason, stories about Notre Dame also focused on the quarterback position. Here the slant tended to be one of curious uncertainty. It was obvious from the 1965 season that the Irish needed a player to replace the graduating Bill Zloch, the stalwart and steady performer who was drafted into playing the position out of sheer necessity.

Two Notre Dame grads turned attorneys, Ed Adams and Frank Maggio, sitting in the stadium several years later used a timeout to engage in ranking their best and worst Irish quarterbacks. When they settled on Zloch as the worst, in their opinion, a fellow in the row in front of them turned and said: "But I tried my best." That is how Bill Zloch should be remembered. And, it was good enough to go 7–2–1 and finish the year ranked eighth. Bill Zloch went on to become a judge in Florida, something the attorneys didn't know at the time. Hearing this story, Ara Parseghian defended his 1965 signal caller: "Bill had more rushing yards than Mike Garrett who won the Heisman Trophy that year when we played Southern Cal. But we had two kids on the freshman team who could really throw the ball."

The ravenous press had been noshing on the decision Ara would have on opening day between two attractive sophomores, Terry Hanratty and Coley O'Brien. The eighteen-year-old Hanratty was six-foot-one, 190 pounds, from Butler, Pennsylvania. The slightly smaller O'Brien, five-foot-eleven, 173 pounds, hailed from the DC area, specifically Arlington, Virginia. Both men were right out of central casting for a Notre Dame quarterback: polite, articulate, handsome, with Irish surnames. For Ara it was an overdue bounty of talent. Either one could have started at any college in America that needed a QB. It was a close call, but late in the week Parseghian finally decided that Terry Hanratty would start. Both quarterbacks would be called upon for heroics before the season ended.

The pre-season polls had Notre Dame at number six and Purdue at number seven. The Irish were five-point favorites going into the game. With a matchup like this, ABC Sports was eager to have the contest open its very first season of NCAA football under the new contract. The decision would become troublesome later on when the network coveted coast-to-coast coverage for the Notre Dame-Michigan State game. NCAA rules prohibited two national games for a single school in the same year. Chris Schenkel, a Purdue grad who still lived in Indiana, and former Oklahoma coaching legend Bud Wilkinson were the announcing team for the game and for the key game each week throughout the season.

So It Begins

The opening kickoff went to Purdue. Three plays and a punt. One of those was a savage quarterback sack by Alan Page. In a season of few signature tackles, this was one that stood out. Greise was wobbly after that. Notre Dame ran three times, once each to Conjar, Eddy, and Bleier, and then punted as well. Next, Purdue ran six consecutive times. When Griese finally completed his first pass it was for a three-yard loss. That prompted another Purdue punt.

On this possession, Notre Dame opened with a forty-two-yard pass over the middle, Terry Hanratty finding Jim Seymour, who was just barely caught from behind on the Purdue fifteen-yard line. Nobody knew it at the time, but history was in the making. Two plays later, Rocky Bleier fumbled an errant halfback pitch on the six-yard line. As Bleier ran parallel to Hanratty at quarterback, the ball bounced off Bleier's shoulder pads as he turned to catch it. It hit the ground and bounced straight into the arms of Purdue defensive back Leroy Keys, who sprinted ninety-four yards, untouched, into the end zone. The Purdue band's "World's Biggest Drum" got an abrupt workout. Early advantage Purdue.

On the ensuing kickoff, Notre Dame's All-American halfback, Nick Eddy, returned the favor and the ball ninety-six yards for an Irish touchdown. Two touchdowns in under twenty seconds. Tie ball game.

There's a story behind that play. Tom Pagna had the team practicing a new "center wedge" alignment for kickoffs that week in practice. It worked pretty well against the prep team, and so it was decided to try it under game conditions. The key players in the center of the formation were Bob Gladieux, Don Gmitter, Jim Seymour, Larry Conjar, and Rocky Bleier. After forty-five years, the players on the field can still remember making their blocks and watching the back of Eddy's uniform ("No. 47") coast into the end zone. One Purdue player sustained a broken leg on the play. On the sideline, student trainer Tom Feske remembers it this way:

133

> *Larry Conjar was the great fullback on that team and was a key blocker on the kickoff team. After Eddy returned the kick for a touchdown and they returned to the bench, I still remember Larry saying to Nick with this huge smile, "Hey, I was looking to knock somebody on their butt, but the hole was so big there was nobody left. I had to lay back just so I could hit somebody [trailing the play] at about the twenty-five."*

The Eddy runback was electric.

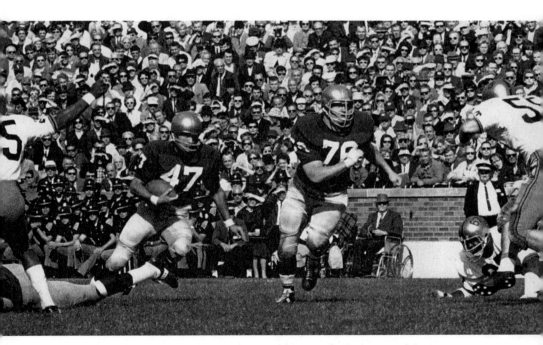

Nick Eddy (47) gets a block from Tom Regner during the first game of the season against Purdue. Eddy returned a kick off 96 yards for a touchdown to even the score 7-7 in the first quarter. *Source:* Notre Dame Sports Information Collection

Looking in the rearview mirror of forty-five years, it may have been the most important play of the entire season. The 1966 Irish team would be built on a stingy defense combined with an opportunistic offense. But ten minutes into their first game, neither the offense nor the defense knew their personality or their potential. Being able to take a football mulligan was important for the psyche of the team.

Thereafter, the momentum of the game favored Notre Dame. The game ended ND 26, Purdue 14. Take away the mulligans by both teams and it would have been ND 19, Purdue 7. The 14 points scored by Purdue would be the most scored against the Irish all season, and 7 of only 17 scored against the first team defense.

Respect

Today the game is remembered as a mild blowout. It was far from being one. Purdue moved the ball for a total 293 yards. Bob Griese was fourteen of twenty-six passing for 178 of those yards. This was a pretty fair afternoon against what was to become the toughest defense in the nation.

Rick Talley, sports editor for Illinois' *Rockford Register-Republic*, commended Griese, "who kept flinging and fighting even though knocked groggy on the second play of the Irish game." Coach Jack Mollenkopf admitted, "He took one heck of a beating out there." Griese eventually came in second in the Heisman balloting (Nick Eddy came in third, Hanratty eighth). Florida's Steve Spurrier finished first. The way the voting works, one has to wonder if Griese would have won the 1966 Heisman had not so much talent been located in the Midwest, specifically in Indiana. Purdue ultimately finished second in the Big Ten, losing only to Michigan State, 41–20. The team took its first trip ever to the Rose Bowl, against Southern California, winning 14–13, and finished a respectable number six in the polls.

In his first game, sophomore Jim Seymour broke two Notre Dame single game records for number of receptions (with thirteen) and yards receiving (with 276). He tied a third school record with three TD receptions in a single game, and he almost had number four on his first catch. Seymour was completely unaware of the dimensions of his afternoon's work. In his polite manner, he was later quoted in the locker room as saying, "Honest, sir, I don't know how many I caught. How many was it?"

Hanratty had an excellent day in his debut at quarterback. He was sixteen of twenty-four, for 304 yards, only 29 yards short of setting an ND single game passing record. His three touchdowns to Seymour went for eighty-four, thirty-nine, and seven yards, respectively.

A strong running game made everything work. Eddy had fifty-two yards rushing, Conjar forty-eight, and Blier thirty. Years later, everyone involved was quick to give most of the credit to the offensive line:

This photo captures the release of the ball from quarterback Terry Hanratty to end Jim Seymour in the opening game of the 1966 season, against Purdue. *Source:* Notre Dame Sports Information Collection

George Goeddeke (center), Dick Swatland and Tom Regner (guards), Paul Seiler and George Kunz (tackles), and Don Gmitter (tight end). In truth, everyone had a day they would remember.

The post-game comments by a disappointed Coach Mollenkopf were both gracious and prophetic. "We weren't prepared for Seymour," was his first statement to the press. "We had no idea how great he is. Man-to-man he is impossible to cover." Mollenkopf later stated, "This might be the best Notre Dame team in twenty or twenty-five years."

Mollenkoph and the Boilers, led by quarterback Mike Phipps and Leroy Keyes (converted to halfback), would beat Notre Dame the following year, 28–21. Jim Seymour would be double covered for the entire game.

Ara's take on the game was succinct. "I was afraid to say how good I thought these kids were." He was named UPI Coach of the Week.

As the Purdue Marching Band (at the time the nation's largest band at 300 members) was on the ND field at halftime doing a tribute show to the 150th Anniversary of Indiana Statehood, it moved from formation to formation—from a birthday cake to an Indy race car to two spacecrafts linking. At this point, the announcer intoned the following over the stadium public address system: "Indiana is the land of the astronaut—with many spacemen being Purdue University graduates. The first Gemini-rocket-docking attempt was piloted by astronaut Neil Armstrong, Purdue bandsman.[1] The space link-up—another first for the United States."

On September 21, 1966, the only link-ups that Purdue would remember would be between the Notre Dame Gemini, sophomores Terry Hanratty and Jim Seymour.

---

1 Author's note: My friend Neil Armstrong would eventually have a day we all would remember, July 20, 1969.

13

SHILLELAGH

You played to win and deserved to. That start was a good one.
One game does not a season make! Not one play of the Purdue
game will count in the Wildcat fiasco.

– The Phantom

The worry was that the Irish would let down after beating Purdue on national television. The second game of the '66 season was scheduled at Northwestern within the confines of antiquated and uncomfortable Dyche Stadium. The joke was that Fred Flintstone had carved his name into one of the benches in the visitor's locker room—when he played there. Mickey Mouse may have been a more appropriate reference.

It was Ara Parseghian's first coaching visit back to Evanston, pitting the Irish coach against some of his former recruits. One year earlier in South Bend, Northwestern had given Notre Dame a competitive game for one half, but the game eventually turned into a 38–7 rout. A letdown so early in the season would have been disastrous for Notre Dame's National Championship aspirations.

Many traditional college football rivalries have oddball internal trophies (Little Brown Jug, Old Oaken Bucket) that are entrusted to

Coach Ara Parseghian shows Captain Jim Lynch the Shillelagh, the trophy which goes to the winner of the Notre Dame – Northwestern game. *Source:* Notre Dame Sports Information Collection

the winning side until their next meeting. Such was the case between Northwestern and Notre Dame where the trophy was the Shillelagh, the Gaelic name for an Irish fighting stick. Physically, these fighting sticks are usually made of hard Irish blackthorn with a knobbed shaft (thorns were removed) and a clubbed end created where the base of the stick had once been a knotted root. When not used for fighting, the shillelagh makes a very nice walking stick and a distinctive ornament for a trophy case. The Shillelagh trophy had resided for five years at Northwestern as Ara Parseghian's teams had beaten the Irish in four consecutive encounters, 1959–1962. But the craggy black club was now ensconced in the Rockne Memorial trophy case at Notre Dame because Ara's Irish had finally won it back in 1965. The Notre Dame head coach had grown accustomed to having the slender hardwood weapon-trophy in proximity.

Agase

But to keep the stick close at hand, Ara's team had to beat the Wildcats and Ara's friend Northwestern Head Coach Alex Agase. Ara and Alex weren't just friends, they were best of friends. Their families took vacations together. Joe Doyle tells a story about one of the dual family trips at a lake when a panicked young Kristan Parseghian was flailing in the water away from shore. Alarmed, both Ara and Alex immediately dove in off the dock and swam to her aid, almost crashing into each other in the process. As Doyle chuckled, "Can you imagine those two big hulks of men crashing into the lake? The fish had to be terrorized." That's how close they were.

Agase was Parseghian's chief assistant at Northwestern. It would have been logical for Alex to move to Notre Dame with his friend. But just like Ara had succeeded Woody Hayes at Miami of Ohio, it was Agase's turn to move up into the head coaching ranks. Ara endorsed the move and was very supportive of his friend. In fact, Ara only took three of his Northwestern assistants with him: Paul Shoults, Doc Urich, and Tom Pagna. Four of Parseghian's assistant coaches at Northwestern remained behind to support Agase.

The Northwestern coach was well liked by the Chicago press. Before the 1966 Notre Dame game, the *Sun*-Time's Jack R. Griffen wrote, "Alex Agase has the build of a bear—a rather good-sized one—and the soft, gentle manners of a Southern gentleman. He likes long cigars, laughs easily, and wishes people would not go around this week feeling sorry for him."

Oldsmobile

As the '66 season arrived, the kicking game was the one area of discomfort among the Notre Dame coaches. It wouldn't be until the ninth game that a satisfactory punter emerged—after many were tried. Walk-on junior Joe Azzaro was determined to move up into contention for place-kicking duties. His was an amazing story. Joe had been severely injured as a high school student in a car accident. Both his feet were crushed. His doctors said he would never play football again. Not to be deterred from the sport he loved, Joe started practicing kicking field goals in his back yard over the family grape arbor. He made his high school team, Pittsburgh Central Catholic, in his senior year—exclusively as a kicker. Of course he was interested in Notre Dame, but under Hugh Devore in 1963, there was no reciprocal interest. Fortunately he had good enough grades to get into Notre Dame on his own.

He became a walk-on Freshman Team member in 1963, and helped pay for tuition by waiting tables in the dining hall in the off-season. He was finally awarded a scholarship for his sophomore year, but a torn quadriceps delayed his progress by another year. In 1965, Ken Ivan proved to be a very reliable place kicker for the entire season. As a senior (with two more years of eligibility) in 1966, Azzaro was fighting for a job. By the week before the Northwestern game, he was in great physical shape and finally getting noticed. Ara coached the kicking teams personally. He would use incentives, like making bets for milkshakes, for improvements in accuracy and distance. He also had the annoying habit of walking right in front of the kickers (mid-stroke) in practice to make sure they wouldn't flinch in game conditions.

The travel squad to Northwestern was limited in size, and there was no room for two kickers on the bus or at the hotel. But Ara strongly encouraged Azzaro and a couple of other guys (Tim Monty and Curt Heneghan) to get themselves to Chicago. Their gear would be taken there on the team bus. It was also mentioned that the coach's personal car, an Oldsmobile, would be parked behind Rockne Memorial and it might be left unlocked, with the keys under the floor mat. Joe could take direction well and arrived with his pals in Evanston, just in time to warm up for the game. He recalls, "We parked right next to the locker room door, no problem." The boy who was told he would never play football again got into the game and scored his first point for Notre Dame in the fourth quarter. That's how he became the regular place kicker for the remainder of the season. Azzaro still remembers, "When we got back to Notre Dame I mistakenly locked the car keys inside the car. It was lucky I wasn't around when Ara returned."

Pile Driving

This would be the third game of the season for Northwestern, and they were off to a disappointing start. Their first game was against an emerging University of Florida program. *NW University Notes* previewed the game, writing, "It will mark one of the few times a Big Ten team has gone south to play a Southeastern Conference foe." Northwestern was thumped by the Gators and the eventual Heisman Trophy-winner Steve Spurrier, 43–7. In their home opener a week later, Indiana upset the Wildcats 24–14, even though they set a school record for passing yards, 297. Nothing would have gotten the Northwestern season back on track better than an upset win over Notre Dame. Likewise, a 0–3 record would be difficult to recover from.

Northwestern had started the season with high hopes. They planned to increase their emphasis on passing from twenty percent to sixty percent based on skilled personnel. They were relying on quarterback Denny Booth, tight end Cas Banaszek, and split end Mike Donaldson. But they claimed experienced runners as well. Ron Rector was one of the leading rushers in the Big Ten in 1965, along with pile-driving fullback Bob McKelvey. Northwestern's concern was interior linemen. Even though they lost to Notre Dame 38–7 in 1965, they had led ND 7–6 with only three minutes to play in the third quarter of that game. Then the game broke open with runs by Nick Rassas, thus ending a four-game Wildcat winning streak. They were returning sixteen seniors, twenty-three lettermen, and only eight of twenty-two positions needed to be filled in 1966.

Notre Dame received the opening kickoff, but they were stymied in three plays and punted. Unfortunately, sophomore offensive tackle George Kunz would be injured and lost for the remainder of the season. Then Northwestern was held to three plays and a punt. On the first play of the second possession halfback Nick Eddy went through a big hole created by replacement right tackle, sophomore Bob Kuechenberg, and ran fifty-six yards for an Irish touchdown. Jim Ryan added the extra point.

Later in the first half, an apparent touchdown pass to Jim Seymour was called back because of an offside penalty. But Northwestern was stymied and linebacker John Pergine blocked a punt that he ran back for twenty-six yards. But the Irish were held. Then the ND defense pounced on a juggled Booth-to-Camble pitch out. This started the first sustained drive by either team. Larry Conjar finished nine plays, smashing over right guard for the TD. The Irish had even more chances to score. But Hanratty was intercepted at the goal line, and later in the second quarter he fumbled. The sloppy half ended Notre Dame 13–Northwestern 0.

Whatever hope the Wildcats had of clawing back ended on the second series of the second half. ND received the ball at their thirty-nine-yard line after a punt. Five runs, two passes, and one penalty later, Rocky Bleier cut back behind left tackle Paul "Barn" Siler for 6 points. Terry Hanratty successfully ran a QB draw for a 2-point conversion. Now it was ND 21–NW 0. After that, the first team defense slammed and locked the door. Tom Schoen ran back an interception thirty-seven yards for a touchdown. Sophomore Frank Criniti had the final Irish touchdown late in the game on a one-yard run after a drive engineered entirely by the second team.

The only Northwestern points came in the fourth quarter against Irish subs, a thirty-two-yard pass from Melzer to Murphy. Everyone on the sidelines remembers Defensive Coach John Ray going ballistic after that touchdown. There he was, kicking the turf, pacing like a wild man, and getting into the face of each defensive player as they reached the sideline. He just couldn't abide any shortfalls on defense, even by the second unit. Maybe it was an overreaction. The game wasn't in any doubt. But it was a big deal to Coach Ray, and he transferred his intensity to the rest of the team. It worked. The Notre Dame defense only allowed one more touchdown for the remainder of the season—in eight games.

Other than this momentary lapse, the defensive unit played with determination. For the game, Northwestern passers were twelve for twenty-six for 119 yards, but were limited to only 40 yards rushing. In the game, ND was penalized for eighty-five yards, so the team actually gave up forty-five more yards to the watchful officials than to the powerless Wildcat running attack. No pile driving was in evidence.

After the game, a disappointed Coach Agase was reflective, saying, "We had a second quarter first down on the seven and if we had scored then it would have been 7–7 at the half. Then the last half would have been a dog fight . . . But, we didn't [score it]."

However, Northwestern was able to finish their remaining schedule 4–3 and land in the middle of the Big Ten standings, ahead of Michigan, Wisconsin, Indiana, and Iowa.

The win was sweet and forcefully addressed the issue of a possible letdown. But the Irish offense had a day of mixed results. Hanratty was fourteen of twenty-three for 203 yards. There were three fumbles (one lost) and one interception. Nonetheless, a 35–7 final score insured the Shillelagh would continue to gather dust in the Rockne Memorial trophy case, steps away from the door to Ara Parseghian's office.

14

THREE AMIGOS

By the third week of football and the fourth week of classes, normal students and football scholars alike would have been seriously engaged in academic work. For most students, football was the main distraction and class work was their main concern. Football players had a more difficult balancing act to perform. They were expected to be outstanding on Saturdays and compliant with academic standards on the other six days of the week. They were ably assisted by their advisor Professor Mike DeCicco and a cadre of faculty members who have always embraced the attitude that every student who cares about learning will be given the requisite attention to succeed. It is part of the unwritten code of decency that envelops the Notre Dame campus.

The academic strength of Notre Dame in 1966, as it is today, was built upon the special relationship between the undergraduate students and a hands-on faculty. Notre Dame has always emphasized the role of good teaching combined with good role models. To put this aspect of the "four-legged table" into clearer focus, three faculty members will be featured. They are merely representative of the scores of committed professors who were at Our Lady's University serving this generation of Domers.

Frank O'Malley, Robert Leader, and Emil T. Hofman were at the pinnacle of their teaching influences in 1966. They knew each other pretty well at the time. Notre Dame has never been a very large institution (compared to what outsiders believe about it), and since the mid-fifties, South Bend has been a modestly-sized town (population 136,000 in 1966) struggling to reclaim the manufacturing momentum it enjoyed in the first half of the twentieth century. The result is that for generations, faculty members have bumped into each other a lot, both on and off campus. Perhaps more to the point, they cleaved to each other in this remote outpost, a satellite of the more urbane Chicago, ninety miles away.

These three friends have the appealing dimension of spanning almost a century of Notre Dame Football. Frank O'Malley was a student at the time of Knute Rockne. Emil T. Hofman presides today on a campus where he has known a full litany of coaching names: Leahy, Brennan, Kuharich, Devore, Parseghian, Devine, Faust, Holtz, Davie, Willingham, Weis, and Kelly. (Nobody in the know counts O'Leary.)

Each teacher has a unique story. To know these men is to find the foundation, the bedrock, of Notre Dame, the academic place.

Frank O'Malley

Frank O'Malley begrudgingly tolerated Notre Dame Football. If he attended the games in 1966, it was a well-kept secret. But he always knew that football was important to the place and the students he loved. Professor O'Malley was a compassionate gentleman filled with respect for words, writers, seekers of Faith, and clumsy Notre Dame men, whom he tirelessly labored to fill with a respect for words, writers, and seekers of Faith.

O'Malley was raised by Irish immigrant parents in Clinton, Massachusetts, where his father was a weaver at the local cotton mill. After high school he worked two years in a local drugstore to pay for college. A spiritual person, he gravitated toward a Catholic college. Thanks to Knute Rockne's football teams, Notre Dame had become the most prominent Catholic college in America. O'Malley started as a student at Notre Dame in 1928 and graduated as valedictorian in 1932. The unique combination of academics, Catholic heritage, and national stature through football captured his heart, and he never left.

He was one of a small group of male professors referred to as the "dons." This meant that they were bachelors and that they lived in quarters within one of the residence halls. Two monastic rooms and a tiny bathroom weren't the attraction for this calling. No, the benefit was the constant interaction with the bright minds that washed in and out of Notre Dame with the regular tides of freshmen and seniors.

Frank O'Malley *Source* - University of Notre Dame Archives

Professor O'Malley was one to collect his students, like stamps or coins, and turn them into lifelong friends. This was especially true of his gifted student-writers. Edwin O'Connor was an O'Malley protégé and life-long friend. O'Connor dedicated one of his books to him, *Edge of Sadness*, which won the 1962 Pulitzer Prize for Fiction. After the publication of *Last Hurrah*, O'Connor became a literary celebrity. But every year in the fall (he did like football), O'Connor would return to Notre Dame to spend a few days with his mentor and friend. He would also be a surprise guest at all of O'Malley's classes. He made his annual pilgrimage-visit in 1966. It was to be his last. His 1967 trip was postponed until the spring. On March 23, 1968, O'Connor died suddenly of a cerebral hemorrhage, only a few days before his scheduled visit. On that day, a distraught Frank O'Malley arrived at his freshman English class (Rhetoric and Composition) and announced the death of his former student and friend. He cried openly, then cancelled class.

Before the annual Thanksgiving break, Professor O'Malley would ask if any students were staying on campus, unable to return home. In the '60s, Notre Dame had emerged as truly a national university. While the majority of students could afford a way home to towns in Illinois, Indiana, Michigan, Ohio, and Pennsylvania for the four-day holiday, many could not. He invited those left behind to join him for Thanksgiving dinner at the Morris Inn, the only hotel on campus. It had a kitchen inhabited by a real chef. For the (un)fortunate few from places like Northfield, Nebraska, and Middlefield, Connecticut, this meal was an unforgettable experience.

The shadow of the cross doesn't seem to fall across mathematics. But it does fall on a person in this field. It will affect the way he teaches and deals with students: the whole approach becomes different.

What the Christian school seeks is not the bland student who blindly follows the fashionable, but the complicated, wondering, worried, struggling person who is trying to put some things together.

—Frank O' Malley

A sensitive man with such a big heart should have been left to live in peace in a remote corner of Indiana. But demons were dispatched. The ever-present incense of O'Malley's cigarette smoke held them somewhat at bay during the day. But the lounges in downtown South Bend's Oliver Hotel and, after Oliver's demise, the LaSalle Hotel, became the Devil's playground. Leaving campus early in the evening and returning back to campus late became a habit that O'Malley struggled with. Frank was always lively and alert for classes in the afternoon, but the students all knew he was a suffering soul. Many a student at Lyons Hall found himself with the awkward task of helping Frank into bed after one of his trips to town.

Mercifully, the demons never were able to claim him. He was an active writer and literary critic throughout his life. In class he made good writers come alive, especially good Catholic writers. He tried to light the pilot light for creative writing in even the most reluctant student. He would encourage the class to "tell stories well, be authentic" and to do it "with color"—even if the words were printed black on white. He hated throw-away words like "majestic" because he couldn't paint or enhance a picture in his mind with them. With an all-testosterone audience, some of O'Malley's teachings stuck. In fact, most of it did.

Other students were jealous when the select few were able to get into one of Frank's classes. For one thing, he was known as "A–B O'Malley" referring to the range of grades he awarded at the end of class. But over time, everyone knew that something special was happening under O'Malley's watchful eye. He required writing assignments for every class and often made students read them aloud. He would find the kernel of good in these and encourage the student to try harder the next time. The lazy student was soon exposed by embarrassment. Every assignment received his written comments, but never a grade. One student was shaken when the comment read, "You know what I think of this." It was a life's lesson in a few simple words from a man who had nothing but love to give. An article that appeared in *The Dome* in 1960 read:

Perhaps no one else has better conveyed that sense to Notre Dame students than witty, incisive English Professor Frank O'Malley, 28 years on the faculty and the university's most inspiring undergraduate teacher. O'Malley plumbs life's most basic emotions, using Charles Peguy to examine the virtue of hope, Claudel to plumb suffering, Kierkegaard to

*emphasize the shallowness of religion without love. When he reaches stu-
dents, O'Malley often changes their lives, teaching them to love learning
and learn love. "The totality of life has hit me," said one of his students
last week. "The act of knowing and the act of being are becoming one.*

For forty-six years Frank O'Malley loved Notre Dame. And for all
those years the students loved him back. His 1974 obituary appeared in
Time Magazine, something quite unusual for a college professor. His colleague Professor Thomas Stritch said, "O'Malley was the most brilliant
teacher of humanities Notre Dame has ever known." Frank O'Malley
will always be a part of Notre Dame. He is buried in the Holy Cross
Congregation's cemetery on the Notre Dame campus. He is one of only
a select few non-CSC brothers or priests to be so honored.

Robert Leader

Robert Leader came to Notre Dame in 1952 by way of Yale University and the University of Illinois. But he almost didn't make it. You
see, Bob Leader was one of the 25,000 Marines wounded on Iwo Jima.
That would make him a war hero in anybody's book. Reporter Robert
Sherrod characterized the assault on Iwo Jima as "nothing less than a
nightmare in hell." But Professor Leader's war exploits were even more
noteworthy. He was a member of the Third Platoon, E Company, the
famous "Easy Company," that climbed and took Mount Suribaci and
then planted an American flag for all of the American forces on land
and on ship to see. About that event, *American Heritage Magazine*
wrote:

> *While these duels were being fought, Leader and Rozek discovered a
> long piece of pipe, apparently a remnant of a rain-catching system,
> and passed it up to the summit. Waiting with the flag were Schrier,
> Thomas, Hansen, and Lindberg, and they promptly set about affixing
> it to the pole. It was about 10:30 A.M. when the pole was planted and
> the Stars and Stripes, seized by the wind, began to whip proudly over
> Mount Suribachi. The date was February 23, 1945. This achievement
> by the 3rd Platoon had a unique significance. Mount Suribachi was the*

*first piece of Japanese-owned territory—not counting mandates like
Saipan—to be captured by American forces during World War II.*

The black and white shot of the flag-raising by AP photographer Joe
Rosenthal became the most celebrated image of the War in the Pacific.
But as historians know, the famous photo was actually taken of the
second flag-raising—after a larger stars and stripes was transported to
the summit. The first flag was quite small. Both flags were hoisted on
the discarded piece of water pipe that was procured by Corporal Bob
Leader. Secretary of the Navy James Forrestal, observing from a ship,
commented, "Raising that flag on Suribaci means a Marine Corps for
the next five hundred years."

Flags of Our Fathers, by James Bradley, is a comprehensive historical
account of Iwo Jima, the flag-raising, and the aftermath for those in
the photo who survived. Bob Leader was featured as one of the last
remaining members of Easy Company and therefore quoted extensively.
Regrettably, Professor Robert Leader, USMC, departed this life in 2006.

A student sitting in Leader's class in 1966 would have known nothing
of his military past or his heroism. Leader rarely spoke of it. Instead,
sitting in the darkened Law Auditorium (once used by Frank Leahy
for film sessions and chalk talks), the student would be informed and
entertained about art history—an unlikely subject for an ex-Marine to
teach if ever there was one. He came to Notre Dame from Champaign,
Illinois, for a simple reason. State universities had less interest in sacred
art than religious schools. Leader was a practicing artist who designed
murals and stained glass for religious spaces and developed a national
reputation in doing so.

What he became over the years was a favorite among the students
because of his spirited banter and wit. That, and the fact that he drove
to work everyday a dusty sage-green Jaguar XKE convertible that was
inconspicuously parked at the rear of the Architecture Building. The
all-male student population coveted that car.

Leader was forever quotable. He once commented that he would prefer
to watch a pretty girl studying the Mona Lisa than to study the Mona
Lisa itself (apparently he wasn't wowed by this da Vinci masterpiece).
That was lively copy at Notre Dame in 1966. After the arrival of female
students into his classes in 1967, not so much.

150

Robert Leader
Source: University of
Notre Dame Archives

There are no revolutionaries with mortgages.

*The years a person spends in a university is one of the few times
in his life when he can really experiment and question.*

*There's something wrong with a student body that doesn't riot at
least once a year.*

—Robert Leader

There are over fifty churches throughout the United States that feature Leader's stained glass artistry, including the Sorin Hall Chapel on
the Notre Dame campus.

Oh yes, he was a rabid Notre Dame Football fan. This was a constant
topic of conversation around the "Old Bastards Table" at the University

Club, which was regrettably torn down in 2008 much to the detriment of the faculty community at Notre Dame.

Emil T. Hofman

Emil T. Hofman arrived in South Bend to teach at Notre Dame for a single semester in January of 1950. He still remembers that first winter as particularly severe with biting cold and lots of snow. Despite those harsh few month, he never left. Faculty stories like his have long ago ceased to be remarkable at Notre Dame. There are so many.

Doctor Hofman is a living manifestation of the Notre Dame four-way: academics, religion, family, and football. Hofman was schooled at Catholic University, where he was mentored by Bishop Fulton J. Sheen, later known for his television presence in the 1950s. Hofman started as a chemistry teacher (for which he is still probably best remembered), advanced to become Dean of the Freshman Year of Studies, and is now Professor Emeritus, which he laughingly characterizes as "still working but for no salary." He enjoys Notre Dame Football immensely, now from the press box, but he has the same intricate working knowledge of the game that most of us have for German operas.

He has been a stalwart proponent of the highest values at Notre Dame for sixty years. As such, he has earned friendship and respect across the campus. This includes the athletic directors, especially his close friend, the late Moose Krause, and the head football coaches, especially Ara Parseghian. He can comfortably articulate the specific roles that the classrooms, the chapels in every dorm, and football Saturdays have in working together, in the formation of Notre Dame students.

Hofman faithfully attends daily Mass. On most days, if the weather cooperates, he also sits outside on a campus bench; everyone knows the one, just south of the steps to the Administration Building with a perfect view of the Golden Dome. Doctor Hofman patiently waits for visitors to join him for a chat. He rarely waits very long. And those who are seated in a conversation with him must accept the constant interruptions from passersby. When kidded that he has evolved into a "babe magnet," he just shrugs his shoulders and replies, "That's the way God meant for it to be." The "T." in Doctor Hofman's name stands for Thomas, his Confirmation name. A little known fact is that his

Baptismal name is Aloysius. Emil (A.) T. has become a Notre Dame icon, and deservedly so.

If you were a freshman in the fall of 1966, the name Emil T. Hofman might have struck fear in your heart. In those days Doctor Hofman taught introductory chemistry (a two-semester course) to all the science, pre-med, and engineering students. This meant two sections of 550 students each (the total number of seats) in the old Engineering Auditorium, at the time the largest capacity lecture hall on campus. This maximum of 1,100 students meant that about two-thirds of the freshman class was exposed to Hofman's tutelage on the first day of classes. Most stayed with him, but some immediately saw the light and transferred to liberal arts or business.

The way Doctor Hofman taught Chemistry was somewhat unorthodox. He had a quiz each and every Friday at the end of class and only one exam, the final, at the end of each semester. It was akin to preparing for a weekly schedule of football games. If you could pass the

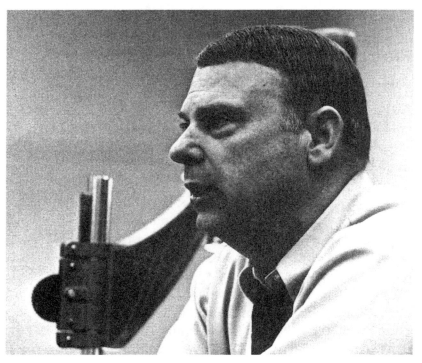

Emil T. Hofman Source - University of Notre Dame Archives

quizzes and correct the gaps in your preparation by the final, you had a good chance of passing. But grading was tough. Emil likes to remind people that Eric F. Wieschaus received only two Bs in his course. But he was forced to change those grades years later in 1995. When filling out the official change-of-grade form, there was a space for "reason." Doctor Hofman entered this notation: "Won Nobel Prize."

Living on the Freshman Quad on Thursday nights during football season was remarkably entertaining, albeit tiring. Of course all the windows would be wide open for ventilation from the stagnant dormitory air. At regular intervals there would be some creative incantation shouted out for all to hear that included the name "Emil T." embedded in it somewhere. Limericks were in vogue. Applause would follow and then a period of absolute quiet followed as the chemistry students would dive back into their class notes. Like Old Faithful it would happen again in about an hour, eliciting the very same reaction from Keenan-Stanford to Zahm to Cavanaugh to Breen-Philips to Farley. This happened well into the early morning hours. Those freshmen not taking chemistry welcomed the crisp cold of November nights that closed the windows, if only because they could finally get a decent night's sleep on a Thursday.

Behind Emil's approach and superb teaching skills there was an effective method. Students learned incrementally, immediately saw their mistakes, and had ample time to correct their thinking. There was only a two percent drop-out rate once students committed to the regimen. This in what is generally considered a weed-out course at most other colleges. Generations of students remember passing Emil T.'s course as a badge of honor. Today the world is blessed with scientists, doctors, dentists, and engineers who were baptized by the fire of the legendary Emil T. Hofman. No wonder that at age ninety he is still beloved by all, a babe magnet for the ages.

15

IT'S DE-LOVELY

The Army–Notre Dame game has made All-Americans because of the attention it has demanded. They are undefeated, they will seek revenge. They have spirit – tradition . . . And a history of never quitting. They are quicker than any team we have thus far played.

Greatness . . . is not a moment, or a play, or another player. Greatness is consistency!! Always giving the same!!

—*The Phantom*

It was a perfect day for football in South Bend: sunny, clear, and seventy-two degrees. The weather during football season in Northern Indiana resembles a meteorologist's version of Russian roulette with at least two of the five chambers of the climate gun loaded with unpleasant surprises. But weather would not be a factor on this day when the Cadets of Army visited Notre Dame Stadium.

On paper, the game appeared to be a good match-up, unlike the last few games in the series between these erstwhile traditional rivals. Army was returning eighteen lettermen on its team. After the 1965 campaign, Head Coach Paul Dietzel had abruptly left West Point to become head coach at South Carolina. So there was a new coaching staff headed by Tom Cahill (who would win Coach of the Year honors). The Cadets were 3–0 coming into the contest, with wins over respectable opponents Kansas State, Holy Cross, and Penn State.

A year earlier in 1965, Notre Dame had prevailed to win by a modest 17–0 margin at the new Shea Stadium, built within site lines of the New York World's Fair. All of the pre-game evidence pointed toward a competitive game in 1966. At a press event in Chicago early in the week of the game, Army publicity agent Frank Walter insisted that the Irish really hadn't been thoroughly tested yet. "I guess I'm the only guy in Illinois who thinks we have a chance on Saturday." Notwithstanding his optimism, by mid-week the Irish were four-touchdown favorites.

Sensitivity

The season marked a benchmark of sorts for the Army team. The *Army Media Guide* highlighted sophomore tight end Gary Steele from Levittown, Pennsylvania, as the first "Negro" to play varsity football for Army. Publicist Walter explained further. "It isn't because we haven't wanted Negroes or Negro athletes at Army; in fact we'd like to have more. It's just that not many have the academic background to meet our requirements."

The insensitivity of this remark is stunning by today's standards. But back in 1966 nothing was made of it. The nation was struggling painfully with racial equality issues, and the protocols for political correctness hadn't been established yet. It wouldn't be too long before offhand remarks like this in athletics would get a person fired. The comment is included here because neither Mr. Walter nor the West Point Administration should be thought of as prejudiced. They were not. It is included to demonstrate how far the country had to move forward in 1966, and how far we have now progressed as a nation. Mr. Walter would have been prescient to have predicted an African-American commander-in-chief within forty-four years. That would have been news.

For perspective, Notre Dame also was struggling to attract qualified minority student athletes, much to the disappointment of all concerned, especially Fr. Hesburgh. South Bend wasn't a particularly hospitable place for minorities, with a history of KKK activities in its inglorious past. Except for parishes in Louisiana, African-Americans weren't Catholic as a rule, and therefore, they viewed Notre Dame with skepticism. Wayne Edmonds playing in 1953 was Notre Dame's Jackie Robinson figure as the first African-American to earn an ND monogram in football. But at first, even Wayne had been refused service at the campus barbershop and was forced to go into town for his haircuts. Georgia Tech would refuse to let Wayne play at its home field in Atlanta in 1953, so the game was rescheduled to South Bend at the insistence of Frank Leahy and the Notre Dame Administration. Wayne blazed the trail for more Black football monogram winners, notable among them Aubrey Lewis, Jim Snowdon, and Dick Arrington. On the 1966 Irish squad, senior Alan Page was the only person of color.

Emblematic of the culture of the day was an incident in Cincinnati involving Notre Dame basketball great Tom Hawkins, a 1959 graduate. When the country club lined up to host a Notre Dame club meeting learned that Hawkins, ND's first monogram winner in basketball, was to be the featured speaker, it told event chair Mike Brady that Hawkins could not attend. To his credit, Brady, a classmate of Hawkins, promptly moved the event. No Hawkins, no Notre Dame club.

Billets

The 3–0 Army team arrived on Friday via United Airlines from New York City. Win or lose, it wasn't returning until Sunday morning on a flight leaving South Bend at ten a.m. But this accommodation was more like a prison sentence than a respite from the strict routine back at West Point; the players were staying at the Hotel Elkhart, twenty miles away. The advertisement for this fine establishment (which appeared in the game program) highlighted free parking, air-conditioning, free television, free ice, and automatic elevators. Undoubtedly, it was the best hotel in Elkhart at the time. Whatever sparse nightlife South Bend had, well, Elkhart had even less.

The other members of the Army traveling party (band, glee club, and upperclassmen) had it somewhat better. They all took a New York Central train leaving late Thursday evening and arrived on Friday afternoon. In Army parlance, they were "billeted and fed at the Joint Services Armory" about a mile south of Union Station in South Bend. The entire trip would cost each visiting cadet only forty-three dollars out of pocket.

A few pranksters from Notre Dame found where the Army mule, their mascot, was "billeted." Overnight before the game, they were able to use food coloring to paint green shamrocks on both of the animal's hindquarters. It wasn't recorded if the mule was actually allowed into Notre Dame Stadium.

In a gesture of hospitality, Saint Mary's College scheduled a mixer for the lonesome visitors the Saturday evening after the game. That was all the socially-deprived, all-male population at Notre Dame needed— more competition from upperclassmen in those well-tailored, snappy grey uniforms.

Playing Dirty

But first there was a football game to be played. Army won the toss. And it was right at that very moment when their luck ran out—for the remainder of the afternoon and hopefully the evening as well.

Tight end Don Gmitter was to comment years later, "They were the dirtiest team we played all year. They had this Cadet hustle and gang tackling, and a lot of it was after the whistle. So we started crunching some people, and they got the idea. After about three minutes they weren't talking any more."

The first Army series was a three and out. After a punt, Notre Dame started on its forty-six-yardline. The scoring drive that followed was executed with military precision. First a pass from Hanratty to Seymour for nineteen yards. Then a pass to Nick Eddy for nine more. Just when Army was thinking pass, they had to stop Larry Conjar on three consecutive runs inside the tackles for fourteen yards, seven yards, and two yards. Then more pounding, a three-yard run by Rocky Bleier, followed by two more Conjar blasts. On the ninth play, Bleier scored on a two-yard run over left tackle. Everyone on offense was warmed up: Hanratty, Seymour, Eddy, Conjar, Bleier, and the offensive line that was moving people around at will, including center George Goeddeke, guards Dick Swatland and Tom Regner, tackles Paul Siler and Bob Kuechenberg, and tight end Don Gmitter.

When you mention this game today, the guys all tell the same story about this first drive. After the fourth carry by Conjar, the Irish broke the huddle with another play called to their bruising fullback. Across the line an Army linebacker yelled, "You guys aren't going to run that play again?" The Notre Dame center George Goeddeke yelled back, "Yes we are, and this time it's on two." The play went for positive yardage. Army had no answer for the Irish attack, even when they knew the play in advance.

After the first score, Notre Dame kicked off to the Cadets. On their third play from scrimmage, halfback Carl Woessner fumbled . . . after running into the massive Kevin Hardy who separated him from the pigskin. Irish defensive tackle Pete Duranko recovered the loose ball on the Army thirty-three-yard line. On the next play Hanratty connected with Seymour again, for a touchdown. With 7:35 left to play in the first quarter, the score was Notre Dame 14–Army 0.

What little offense Army was able to generate came on its next series. It ran nine plays and had a pair of first downs before it was forced to punt to Jim Smithberger on his own twenty-four- yard line. Six plays and two penalties later, Terry Hanratty ran seven yards around tight end Gmitter for another TD. It was a mechanical seventy-six-yard drive. The first quarter ended ND 21–Army 0. By the end of the half Notre Dame would score two more touchdowns.

That score at the half, 35–0, was the way the game ended. But it could have been more lopsided. The student publication *Scholastic* wrote: "The score was 35–0 and it might have been 100–0 if Ara Parseghian, the humanitarian who coaches here, had left his Hanratty–Seymour battery and other regulars in the contest for the second half." Offensive starters were pulled at the half and defensive starters were pulled at the end of the third period. The second half became a "Saturday scrimmage," an opportunity for the Notre Dame coaching staff to get more reserve players into game situations. This experience would prove valuable later in the season. The second team offense led by Coley O'Brien was able to gain 125 yards in the second half using a substantially-reduced playbook.

The *New York Sunday News* declared the game "the most lopsided of the twenty-six triumphs by the Irish in the series dating back to 1913."

Army coach Tom Cahill provided an honest assessment of the game. "The thing that beat us," he said, "was their balance. You try and stop them one way, and then they beat you another. From the scouting reports we were well prepared, but we just couldn't stop them." If he mentioned the Notre Dame defense, those quotes didn't make the Sunday papers. But defense was the story of the game.

The printed stats for the game supported Coach Cahill's terse summary. Touchdowns: Bleier, Seymour, Hanratty, Eddy, Eddy. Terry Hanratty was eleven for twenty passing. Seymour had eight receptions for 155 yards. The running game was balanced: Eddy seven runs for thirty-seven yards, Bleier six runs for thirty-six yards, and Conjar seven runs for forty-four yards. Those players saw little or no action in the second half.

In the third game of the season, Notre Dame, led by the defense, pitched its first shutout. That felt good. John Ray, the brooding human thunderstorm, displayed no lightning. There would be five more shutouts before season's end.

This photo captures the Notre Dame starting backfield in 1966, l-r) Rocky Bleier (28), Larry Conjar (32), Nick Eddy (47), and Terry Hanratty (5). Only Conjar would stay healthy enough to play in all ten games. *Source:* University of Notre Dame Archives

The ever-respectful Parseghian carefully skirted a critique of the Army team or the notion that the game may have been a mismatch. "I don't know when I've had the luxury of coming into the locker room at halftime and not be worried. So I said to myself, we'd better enjoy it." Then Ara used the game to express some coaching concerns about his sophomore second unit: "They need lots of work."

Parseghian, a serviceman himself, always had tremendous respect for the service academies. After the game, a small contingent of Domers walked across the playing field with a banner reading, "ARMY ROTS— SEE?" That didn't last long. The sentiment on the ND campus was still overwhelmingly pro-Lyndon Johnson, pro-troops, and pro-war. It is worthy reminder that from the 1965 Army graduating class, twenty-six would lose their lives in Vietnam.

For those fans listening to updated scores on the radio, on the same day, number-one-ranked Michigan State beat Michigan 20–7 at East Lansing. The stage was being set.

During halftime, the Notre Dame Marching Band did another show celebrating 150 years of Indiana statehood. It featured a medley of songs by composer Cole Porter from Peru, Indiana: *Night and Day, Montmart, Blow Gabriel Blow, Begin the Beguine*, and *It's De-Lovely*.

For the Irish the entire day was "de-lovely." The Army team, however, was sentenced to another night in Elkhart.

16

ON THE FIELD FOR
THREE PLAYS

The irony of writing about the 1966 Fighting Irish nearly a half-century after the fact is that there is so little reference material available regarding the most significant aspect of the team, the defense. Consider the hundreds of column-inches of copy that have been written over time about the National Champs and the "Game of the Century," yet so few articles are able to provide insight into either individual plays or the individual players on the defensive side of the ball.

Even the squad's end-of-year statistics are dominated by offensive numbers with only a couple of defensive categories even tabulated: tackles, kicks blocked, fumbles recovered, and passes intercepted. So be forewarned, this will be a short chapter—but not because it deserves to be. To the contrary, it's about a very important subject if you want to understand Notre Dame Football in 1966. Very important.

Those who are at all familiar with the 1966 team can recite the single most impressive statistic—that in ten games the first team defense allowed only 17 points (7 to Purdue, 10 to Michigan State). As remarkable as that is, the second team defense only allowed 7 points (to Northwestern, late in the second game of the season) and that group played a lot, often for most of the fourth quarter. Ask them about it today and the subs aren't surprised. Mostly they remember playing against the number one offensive unit all week . . . in practice. So they were well prepared.

Rounding out the 38 total points scored against the Irish, one touchdown was against the offense (Purdue) and one was against special teams (Navy). Overall, there were six shutouts in ten games. This remarkable defensive record transpired against some very good teams, including four Top Ten opponents (Purdue, Oklahoma, MSU, and Southern California). Any offensive unit would have tremendous latitude to be aggressive when there were reasons to believe the other team would have trouble scoring at all. This was the luxury Ara Parseghian enjoyed in '66. The defensive unit only allowed an average of 2.4 points per game.

Tom Rhoads summarized the defensive attitude. "Our goal was to only be on the field for three plays. We were really pissed when it took more than that to get back to the bench. We wanted to be done for the day by the beginning of the fourth quarter. We'd know we were done for the afternoon when we heard Officer Tim McCarthy give his safe driving tips."

Officer Tim McCarthy provided a safety tip between the third and fourth quarters beginning in 1964. These were so corny that they were anticipated by the crowd in the stands, and apparently by the team as well. One of his most memorable was, "Remember, if you have one for the road, you'll get a trooper for a chaser."

The Toughest Sixty Minutes

The rules for earning a varsity football letter, the prized monogram "ND," were quite strict in 1966. A player had to have accumulated sixty minutes of playing time over the course of the season, or cumulatively in their respective career. The individual player statistics were kept by student managers, who meticulously watched game films, recorded who was on the field, and counted the seconds between individual snaps.

From this accounting process emerges one of the most stunning but well-disguised statistics from the Michigan State game. Against the second best team in the nation, the starting eleven members of the defensive unit played every single down with only two substitutions made (amounting to less than one minute combined playing time). Nine of eleven defensive players were in the game for the full thirty-three minutes, twenty-eight seconds. The other two only missed a single play.

The names of these outstanding defensive players are familiar to many, in part because of their professional careers after graduating from Notre Dame. But all deserve recognition for being part of what might be the finest defensive team in the history of college football (Michigan State could legitimately claim recognition here for their 1965 unit), and without question the best defensive unit in Notre Dame Football history. You won't hear much debate about that.

Notre Dame played a 4–4–3 defense in '66. The front four were Alan Page, Kevin Hardy, Pete Duranko, and Tom Rhoads, who were backed up by Harry Alexander, Alan Sack, Eric Norri, and Chick Lauck. The line-backing corps was led by Jim Lynch, Mike McGill, Dave Martin,

The Notre Dame defense allowed only 24 points over the entire 1966 season. Photographed are the defensive line and linebackers. First row: (l-r) Ed Vuillemin (35), Alan Page (81), Kevin Hardy (74), Pete Duranko (64), and Tom Rhoades (87). Back row: (l-r) Defensive Line Coach Joe Yonto, Dave Martin (56), John Pergine (50), Captain Jim Lynch (61), John Horney (51), Mike McGill (60) and Defensive Coach John Ray. *Source* – Notre Dame Sports Information Collection

163

John Pergine, and John Horney, who were backed up by Alan Van Huffel, John Lavin, and Ed Vuillemin. The starting defensive backs were Tom Schoen, Tom O'Leary, and Jim Smithberger. The second string was Dan Harshman, Mike Burgener, and Tom Quinn.

Mining the final end-of-season statistics for data is revealing. There were twenty-six pass interceptions, led by Schoen (seven), Pergine (five), Smithberger (four), Lynch (three), Burgener and Harshman (two each), and O'Leary, Martin, and Horney (one each). There were eleven fumbles recovered, led by Alexander and Martin with two each, followed by Duranko, Hardy, Horney, Jeziorski, Lynch, Pergine, and Smithberger with one each. Martin and Pergine each had one blocked kick.

Tackling, bringing to the ground a conditioned athlete intent on forward progress, is one of the most difficult maneuvers in all of athletics. Yet, of all the 633 plays run against the Irish in 1966, there are very few signature tackles to be found in historical game records. The inescapable conclusion is that the defense played as a unit, with lots of gang tackling. The leaders in double-digit tackles were Lynch (106), Pergine (98), Hardy (79), Duranko (73), Page (63), Martin (62), Smithberger (54), O'Leary (46), Rhoads (41), McGill (40), Schoen (30), Lavin (21), Sack (17), Burgener (15), Harshman (14), Quinn (13), VanHuffel (12), and Jeziorski (10). The ultimate leader in game minutes was John Pergine, followed closely by Dave Martin and Alan Page, each man with over 250 minutes played.

Upon close examination, three additional statistical anomalies jump off the page. Notre Dame was only on the receiving end of kickoffs on thirteen occasions (two of those were run back by Nick Eddy for touchdowns). This is yet another testament to the defense. And there was only a single field goal scored against the Irish in 1966 in five attempts. Opposing offensive teams were rarely close enough to even attempt a field goal, again a tribute to the defense. The lone exception happened at Michigan State—and it took a remarkable, barefoot Hawaiian with the wind at his back to hit that forty-seven-yarder. Last, and in many way the most impressive stat of the season, was that zero points (of any kind) were scored against the Irish in the third quarter.

An unheralded and immeasurable service the first team defensive unit provided was to sharpen the skills and the focus of second team offensive players, many of those players rising sophomores. Without capable and prepared substitutes who were able to fill in for sudden vacancies on the offensive side of the ball, the 1966 season would have ended differently, especially in the final two games. Every player acknowledges that the toughest defensive team they played against all season was wearing familiar gold helmets—on the weekdays.

The Meanest White Man

When a first draft of this chapter was sent to some of the players for comments, Harry Alexander responded that he believed something was missing. But he couldn't quite put his finger on it. Upon reflection, the missing element had to be the overwhelming presence of defensive coach John Ray. Alan Page called him "the meanest white man I ever knew." He meant it as a compliment, a term of endearment decades later.

Ray was every bit the tactical innovator on the defensive side that Parseghian was on the offensive one. If he hadn't been, Ara wouldn't have hired him. He was smart, quick, and disciplined. He had to be that way to keep up with the head coach. While Ray possessed the enduring qualities of competence and character, that's not how the players remember him. Ara could communicate volumes with an offhand glance known as "the look." Although Ara had a full range of emotions, he effectively employed subtlety. There was nothing subtle about his defensive coordinator who doubled as the position coach for the linebackers.

John Ray's personality and demeanor was one dimensional. He was a human thunderstorm. He constantly demanded respect because of the wrath he could inflict. Even from afar, the brooding dark clouds of Ray's presence provided fair warning that he was not to be taken lightly. "No man on defense is worth a time out, so if you are hurt get yourself off the field in a hurry." Messages like that were constantly drilled into the defensive mindset.

Then there was the constant rolling thunder, the litany of criticism, designed to sharpen focus and command attention. Jim Lynch tells a story about Ray sidling up to him (out of earshot of everyone else) in practice after he missed a tackle and saying, "You're the captain? What a disgrace. We ought to have a new election. You're a disgrace to the uniform." Comments like that were meant to get the juices flowing— and they worked. The thunder, running commentary by the gravelly-voiced Ray, was incessant.

That thunder immediately turned into full-fledged cracks of lightning with the slightest provocation induced by stupidity. Penalties were venial sins. Scores against the defense were mortal sins. Ara demanded playing smart. When a defensive player had a miscue, Ray took it as an affront to the head coach and to the entire team. Much of it was tied to his personal pride and his desire to please Ara. The outburst that is still remembered in vivid detail (language unprintable) happened when the second team defense gave up a touchdown to Northwestern late in the second game of the 1966 season. John Ray exploded. It was an entire thunderstorm in a couple of short minutes that the guys still talk about. The game wasn't even close, but that wasn't the point. The upshot was that the second unit never allowed a score of any kind after that.

John Ray expected perfection. In 1966 the Notre Dame defense came as close to perfection as any team in modern college football history ever will.

17

DRIZZLE, COLD, WIND, AND CLOUDS

Congratulations on your Army win. 3/10 of your season is over. Of all the games the Irish have played and will play, only one is what I worry about as a "sleeping giant" – North Carolina.

No slogans – no wisdom – just work to get number 4 in our path to being the best. Life is short – what we do with every day or every game is to all of us – v i t a l ! ! Opportunity knocks - - - - 10 times. We've answered her first three!

—*The Phantom*

When colleges play a preponderance of their football games in the Midwest, they have to be prepared for the inevitable inclement weather: wind, rain, snow, and cold. Therefore, teams in 1966, especially those in the Big Ten Conference, were built around success at the running game first and the passing game second. Teams from the South didn't have to follow the same formula because their weather was predictably milder. On October 15, 1966, on what should have been a beautiful fall day in the Midwest, the fortunes of the top two collegiate football teams in the land would forever be affected by the weather. It rewarded one and punished the other.

At Notre Dame Stadium the conditions were the worst anyone had seen for many years. It was a bone-chilling day with sustained winds at twenty-four miles per hour and gusts to forty miles per hour. Mark Carmichael writing for the *South Bend Tribune* termed it a "crew of 'horsemen' named Drizzle, Cold, Wind, and Clouds." This was an historic reference to the greatest sports lead of all time written by Grantland Rice. "Outlined against a blue-gray October sky, the Four Horsemen rode again. In dramatic lore they are known as Famine, Pestilence, Destruction, and Death. These are only aliases. Their real names are Stuhldreher, Miller, Crowley, and Layden." That day in 1924, Notre Dame was playing Army at the Polo Grounds. On this day in 1966, it was Notre Dame Stadium, and the Tarheels weren't ready for the game conditions, or for the Irish.

North Carolina was a very respectable team coming into the game. They had a 2–1 record. They opened their season with a 10–7 loss to Kentucky. This was followed by a 10–7 win over in-state rival North Carolina State and a surprise 21–7 besting of the Michigan Wolverines. Their schedule allowed them two weeks to prepare for the Notre Dame game. There was no way they could have prepared for the weather they would encounter.

Carolina was built around a passing attack and their talented quarterback Danny Talbott. According to Jack Griffin of the *Chicago Sun-Times*, "This fellow does everything except take movies of the game." Tarheel coach Jim Hickey proclaimed him, "the first really classic runner we've had since Charlie 'Choo Choo' Justice." Talbott was named ACC Athlete of the Year in 1965. The boy had talent. Nonetheless, Notre Dame was a twenty-five-point favorite before the game.

Unfortunately for NC and Coach Hickey, Mr. Talbott didn't see much of the game. About midway through the first quarter, Talbot was forced to leave with an ankle injury. Three plays later, the relentless Irish defense sent number-two quarterback Jeff Beaver out with a dislocated shoulder. The visitors were powerless to compete after that. Despite, or because of the weather conditions, Notre Dame literally ran away with the game.

By halftime the Irish were out in front by a 20–0 score. Larry Conjar finished off two sustained scoring drives of seventy-three and fifty-five yards with one-yard bursts through the line. There was virtually no passing given the wind. Newcomer Joe Azzaro was able to convert 2 points after touchdown, quite a feat under the game conditions. They would be the only PATs for the day. The first half scoring finished with three consecutive Hanratty passes, the final one a fifty-six-yard scoring pass to Seymour, most of that distance coming from the run after the short pass. The wind was really gusting and swirling on the floor of Notre Dame Stadium.

The third quarter began with an Irish drive finished by a Nick Eddy twelve-yard touchdown run. The Notre Dame defense remained stingy. Carolina only had five offensive plays from scrimmage in the third stanza. In one of those, John Pergine intercepted third-string quarterback Tim Karr's pass at the 3:22 mark. After an efficient sixty-seven-yard drive, all on the ground, sophomore Bob Gladieux scored from five yards out.

That is how the score ended: Notre Dame 32–North Carolina 0, Wind 20 mph. Between them, Eddy and Conjar ran for 172 yards and three touchdowns. In contrast, quarterback Hanratty was five of eleven for ninety-six yards, but fifty-six of those were on the one scoring pass to Seymour.

Thank You, Woody Hayes

It is convenient—often too convenient—for sportswriters to lob luck–of-the-Irish moments into game accounts. Therefore, it is with reluctance that one such event is inserted into the narrative. But it must be discussed, since it is the turning point for the entire Notre Dame season in 1966.

The Irish were having their way with North Carolina in the adverse weather, largely because the team was structured and the playbook was designed to deal with weather contingencies in the Midwest. Once North Carolina lost their star player, and then his backup, the Heels were completely unable to cope. The result was a rout in favor of the Irish.

But in Columbus, Ohio, quite another scenario was being played out in essentially the same weather conditions with perhaps an added dose of rain. Both the visiting MSU Spartans and the hometown Buckeyes were prepared to play in the mud, both on offense and on defense. The result was a very close game that Michigan State eventually won by the slimmest margin, 11–8. And it took a trick play by the Spartans in the fourth quarter to preserve the win.

Fortunately, the pollsters (sitting in dry offices without the benefit of instantaneous game highlights on TV) simply compared the Notre Dame score with the Michigan State score and then flipped the rankings of the two teams. Notre Dame became the new number one, Michigan State, number two. It was this advantage that would sustain the Irish through a difficult November, both on and off the field. It was on this day that becoming the undisputed National Champions became a possibility. It was on this day when the Irish became masters of their own destiny.

In 2010, when asked if he ever thanked Coach Woody Hayes and the Buckeyes for their assistance, Ara rolled his eyes with an expression that signaled, "You've got to be kidding." But he understood that behind the question was a legitimate historical inquiry. So he carefully crafted a thoughtful response. "You know, when you are in the middle of a season all you can think about is winning your games. If you lose once at a place like Notre Dame, your season is finished, because all we ever had to play for was the National Championship. Even when we were named number one, the coaches never paid much attention. We always knew we had to win the next game."

The players all recognized what they had accomplished when they moved up to number one. The atmosphere on campus moved from electric to supercharged. Before the season was over, all that energy and enthusiasm would be called upon. That, and a cool head coach focused on winning every game and doing what was required to stay in front of the other horses in the race.

Oddly, when it was raised forty-five years later, very few of the players even knew about the Ohio State–Michigan State score and its connection to their season. Perhaps it shouldn't be surprising, because they followed their coach's lead.

18

KIDDIE CORPS

O ne of the most enduring visual images from Notre Dame's 1966 football season is the cover of *Time Magazine* (October 28) depicting head shots of sophomores Terry Hanratty and Jim Seymour in a composition, as if in a huddle, that included fragments of other uniforms (the back of No.75 is Bob Kuechenberg). It is remarkable for a number of reasons.

It is among the first *Time* covers to feature college students, and all of those covers were of football notables (players like Red Grange, Dick Kazmaier, Johnny Lattner, Roger Staubach). It is believed to be the first cover depicting teenagers. Only covers depicting Shirley Temple and Princess Elizabeth (now Queen Elizabeth II) as a child have verifiable younger subjects (unlike military action photos). Since Hanratty is younger than Seymour, this could make him the youngest male to be on a *Time* cover up to that point in time. This was pretty heady stuff. Later in the '60s, as protests against the Vietnam War combusted, images of college students became more prevalent, but for very different reasons.

Notre Dame Sports Information Director Roger Valdiserri provides an interesting backstory to this cover. *Time* officials called his office looking for photographs to use of the two sophomores. Valdiserri thought putting two underclassmen on the cover of a national news magazine was a terrible idea, and for good reasons. First, the two had played in only a few games. The team had a group of seasoned veterans; some had played in 1964 when a National Championship was almost realized. A case could easily be made that those players were more deserving of national recognition. But Roger was most worried about internal team chemistry. He took his concerns up the chain of command, from Ara to Moose Krause, to Father Edmund Joyce. All of them agreed that two boys with a couple of games under their belts should not be on the cover of *Time.* Therefore, the request for photographs was denied.

Then magazine officials informed the University that they were going to proceed nonetheless—using original art if necessary. Notre Dame held its ground. So did *Time,* and the cover was published. The team was informed of the sequence of events and the cover became a symbol of unity, not a divisive force. Captain Jim Lynch reflects, "Hanratty and Seymour were key to our success, along with a great sophomore class." Still Terry and Jim would take their share of ribbing—mostly good natured, thanks to advanced warnings by Valdiserri.

Imagine, when the magazine ran with the cover story, Hanratty and Seymour had only played in *four* games at Notre Dame. This speaks loudly to the power of Notre Dame Football as being part of the American consciousness in 1966. The cover also prompts an interesting trivia question. How many people associated with Notre Dame have ever been on the cover of *Time?* The answer is eight, on seven covers. The names, in order of appearance, are: Knute Rockne (1927), Frank Leahy (1946), Johnny Lattner (1953), Reverend Theodore M. Hesburgh (1962), Ara Parseghian (1964), Hanratty and Seymour (1966), and Joe Montana (1982). It is interesting to note that Notre Dame graduate Condoleezza Rice (master of arts, 1975) was never on the cover of *Time* as Secretary of State, an unfortunate oversight. Reading the list above, the contention that football is a core strand of Notre Dame DNA is blatantly obvious.

The manner in which Terry and Jim burst onto the scene certainly contributed to their notoriety. One game, against Purdue, did the trick. The passing combination of Hanratty to Seymour is all most people remember about that season opener forty-five years later. Together, the two underclassmen broke two Notre Dame records, tied a third, and almost broke two more. Throw in a national television audience and the stuff of legends emerges. Two of Seymour's records still endure at

Notre Dame: 276 receiving yards in a single game (Purdue) and 5.3 receptions per game.

When Terry Hanratty arrived at Notre Dame, he wasn't thinking about becoming a big man on campus. His older brother Pete had preceded him to South Bend on a partial track scholarship, so he wasn't even the big man in his own family. His mother was raising four children by herself back in Butler, Pennsylvania. "I pushed him in sports all my life. I wanted him to play baseball, but I always told him, if you want something out of life, you can get it through sports," Mrs. Hanratty said. She was already impressed with Notre Dame by the time Terry was being recruited. Terry's father was once an amateur boxer who won sixteen of seventeen bouts, so the sports genes were also well established. But

Sophomores Jim Seymour (l) and Terry Hanratty (r) gained notoriety in their first game at Notre Dame against Purdue. Two Notre Dame records were broken, one tied and two more almost fell in a single afternoon. They became the first teenagers on a *Time Magazine* cover and two of only eight Notre Dame people to ever achieve this placement. *Source*: Collection of Mark Hubbard

Terry was recruited heavily by both Penn State and Michigan State. Having two boys together in South Bend would be a mother's dream, and convenient for all concerned. Coach John Ray finally persuaded Terry to follow his brother to Notre Dame, at least for a visit. When Ara was brought into the conversation, the die was cast. So that's where he went. It would become a very good decision. For all three seasons that Hanratty played for the Irish, he was among the top vote-getters for the Heisman Trophy, finishing third in 1968. He won the Sammy Baugh Trophy in 1967.

Jim Seymour was raised in large family in the Detroit area, five boys and one girl. He attended Shrine High School in Royal Oak where he played under Al Fracassa (still coaching in 2010), the most successful high school coach in Michigan history. Jim had no burning desire to attend Notre Dame. His older brother John had played halfback for Army for three years. In fact, Jim had committed to the University of Michigan and Head Coach Bump Elliott. But one day during his senior year, he was called out of class and ushered into an office to meet Notre Dame assistant coach Paul Shoults. At the end of that session, Jim was invited to visit Notre Dame. As he tells it, he still had no interest in going to South Bend. But he selfishly accepted the invitation. The attraction was visiting family friends, the Saracinos (his buddy Dan Saracino eventually became the admissions director at Notre Dame and held that position until 2011), who had moved from Detroit to nearby Mishawaka, Indiana.

In Jim's words, "As soon as I met Ara, I knew I wanted to play football for him." But there was this little situation that had to be resolved back at home. So Seymour verbally committed to Notre Dame, but asked for the time to unravel the commitment he had already made to Michigan before it could be announced. When he had a conversation with Michigan assistant Bob Halloway the following Monday, he was read the riot act. A day later, a cooler Bump Elliott called Jim to wish him well with the words, "You'll never regret your decision." It was a time of more civility among college coaches, especially the good ones. Today, Jim still thinks of Ara as a second father figure. "I'd like to be remembered as one of his favorite sons," Jim says.

Freshman Jim Seymour arrived at Notre Dame and was assigned to a room in Keenan Hall with another football recruit, Chuck Landolfi. Jim has two lasting memories from that year of football practices. The first was getting his "head bashed in every day" by the 1965 varsity defensive backfield, led by All-American Nick Rassas, with Tony Carey and Tom Longo. That was good practice for what was to come in 1966. It would be the best group he would ever go against as a receiver in college.

The other memory concerns the often-recounted stories that Hanratty and Seymour would practice together in the old Fieldhouse during the '65 off-season. Some believe it was just a legend. But the stories are true. Someone provided the boys a key, and the two would work out together on the poorly-lit dirt floor while the winter winds blew outside. The passes from Hanratty had to be hard and flat to avoid getting entangled in the structure's overhead tie rods. Seymour had great hands and became comfortable catching the "heavy ball." At the time, practicing inside was considered an exceptional privilege at Notre Dame, especially for freshmen. For Hanratty and Seymour, it was a form of sweaty entertainment—tossing footballs inside, in private, while everyone else was snowbound. The two guys got to know each other's moves and tendencies pretty well. They remained close.

The *Time* cover was immediately followed by another cover for *Sports Illustrated*. On November 7, 1966, *SI* ran a Notre Dame cover with a story titled "That Legend is Loose Again," by Dan Jenkins.

The campus is imposing enough just lying there, all leafy and self-haunting. The dome pokes into the Indiana sunlight like a giant golden skullcap, the black robes move quietly through the rust and amber trees, and the whole scene hits you with a great, intolerant splat of tradition, mystery and nostalgia. But Notre Dame has always done this, ever since Knute Rockne told his hired help to run that ball, pass that ball, kick that ball and fight-fight-fight, his speeches marking either the end or the beginning of pep talks. Now give the Fighting Irish another powerful football team, and one with something extra special – The Baby Bombers. Why, you haven't got a chance. The most accusing, cynical, irreverent infidel among us would be choked into submission by what Notre Dame is and what Notre Dame was. So here lies me, another simple, limpid captive whistling the Victory March as I struggle up to write.

Even the jokes don't help you very much. Go ahead and try them. Ask if the Gipper ever had a last name, by the way, or if the Four Horsemen have cut a new folk album lately. Why did the university swipe its fight song from Webster High in Oklahoma City? How many students are trapped in the underground steam tunnels trying to escape for dates? Ask if the school developed that synthetic rubber only because it might produce better shoulder pads, if it founded the first germ-free laboratory in order to manufacture halfbacks who wouldn't fumble, if the Sacred Heart Church is where everyone goes to seek forgiveness for beating Purdue only 26–14, if it really takes graduates three years to get married because girls figure it will be at least that long before they recover from the pep rallies. And ask if a perfect 10–0 season would be what Father Hesburgh ordered when he said his goal was "the attainment of excellence."

Thus begins the *SI* article, ostensibly about Hanratty and Seymour, that appeared just one week after the *Time* cover story. Mr. Jenkins couldn't help himself. The article is self-indulgent, a pattern that unfortunately would repeat itself one more time in print regarding Notre Dame before the season ended. You wouldn't even have had to be in Indiana to have written the lead paragraph, or most of the article for that matter, just a library somewhere. Most students on campus wouldn't even recognize some of the hyperbole or find the attempts at humor very funny.

The most accurate words are "accusing, cynical, irreverent infidel." An editor in New York wanted a story about the new kids at Notre Dame, and Jenkins got the assignment. He spent the entire first page doing his self-styled background on Notre Dame, but he obviously didn't *really* understand Notre Dame. After the histrionics were passed like a kidney stone, the accompanying article eventually mentions the sophomore duo and allocates almost equal space to each player. The cover should have done the same.

The University's policy of not supplying photographs continued. So a young Walter Iooss Jr. was assigned to visit campus for the North Carolina game and capture a suitable cover shot. The artistic composition is an interesting juxtaposition of positive and negative space. Most of the real estate is covered by royal blue hooded capes (this is why it had to be the North Carolina game, because the capes were only used twice in the season, later at MSU). The images is a bench scene dotted with gold helmets and only two recognizable faces. Terry Hanratty is most visible in the foreground and is identified by name on the cover. The other player is Freddie "Boom Boom" Schnurr. This cover would make Hanratty the first identified athlete to be on the cover of both *Time* and *Sports Illustrated* in the same week. It has happened since (Secretariat comes immediately to mind), but it is not a frequent occurrence.

Source: University of Notre Dame Archives

The sports media machines were now in full gear, working overtime toward what was looming as the "Game of the Year" in East Lansing. Many different names were floated for the new Notre Dame passing combination: Dynamic Duo, Baby Bombers, Torrid Twosome, Mr. Fling and Mr. Cling. The one that is most historically appropriate—the Kiddie Corps—comes from the *Chicago Sun-Times*. It allowed for the inclusion of the entire sophomore class of Notre Dame gridders. Names like Winegardner, Stenger, Kunz, Norri, Tuck, Kuechenberg, McKinley, Monty, Belden, O'Brien, Criniti, Dushney, Gladieux, Landolfi, Lavin, Quinn, Skoglund, and Vuillemin would have important roles in 1966 and play many downs of football for Notre Dame over their three-year careers.

When the *Time* cover appeared, both Hanratty and Seymour were unprepared for the fallout. A few weeks later the student magazine, *Scholastic*, did a parody of the cover as part of its coverage of the season.

Every person on campus was aware that two of their own had become national celebrities. Fingers started to point the guys out as they walked across campus to classes and practice. The boys—and that's what they were—just wanted to play football. That, and being respected by the upperclassmen on the team, were still important. Today, Hanratty reflects back, "We got a lot of ribbing from our teammates, but everybody was great about it. Jim and I didn't wear it on our sleeves. We were probably more embarrassed about it than anything else that out of all these guys, they pick two youngsters. There were many guys much more deserving than we were at the time."

According to Jenkins, Ara tried to manage the situation as best he could:

"Well, they're great kids. They're handling it real good. That's the thing—they're such great kids. But, geez, the stuff going on. Everybody wants 'em to pose for a magazine cover, everybody wants a private interview. I'm tripping over television cable right here on my own practice field.

A lot of pros think Seymour could start for them right now. Well he's a good one, all right. We knew he was good. We knew Hanratty was good, too. But we were afraid to think how good. I'll tell you, I still don't know how good they are."

Jenkins continued, writing:

Who are they, anyway, these two teenagers who had pumped so much unexpected drama and excitement into the 1966 collegiate season? Basically, they were just a couple of kids who had nothing more startling to reveal in their character than politeness and wonderment, nothing more Dome-shaking to say than, "No sir, I sure didn't expect anything like this to happen."

Here, Jenkins got it exactly right.

The Purdue game provides some intimate insights. Jim's mother was quoted at the time as saying, "I was so frightened in that opening game. I was afraid he would look bad. And after he caught the first two, I said, 'Sit down, that's enough.' Shows you how good a judge I am."

Nancy Garvey Seymour, Jim's wife, also remembers the time. "The Purdue game was memorable for me, too," she says, "because I watched it with my dad and boyfriend, not knowing that the receiver they were cheering wildly for was my future husband. I eventually took my friend up on that blind date with Jim a few days later just so that I could say I went out with him. And . . . forty-two years later . . . what a good life we've shared."

Proof that a little notoriety isn't all bad.

What does a guy do after playing in his first college game, with his team winning on national television? He calls his mother, of course. Terry's mom had an interesting experience back in Pennsylvania. A local appliance store thought it would be a great promotion to bring a color TV console over to her house so she could watch the game, the store getting a photo and little ink along the way. By the time Terry called his mother from the pay telephone in the hallway of Walsh Hall, she was disappointed that they had already taken the TV back to the store. She wanted to watch *The Perry Como Show* later that evening, in color. Incredibly, this was the very first time that Mrs. Hanratty had ever seen her son play in a football game, at any level. But she had some motherly advice that Terry has never forgotten. She observed Bob Greise coming over after the game to congratulate her son. "I hope you will be polite like that someday." There was no need to worry.

Suddenly bags of mail started to appear at the Notre Dame post office addressed to Hanratty and Seymour, many of the senders wanting autographed copies of the cover(s). It got so bad that, for a time, Hanratty's and Seymour's roommates were enlisted to sign the covers and get them sent back while the guys were at practice. If you are holding one of these magazines from 1966, it may or may not be authentic. However, what "Hanratty to Seymour" meant to the 1966 team was quite authentic. *Time* got it right putting them on the cover.

19

WIND COMES SWEEPING DOWN THE PLAIN

We have completed 4/10 of the season. Each part of the next 6 parts will offer a different type of challenge. This week it is the Oklahoma Sooners!

They are undefeated.

They have momentum.

They have their home town to play us.

They are the quickest team we will play.

Their strength is in their hustle, speed, and desire.

They gang-tackle and pursue like no other team in the country

They look to Notre Dame to thrust them into national prominence.

It is an old rivalry. Admittedly we will not be as quick.

We are Notre Dame—on the football fields— across the nation— if we are, pray God to let us give our best to be worthy.

—The Phantom

oe Doyle's lead to his Sunday morning column in the *South Bend Tribune* went as follows: "In this land where wind comes sweeping down the plain, Notre Dame whooshed on again Saturday afternoon, crushing the challenge of No. 10 ranked Oklahoma with a 38–0 downwind victory."

The week before the game, practically nobody would have guessed the result. Undefeated Notre Dame was newly installed as the number one team in both major polls. But Oklahoma was also undefeated and nationally ranked at number ten.

For the Irish, the game would be in extremely hostile territory. The fans in the Sooner State remembered Terry Brennan's team coming into Norman in 1957 and winning a stunning upset 7–0, thus ending the longest collegiate winning streak of forty-seven games. Reportedly, movie theaters interrupted their afternoon matinees to announce the score of the game. That victory would never be forgiven, and it was still too painful to specifically reference it in print eight years later. According to *Sooner Notes*, "Although Coach Bud Wilkinson's National Champions of 1956 trimmed Notre Dame 40–0, the Irish won the remaining five (of a six game series), four of them by one touchdown. Always physically bigger, they usually out-hit, and out-tough the Sooners." Still, you have to admire the manner in which a Southerner can turn a phrase. Again, *Sooner Notes* describing their own 1966 team, "They've motored through four opponents like a barber's clippers through a farmer's hair."

The national press corps was having a Smith-Corona field day writing their own what-if stories about games, past and imminent. This intersectional rivalry had all the bountiful copy elements for thirsty beat writers who were more accustomed to squeezing a glass of orange juice out of a single orange each and every week.

Still, some of the verbiage stretched a little too far. Frank Boggs proffered that Ara's winning percentage at Notre Dame (20–3) was .869, but that Oklahoma's Jim Mackenzie's was even higher (by the smallest fraction). That's not to say that the Sooners weren't well coached. An impressive list of assistants went on to notable careers of their own, including Pat James, Homer Rice, Chuck Fairbanks, and Barry Switzer.

Getting There

Getting to Norman, Oklahoma, had never been an easy journey for visiting teams. In 1966, the trip from South Bend was more difficult than it should have been. Notre Dame's charter jet from South Bend direct to Norman on Friday morning was diverted less than a half-hour after takeoff because of an auto-pilot gyroscope failure. Sophomore Coley O'Brien, a seasoned air traveler, remembers the landing. As the jet was descending into Chicago, it hit an air pocket and the plane lurched wildly as the bottom fell out. He was shaken. Larry Conjar, a newcomer to air travel, didn't care for it at all and was even more shaken.

The United 727 sat on the tarmac at Chicago's O'Hare Field for nearly two hours while repairs were made. The players, some still recovering from their anxieties, weren't allowed off the aircraft.

Arriving in Norman, Oklahoma, much later than expected, the team erupted into applause when the plane finally touched down. Then one of the two buses meeting them at the airport couldn't be started, so the entire team had to pile onto a single bus headed to the hotel. It was after dusk, so the Irish weren't able to do their scheduled light workout in the non-illuminated Memorial Stadium. The Friday meal at the hotel was another disruption. The servers were rude and clumsy. Ara himself ordered them all out of the dining room. The entire day was very frustrating, not the way to begin a road trip. In the end, it didn't matter.

Urinating

Coley O'Brien thought he was just a little under the weather because of the stressful landing in Chicago and the overall discomfort of the trip. He didn't sleep much that night. His roommate, Terry Hanratty, finally asked him what was wrong as he kept going to the bathroom to urinate. Coley didn't know, but figured it would pass. The continued experience of feeling sick prompted O'Brien to seek medical attention as soon as he returned to South Bend. It didn't take long for the doctors to diagnose diabetes in this otherwise totally fit young athlete.

Cheetahs

Except for overcast skies, the small traveling squad from South Bend had a near-perfect day, much better than the Sooner team and their 63,439 fans ultimately witnessed. But things started slowly. The first quarter of the game was a scoreless stalemate. The visitors from Indiana had only one offensive possession.

Part of the reason for Notre Dame's slow start was the fast start by the Sooner's star noseguard, Granville Liggins. He was a disruptive player to say the least, especially as a pass rusher.

Granville Liggins wasn't an unexpected surprise. Even as a sophomore his reputation was growing and the films didn't lie. He was fast, he was quick, and he was fearless. To prepare for his disruptive presence, a prep team player, Leo Collins, had been assigned all week to mimic his unpredictably aggressive behavior. He got the nickname "Vanilla Cheetah," a name his teammates still call him at team functions. The name has significance.

At Oklahoma, Liggins was being referred to as the "Chocolate Cheetah." The political correctness of this nickname is dubious by today's sensitivities. However, at the time, just having an African-American on the team was a mark of substantial racial progress in Oklahoma. In 1953, Frank Leahy was forced to find a hotel forty miles away from Norman that would accept the Irish team with its first African-American, Wayne Edmonds. It is a credit to the University of Oklahoma, generically considered a Southern school, that only thirteen years later it had integrated the football team and had a player of the stature of Liggins who was accepted, respected, and known with affection by his teammates.

But Liggins' new nickname didn't stick for long. He recalls, "I met with the PR guys at Oklahoma and they started calling me the 'Chocolate Cheetah.' But I didn't like it too much, so they finally came up with Granny."

On the second Notre Dame possession, Liggins was injured on what has been described as a chop block (legal at the time) off a trap play. Watching the play the following day in films, Ara Parseghian uncharacteristically erupted. Assistant coach (offensive line) Jerry Wamphler caught the brunt of it. Ara had been lobbying for a rule change to ban chop blocks. He didn't like young men being injured in plays that could be designed as legal muggings. Maybe something like this had happened to him as a player, and that made it even more personal. But he was really mad about that play. If it happened again, he'd hold the line coach responsible. Asked about it years later, Wamphler said, "I wasn't worried that Ara would fire me. I was worried that he'd kill me."

Granville Liggins is a noteworthy figure for a number of reasons. A year later, in 1967, he became a consensus All-American. Not having the height or weight to compete in the NFL, Granville went north and had an outstanding career in the Canadian Football League. Eventually he became a Canadian citizen and is known as a leader for racial equality in his adopted homeland

With Liggins on the bench, Notre Dame marched seventy-nine yards into the end zone for the first score of the game. The drive was composed of four passes, the longest to Rocky Bleier for twenty-nine yards, two more Bleier runs, and a dive by Nick Eddy from the two-yard line.

Longest Fifty Yards

When Notre Dame next went on defense, linebacker Mike McGill injured his leg while being blocked. Was it a payback for Liggins? After forty-five years, it is impossible to know. McGill believes it was a clean block. But the aftermath of this event sticks out in the memories of every Irish player on the sideline. Coach Johnny Ray had always preached that a defensive player "wasn't worth a time-out." If one of them got hurt, it was their responsibility to get to the sideline as quickly as they could. The large but very athletic McGill hopped on his remaining good leg over fifty yards across the field to the Notre Dame bench and collapsed. The courageous act by McGill really got the team going. Unfortunately, his injury turned out to be season ending.

On their next offensive possession the Irish were surgically efficient, and with the same result. Terry Hanratty connected with Jim Seymour for a twenty-two-yard gain. That was followed by three running plays to soften-up the Oklahoma defense. Then Hanratty threw to Eddy over the middle for an eight-yard gain that was followed by another couple of bursts behind the overpowering Notre Dame offensive line, finishing with a two-yard keeper by the quarterback. A Joe Azzaro field goal capped the first half scoring. After a scoreless tie in the first quarter, ND had scored 17 unanswered points in only nine minutes, and confidently went to the locker room at the half leading 17–0.

Here Come the Christians

By halftime the outcome of the game had become obvious, at least to many of the out-of-town writers viewing the action from the press box. The Sooners emerged back onto the field for the second half, being announced by a booming blunderbuss (rifle) fired by their mascot dressed in traditional frontier attire. As the Sooners ran toward their bench, one writer remarked with droll irony, "Here come the Christians again!"

The Irish promptly added 21 points in the third quarter before the reserves were called in. The first sequence of plays in the second half was costly for Notre Dame. After receiving the kickoff, the Sooners fumbled two plays later. The ball was recovered by Dave Martin on the Oklahoma twenty-one.

On the first play, Hanratty overthrew to a wide-open Jim Seymour in the end zone. Jim stretched to catch the ball and came down awkwardly on his ankle. It prompted the first injury time-out Notre Dame had taken in two years. No. 85 left the game and would remain sidelined for another two games. When he did return, Jim required constant physical therapy and wore George Gipp-style high-top cleats.

Joe Azzaro salvaged the drive with a thirty-two-yard field goal. Some of his kicks caused alarm at Memorial Field. The stadium was a horseshoe with an open end. In that end zone were temporary stands and the scoreboard. When Azzaro kicked in that direction, the ball went high and deep—so high and deep that it broke light bulbs in the scoreboard. With glass raining down on them, the fans below went scrambling. One of those fans wrote a letter of complaint to the president of the university. She received a cordial response. Yes, they would put wire mesh over the scoreboard lamps. But the president reminded the woman that "it ha[d] never happened before, and probably [would] never happen again." The woman sent this letter to Azzaro, and he has kept it all these years.

The scoring continued, all on running plays. Eddy knifed in for a one-yard TD. Bleier scampered nine yards for another. Late in game, reserve quarterback Coley O'Brien, a nimble runner, scored on a five-yard sweep. Azzaro scored a total of 8 points during the game on a field goal and five PATs. Only two weeks earlier he had driven himself to Northwestern. Larry Conjar carried eight times for fifty-one yards. Hanratty was eleven of seventeen passing for 129 yards. None of the offensive starters played much in the fourth quarter. There was no need. The game had gotten chippy. The Irish coaches tried to avoid injuries to more key players after watching *Time* cover boy Jim Seymour limp off the field and Mike McGill courageously hop fifty yards to the sideline.

In summarizing the game, the UPI lead sentence wasn't nearly as lyrical as Joe Doyle's. But many more people across the country saw it on Sunday morning as they read the game account in their hometown papers. "Notre Dame used the pinpoint passing of teen-age terror Terry Hanratty and an overpowering defensive line to crush Oklahoma, 38–0, today."

The stout Notre Dame defense collected its third shutout. Oklahoma only had thirty-nine yards rushing and one hundred nineteen yards passing (eleven of twenty-five). The Sooners never got closer to a score than the ND twenty-seven-yard line, and that happened late in the third quarter. After so many intervening years, defensive statistics are much harder to find in archives than those for the offense. Remarkably, the hand calculations for this game are still in the files at Notre Dame, so they are included out of respect for this fine defensive effort.

Tackles made by defensive line: Pete Duranko 8, Alan Page 4, Kevin Hardy 3, and Tom Rhoads, Paul Snow, Chick Lauck 1 each.

Linebackers: Mike McGill 5, Jim Lynch 4, John Pergine 4, Dave Martin 3, Ed Vuillemin 2, John Horney and Jim Kelly 1 each.

Defensive backs: Jim Smithberger 3, Tom O'Leary 3, Dan Harshman 2, and Tom Schoen 2.

Four turnovers were recorded by the Notre Dame defense, a fumble recovery by Martin and three interceptions by Lynch, Smithberger, and Harshman.

Defensive tackle Pete Duranko earned one of the game balls along with offensive guard Tom Regner.

We're Number One

In the locker room after the game, the Notre Dame players were uncharacteristically boisterous. Team chants of "We're number one!" erupted spontaneously but died down quickly when the press was invited in.

Nick Eddy was generously quoted as saying, "Oklahoma has a good team with exceptional speed, but I think when they lost Liggins they lost a little momentum and then when we scored late in the second quarter they lost some more. We sure were unhappy the second half and we wanted to do a job on them."

Unhappy with what? Eddy continued, "We thought they were playing a little rough."

Kevin Hardy added, "When teams get down within scoring range, we tighten up. That's what we did today."

The total offensive yard stat was impressively unbalanced, especially for a number one team playing a number ten team: Notre Dame 430 and Oklahoma only 158.

Asked if the Irish should be rated number one, Coach Jim Mackenzie answered, "If they're not number one, it's just because enough people who cast ballots haven't seen them." Oklahoma guard Ron Winfrey said, "They're number one in the country as far as I'm concerned, unless it's the Green Bay Packers." Winfrey drew the assignment of blocking either Kevin Hardy, the 270-pound junior, or Pete Duranko, the 240-pound senior, all afternoon. So his opinion was convincing. "Their size and strength was expected but their quickness surprised me a lot."

According to Ara, he hadn't foreseen the outcome.

We didn't expect this. I don't know what made the difference. I thought it would be a hard-fought defensive battle. You never know if the breaks are going to go for you or against you. But I never expected that score. Hanratty hit some clutch passes, and that opened them up for our running game. I'm proud of the way halfback Nick Eddy performed, too. And halfback Bob Bleier—he's been a very steady player and outstanding runner all year.

Drumbeat

For scoreboard watchers, Michigan State beat Purdue 41–20 at East Lafayette. Those were the two best teams in the Big Ten in 1966. It wasn't as big a mismatch as the score might imply. In the *New York Times*, the legendary Red Smith (a Notre Dame grad) wrote, "At a conservative estimate, Purdue contributed 21 points to Michigan State and subtracted 7 from its own score." So by Smith's accounting, Purdue should have won the game 27–20.

The follow-up Associated Press story on October 23 officially started the drumbeat toward November 19 in East Lansing. "Notre Dame and Michigan State have at least three things in common—a top-ranked football team, a perfect record and a problem. On Nov. 19 the Irish and Spartans meet in a game that could quite possibly decide the National Championship."

20

THROW STONES

50% of your season is over. You are now #1 in the country. The 5 remaining teams will each week represent an aroused group to steal the mark you've made.

If we can keep our heads, never feeling superior, still working to be so, if we can dedicate ourselves to each week's opponent—as they come, we can be number one—all the way.

—*The Phantom*

Rumor

A familiar rumor was swirling around again, as it seems it always did the week before the Navy game. Notre Dame was going to drop Navy from future football schedules. Anybody who knew the history between the University of Notre Dame and the United States Navy would discount the rumor immediately. Anybody who knew Father Theodore Hesburgh would discount it permanently.

Once World War II started, there weren't lots of young men available to attend college—translation: few paying customers. Enrollment at places like Notre Dame plummeted, but the expenses of maintaining a faculty and a physical plant hung around. By the fall of 1942, Notre Dame was in severe financial distress. But what Notre Dame had was exactly what the US Navy needed—a place in the heartland with dormitories, dining halls, classrooms, and a winning tradition. So the Navy V-12 officer's candidate school was located on campus to process the high demand for "ninety-day wonders" into the Navy officer corps. The added revenue was enough to balance the University books and bankruptcy was averted. A grateful Notre Dame was committed to playing a willing Annapolis team for the rest of time. Navy would use these games at large stadiums in major metropolitan areas as both revenue generators and public relations opportunities. So the Navy home games moved around from Washington D.C., to Philadelphia, to Cleveland, to Baltimore, and to New York. It is a traditional annual game that continues today. The relationship with Navy will never be severed. Never.

Leaning Tower of Pisa

The semiannual away game with Navy in 1966 was scheduled for John F. Kennedy Memorial Stadium located in South Philadelphia, a short distance from the Philadelphia Navy Yard. For years this was considered the neutral site for the annual Army–Navy game. If you fly commercially into Philadelphia today, and the wind is westerly, you will get a bird's-eye view of the Navy Yard, ships being repaired in dry dock, and an impressive mothball fleet at anchor. Today, JFK Stadium is gone, replaced by newer venues in the city's sports complex—one each for baseball, football, basketball, and hockey.

The old stadium had only one endearing quality—its size. At the time, it was the largest field available to host a football game on the East Coast. The recorded attendance for the 1966 Notre Dame game was 70,101. If you were at this game, consider yourself the one. The entire brigade of over 4,000 midshipmen were brought up from Annapolis. Notre Dame contributed more than just fans from its campus. The Notre Dame Band and 290 Naval ROTC cadets made the trip to celebrate the twenty-fifth anniversary of the Reserve Officer Training Corps. That show of support stopped all the rumors, at least for another year.

The logistics for playing at a stadium used only once or twice a year were challenging. Normally when teams visit an on-campus stadium, there is an infrastructure to utilize for communications, medical concerns, transportation, and miscellaneous team needs, right down who delivers the bottles of Coke. Emergencies can be covered. If you run short of athletic tape, the home team can supply some. Not in Philadelphia. Anticipating every contingency fell to the student-manager team of seniors, Al Kramer, Jack Sullivan, and Kevin Moran, with juniors Michael Finnerty, Dave Kabat, and Tim Colgan.

Mike Finnerty reflected on his time there.

That old stadium was in sad shape. The NE tower of the stadium was like the Leaning Tower of Pisa. Likewise, the locker room had a tilted floor. There were numerous cracks under the seating areas and we were warned that if it rained there would be falling water in the locker room. While we were setting things up, our counterpart Navy managers made a friendly visit to our locker room. We exchanged a bunch of our ND green T-shirts for their Navy gray NAAA-marked [Naval Academy Athletic Association] T-shirts.

Twenty-Six-Point Favorites

Things were hectic the Friday before the game. Ara had tried practices on Friday mornings before the team left South Bend and liked the results, so the team and their trunk-loads of equipment left South Bend by air on Friday after a team lunch at one thirty p.m. Upon arriving in Philadelphia, the team had a tour of the stadium while the managers went to work converting the empty shell of a locker room into a functioning workplace. The team stayed across the Walt Whitman Bridge in New Jersey at the Cherry Hill Inn. On Saturday, the team Mass was at nine a.m., followed by the pregame meal at nine forty-five. Buses to the stadium were boarded at eleven. After the game everyone would go directly to the airport and fly back to South Bend.

Given how handily the Irish had dismantled the nation's number ten team in Norman the week before, it was a bit surprising that they were only twenty-six-point favorites against Navy. The Middies, 3–3, had already played six games: Boston College, SMU, Air Force, Syracuse, Pittsburgh, and William and Mary. Navy Head Coach Bill Elias and Ara were good friends and joked about their shared Middle Eastern heritage (Elias was Lebanese). They had played against each other in high school, Akron South against Martins Ferry (Ohio) High School. In the Air Force, Sergeant William Elias had logged eighteen combat missions over

Germany in World War II, so his toughness wasn't in any doubt. The Navy coach was determined but realistic before the game. "We have to play like David played Goliath," he said. "We're going to throw stones."

On a perfect day in Philadelphia, sunny, clear, and seventy degrees, some key Irish players were listening to the game (there was no TV coverage) on their radios back in South Bend. Jim Seymour had his right foot in a cast to immobilize the sprained ankle from the broken play at Oklahoma. It was announced earlier in the week that Mike McGill was lost for the season and would undergo surgery for torn ligaments in his knee. QB Coley O'Brien was in a South Bend hospital having tests for chronic fatigue.

The game plan would require adjustments. Notre Dame would be forced to run more. Some lineup changes were being tried by necessity. Curt Henaghan (still working himself back in shape) and Paul Snow would alternate at end, replacing Seymour. John Pergine would move from inside to outside linebacker to fill McGill's void. Kevin Rassas would start at inside linebacker.

Better than 1947

The service academy teams have a reputation of always being well conditioned and scrappy for a full sixty minutes. On their first offensive series, Notre Dame players would be rudely reminded of that fact. Terry Hanratty would be knocked down hard as he was getting off a pass. He was nursing a sore shoulder and this just aggravated the injury. The first drive stalled and Joe Azzaro kicked a forty-two-yard field goal to start the scoring.

The first Notre Dame drive resulting in a touchdown was split over quarters one and two. A John Pergine interception (tipped by Tom Rhoads) plus a penalty moved the ball to the Navy twelve. Larry Conjar picked up five yards at the end of the quarter. Then he crashed over right guard on the first play of the second quarter for seven yards and the touchdown.

After they received the punt, Navy started to move the ball, collecting three successive first downs. They got the ball as far as the Notre Dame twenty-eight-yard line. It would be their deepest penetration of the afternoon. Then Alan Page made his presence known, sacking quarterback John Cartwright on two successive plays. The gun-shy Cartwright would be ineffective after that, throwing five of fourteen for a meager twenty-eight yards, with three more interceptions. Junior John Pergine, now at outside linebacker, had three interceptions, and Tom O'Leary had one. The Notre Dame defense controlled the game.

Nick Eddy exited the game early with a mild ankle sprain after thirteen carries and fifty-seven yards total. He was replaced by sophomore Bob Gladieux. It was a very physical game against a tenacious opponent—typical of the rivalry. At the half, ND was ahead by a modest 10–0 margin. Maybe David still had a chance against Goliath.

But the Notre Dame running game eventually wore down the Navy defense while the ND defense was absolutely unyielding. Navy would only have five first downs for the entire game. Coming out of the locker room, Notre Dame didn't throw a single pass in the third quarter. They had two scoring drives exclusively using runs. Hanratty scored on a one-yard sneak. Gladieux scored from forty-five-yards out. The hurting Hanratty gamely attempted seventeen passes, completing only four, with two interceptions.

The Navy defense accounted for the Navy's only score. Middie John Bergner blocked an attempted punt by Bob Gladieux on the ND twenty-five, pursued the ball to the five-yard line, and then ran it in. John Church kicked the PAT. John Ray had another ballistic moment on the sidelines—and his defense wasn't even on the field.

On the next possession, the chastised Irish marched seventy yards for their final score of the game. The touchdown was set up by three successive runs, Conjar for twenty-three yards, Gladieux for ten yards, and another dose of Conjar for thirty. Terry Hanratty scored the points from six yards away, running hard to the left and stiff-arming two Navy players. That further aggravated the sore shoulder.

As the obvious defensive star of the game (three interceptions), John Pergine was the most-quoted player. "[It] felt good to be a quarterback [running with the ball] again, but I don't care, inside, outside, just get me in the game . . . We play every game like it's for the National Championship. Because it is."

Navy's Bill Elias had nothing but praise. "Notre Dame is the best team I've seen since I've been in college coaching." Better than the 1947 Irish? "Heavens, yes."

Total yardage at the conclusion was ND 327 and Navy 64. Apart from the lopsided statistics, the Middies had physically held their own against the number one team in the land. A battered and bruised Notre Dame team boarded the buses outside JFK Stadium and headed for the airport. David hadn't slain Goliath. Final score: ND 31–Navy 7.

But the stoning by Navy had been relentless.

21

HOMECOMING

T he University of Notre Dame is a cocoon. It is one of the reasons people go there to begin with and it is one of the reasons graduates keep coming back—to live in a simpler environment where everyone attempts to treat each other with respect and decency.

While the protective aspects of the campus are quite evident today, the real sense of isolation was much stronger felt in the 1960s. The campus itself is on the outskirts of South Bend. Since almost none of the students had cars, the only escapes were how far your feet or the city buses would take you. Leaving campus wasn't a regular event.

Media Matters

Inside the invisible walls, the forces of isolation had helpmates. Newspapers were the dominant print media, but it was rare for a student to have a subscription or to buy one at either the Pay Cafeteria (South Dining Hall) or the Huddle. The campus daily newspaper, *The Voice*, was disbanded early in the fall of 1966, so even a condensed version of national or international news was missing. *The Observer*, which continues to be the student paper, didn't really get going until the second semester of '66.

There were always attractive offers, the ubiquitous postcards, to receive mailed subscriptions to magazines, especially *Time, Newsweek, US News and World Report,* and *Sports Illustrated.* Some students tried some of these publications for a while, but the only one with staying power was *SI.* The all-male population also discovered that federal laws required that *Playboy* be delivered with the U.S. mail. Some students tried this for a time. But when the campus mailmen got lazy and left all the magazines in a pile outside the dormitory mailbox areas, the *Playboy*s disappeared quickly. Nobody ever stole *Newsweek,* and you didn't have to steal *Sports Illustrated* because almost everyone had a subscription.

Television was coming of age. In 1966 it was still the rare student who had a small black and white TV in his room. If you wanted to watch TV, the only place to do it was in the dorm lounge (one TV per hall). A few of these halls in 1966 actually had color units—gigantic wooden cases that were hung from the ceiling with sturdy steel chains (or they may have disappeared like copies of *Playboy*). Johnny Carson was very popular at ten thirty or eleven thirty, depending on what side of the time change Indiana was saluting at the moment (this vagary was only recently corrected so that South Bend is consistently on eastern time, or eastern daylight time).

You'd be more likely to find a radio in a student's room than any other appliance—clock radios, portable radios, radios embedded in portable stereos. There was only one band—AM—unless you had a special unit to get classical music on FM. Nobody did. The fare was limited to a couple of traditional middle-of-the-road stations in South Bend. If you wanted contemporary music, and everybody did, you were forced to listen to Chicago stations. The " eighty-nine . . . WLS . . . Chi-cago o o" sounder is permanently seared in the cranium of every student from that generation.

The World Turns

Most of the college students in the 46556 zip code had no way of being up to date on current events. In fact, most could care less. They were there to study and cheer for their football team. Living in the post-Kennedy-assassination world meant half the population hoped for a return to Camelot while the other half prayed for it. The occasional sighting of a female on campus or a beer sneaked illegally at a bar within walking distance of campus were the only reminders of the lives left behind, sacrifices made to participate in the campus-wide fraternity known as Notre Dame.

Yet, changes were in the wind in the world outside, hopes and prayers notwithstanding. There were issues that would eventually become all consuming to a nation—race and the Vietnam War. These issues would exist outside the cocoon in 1966, but they would find their way in with a vengeance by the fall of 1967. Nineteen sixty-six was a great year to hope and pray without distractions for a National Championship at Notre Dame.

Home-Thoughts from a Broad

Notre Dame students from the '60s will recall a twice-daily event that eclipsed all others in importance, except eating. This was the delivery of mail to the communal boxes located near the entrances to all the dormitories. Homecoming for most students came by way of the US mail. The cost of a first-class stamp was five cents. There were magazines, like the ever-popular *Sports Illustrated*, letters from home (some with small amounts of welcomed cash enclosed), and those tantalizing letters from girlfriends, either one or many. The girlfriend letters were easy to spot through the mini-portal glass doors to the individual mailboxes because they arrived in pastel-colored envelopes. The danger for the student delivering the mail was that he'd be asphyxiated by the toxic aroma from the canvas bag as it was opened—the combination of all the perfumes that had been lathered onto the pastel contents.

Homecomings, in the physical sense, were quite another dimension for the fortunate few. It became customary for visiting parents to take their sons off campus for an edible meal, along with as many of his friends as could be accommodated. The favorite places for this ritual tended to be Rocco's and Rossi's Sunny Italy, both restaurants close to campus, accommodating to large groups and generous in their portions of Italian fare, which was virtually nonexistent in the dining halls.

The most extraordinary of homecomings was the visit by a girlfriend from out of town for a football weekend. For the select few students that actually experienced this, it was an exercise in logistics. First, there were no places to stay, at least affordable places to stay. There was a paucity of hotel or motel rooms in South Bend, and even in all the surrounding towns, rooms were reserved months in advance by alumni with football tickets. The option of having a girlfriend stay with a girl friend at Saint Mary's was challenging. It took a little juggling to keep all the "friends" straight. It worked best if a guy at Notre Dame could provide shelter for the out-of-town boyfriend of a Saint Mary's girl in trade. There were precious few of these situations.

To fill the void and meet the market demand for overnight accommodations for visiting women, an informal network was established by homeowners located just off campus in a neighborhood known as Harter Heights—this being the streets south of campus off Notre Dame Avenue (Angela, Peashway, Pokagon, Napoleon, St. Vincent, and the crossing streets). If a family had a vacant bedroom (and sometimes they would create one) it was put into the pool and guys made advance reservations. The cost was around twenty dollars per night. The added benefit was that the visiting girl could honestly claim to parents to be staying with a family and not in some fleabag motel shacked up with a love-starved Notre Dame man. It was all quite above boards. The guys could pick up and deliver their dates by walking to and from campus. Buses weren't romantic. So all the things to do rarely included venturing into South Bend proper.

One of the primary roles of student government was to schedule big-name talent for concerts on the Saturday evenings after football games. In 1966, these acts included The Brothers Four (Purdue), The Righteous Brothers (Army), The Temptations (North Carolina), Ray Charles (Pittsburgh, Homecoming), and The Clancy Brothers (Duke).

One game a year was actually designated as Homecoming. This meant that dormitories would create elaborate floats or displays on their front lawns. Prizes were awarded. Some floats were creations requiring advanced engineering. Others were mostly paper maché. The ever-present danger in South Bend was rain—like that never happened. Hours and hours of time were consumed in these float-making endeavors, a release from the pent-up frustrations that most guys had from being away from home with perfumed mail as the only touchstone of reality.

Occasionally girls flew in for the weekends. But Notre Dame students and the parents of students weren't likely to have the means to do this. Buses were the likely mode of transportation, unless the point of origination was a city on one of the train lines serving South Bend's Union Terminal. This opened up most of the East Coast from New England, New York (including upstate), and Pennsylvania. Folks from Chicago had another rail option, the South Shore Line, leaving from the Loop at Randolph Street. This train was nicknamed the "Vomit Comet." There isn't a Notre Dame man from this era that didn't take this train at some time or another. None of them would dispute the aptness of the moniker. Some also renamed the train "Orange Peril" after an incident when the train couldn't stop at the LaSalle Hotel and rumbled over the hill and across the bridge to the end of the line into a collision with the steel barrier at the end of the tracks.

If a fellow with a female visitor worked it just right, the sequence for the weekend went something like this:

FRIDAY:

1. Pick up (name) at (name of transportation center).

2. Drop off luggage at Mrs. (name)'s house.

3. Go to pep rally in Fieldhouse.

4. Introduce (name) to all my jealous friends outside Fieldhouse

5. Walk to Rocco's for dinner

6. Drop off (name) at Mrs. (name)'s house.

SATURDAY:

1. Go to class.

2. Pick-up (name).

3. Have lunch at South Cafeteria (the Pay Cafeteria).

4. Walk to game.

5. Get (name) into Stadium in any fashion.

6. Move (name) into student section to meet jealous friends.

7. After game eat at the Huddle.

8. Go to concert at Stepan Center.

9. Return (name) home.

SUNDAY:

1. Pick-up (name) and walk to campus to attend Mass at Sacred Heart.

2. Have lunch at Pay Cafeteria.

3. Put (name) in cab to return to transportation center.

4. Start doing homework.

The student magazine *The Scholastic* could have published this agenda. Photos for scrapbooks and making out were viable options to the traditional routine, but not part of the official itinerary.

By Monday morning, everyone was still waiting by the mailboxes for the regularly scheduled homecoming to arrive. For almost everyone, the perfume was the only thing to keep you going until Christmas break.

22

MALPRACTICE

Why can't the Regners, Goeddekes, Conjars, Seilers – recognize that 4 weeks more can immortalize their playing careers, that we have a chance that few others will ever realize in their lifetimes. If we can grasp this – if we choose to give our best – four more weeks – one week at a time, Notre Dame and her men and their futures will light up with luster. Intensify – everything you do.

—*The Phantom*

The athletic director at the University of Pittsburgh, Frank Carver, set up his team's impending game with the Irish as follows: "The miracle at Notre Dame is the manner in which they can consistently come up for every game against opponents to whom, without exception, the Notre Dame game is The Big Game." As the 1966 season played out, every game, including one against a weaker opponent like Pitt, had become a big game for Notre Dame as well. The run for the National Championship in November started with a home game against the Panthers. Then came Duke, Michigan State, and Southern California.

Early in the week before the game, the oddsmakers had the Irish as 39-point favorites. Closer to the day of the game they sobered up and removed the odds altogether. In South Bend the worry was that the team would be lethargic. Even a close game with a weak opponent could swing the polls back toward putting the Spartans ahead of the Irish, something that would make a push toward number one that much harder. The lesson MSU learned in Columbus wasn't lost on anyone with trepidation about the future.

This was the designated Homecoming game at Notre Dame. Floats and dormitory decorations were in full swing being constructed across the quads until Wednesday. That's when four inches of fresh snow were dumped on campus and the temperatures plummeted into a sudden winter. Paper machè was soaked and the two-by-four skeletons became icy winter sculptures. Fortunately the spirits for the weekend were unusually high throughout the sudden change in weather. There were visits from girlfriends, a Ray Charles concert, and a number-one-ranked football team to get behind with a show of solidarity that came with rekindled school pride. Call it tradition.

One piece of news did emerge that concerned the Notre Dame coaching staff. It was finally determined after medical tests that backup quarterback Coley O'Brien was a diabetic. O'Brien would need individual medical attention to continue playing, including his own personal doctor at all remaining games.

Russ Franke of the *Pittsburgh Press* provided a telling pregame quote from the Panther's head coach: "Dave Hart said Notre Dame is the best team he has ever seen in college and is worried about 'getting buried.' Notre Dame will try to put on a show for their homecoming people, they'll try to make mincemeat out of us."

The clarity of thought with which the head coach saw the game unfolding early in the week didn't carry over to game day, unfortunately. He may be partially forgiven based on the demanding schedule his team had to face in 1966, which included bouts with UCLA, California, West Virginia, Navy, ND, Miami (Florida), and Penn State. That, combined with memories of the 69–13 walloping that Pitt endured at the hands of Notre Dame in 1965 before a home crowd.

To begin the game, Pitt won the coin toss and elected to defer until the second half. Notre Dame elected to receive. Ordinarily, this event wouldn't even deserve a mention—except that in this case it had a direct bearing on how the game unfolded.

Given the pregame men-versus-boys scenario that had been woven by the press, the first half was a disappointment. The two teams traded possessions and punts until the clock read 4:59. That's when Terry

Hanratty rumbled around the right side for three yards and the game's first touchdown. This was followed by a Joe Azzaro PAT. The Irish controlled the ball twice more after that, but interceptions stopped both drives before they could get started. Going into the locker room at intermission, the score was Notre Dame 7, Pittsburgh 0. So far, Pitt wasn't "getting buried."

Coming out of the locker room, Pitt Head Coach Dave Hart made one of the most interesting and unexplainable coaching decisions of the season. Because they had deferred at the coin toss, it was now Pitt's option to determine how it would start the second half. Hart elected to kick off to the Irish, *for the second time in the game*. Who knows what was behind the call. But Hart very quickly wanted that decision back. Nick Eddy received the opening kick at the ND fifteen yard line. He headed right for ten yards then swerved left. He was grabbed twice around the ND thirty, spun away, and broke a tackle. After one more fake and a cut, the final Pitt defender missed the tackle at the Pitt twelve and Eddy coasted into the end zone. Azzaro missed the PAT, so Notre Dame now had a 13–0 advantage.

What was Coach Hart thinking? Today it is impossible to find an explanation buried in the accounts of the game. One decision, one play, and then Pitt's underdog team needed two scores just to catch the heavily-favored Irish. It was the coaching equivalent of malpractice.

It is also interesting to note that this was the seventh game for the Irish. They had only received a total of ten kickoffs: one for each of seven games, and then three more times—one after both touchdowns by Purdue, and one by Navy. So this was only the eleventh kickoff to the Irish receiving team. On two of those, Nick Eddy ran for touchdowns. When Eddy's running yardage is viewed today, it should be remembered that in 1966, run-back yardage was not included in a player's overall rushing yardage for the game. If ever there needed to be an explanation as to why Eddy was considered the premier collegiate running back in 1966, Coach Hart probably could have provided the answer.

The game turned in favor of the Irish after the Eddy runback—in a lopsided fashion.

Tom Schoen fielded a punt at the ND thirty-seven-yard line, got a block from Alan Page to clear an alley in front of the Notre Dame bench, and ran it in for a touchdown. A 2-point conversion was attempted. It was a successful pass from Hanratty to Paul May. ND 21–Pitt 0. On the next Notre Dame possession, Larry Conjar lunged in from one foot out for the TD. This time the 2-point conversion failed. ND 27–Pitt 0. After stopping Pitt again, a three-yard (really) punt gave the Irish the ball back at the Pitt twenty-yard line. Hanratty threw one to Bob Gladieux for a touchdown. Another 2-point conversion failed. ND 33–0. Moments later, Dave Martin recovered a fumbled lateral at the Pitt nineteen. This was followed by runs by Ron Dushney and Gladieux. Then Gladieux crashed for five yards into the end zone. Azzaro kicked the point after. ND 40–Pitt 0. That's how the game ended. The Irish beat the early point spread by a single point.

The remarkable Notre Dame defense had shut out another opponent, their fifth. The leaders in tackles for the game were Lynch (eighteen), Hardy (fifteen), Horney (fourteen), Pergine (thirteen), Duranko (ten), Page (nine), Rhoads (seven), and Martin (six).

Fans visiting Notre Dame Stadium that day were inconvenienced for the first time by the eruption of a construction site on the eastern side, directly across Juniper Road. Excavation for the new Athletic and Convocation Center had been started at the expense of hundreds of prime parking spaces. It would take two full years to finish this facility, one that Notre Dame desperately needed just to stay current with prominent collegiate sports programs. Funds from a loyal alumni base made it possible.

In the Pitt game program, President Theodore Hesburgh, CSC, was eloquent, as usual, in describing his University in 1966. "Notre Dame, as a Catholic University, is at a crossroads in a very special way. We are clearly, openly, and unashamedly interested in the spiritual and moral dimensions of man's main problems . . . all that bears on total human development in our times. These great areas of knowledge, in all their human, spiritual, and moral dimensions, are our deepest concerns."

With world-class leadership at the top, a generous Notre Dame Family, and a number-one-ranked football team, the Notre Dame table was about as stable as it had ever been. It was an official Homecoming to remember.

23

SIXTY-FOUR

Seniors: no game is as important as your game with Duke – your last appearance for Notre Dame on your home field!

—*The Phantom*

When the 1966 Notre Dame Football schedule was assembled, probably a decade earlier with one notable substitution, there was no consideration or thought of how it would factor into the mosaic of a team chasing the National Championship. There was a simple reason for this. Notre Dame thought of themselves as playing for the National Championship every year, and therefore the only reliable formula was to win every single game. The sequence of games shouldn't matter. But the order of the opponents could emerge as being quite important to the end result due to location, weather, injuries, and that nebulous factor—momentum. So the scheduling of Duke as the eighth game in '66 did become a factor. Fortunately, it was one that didn't hurt the Irish.

This was because their ninth game was at Michigan State, and by this time it was being designated as the "Game of the Century" and would in all likelihood determine the National Champion in college football.

Michigan State was looming as one of those must-win games. Like most teams that late into the season, the Irish were physically banged up and had been that way since road trips to both Oklahoma and Navy. They didn't need a tough matchup the week before MSU. They needed a game that could provide time for injured players to heal and for green players to get valuable game experience. That's exactly what they got with Duke on the schedule. The Spartans also had a soft spot in their schedule, playing a weak Indiana team on the road.

Duke and Notre Dame had only played each other on two previous occasions. They each had one win. The most recent encounter was in 1961 at Duke Stadium where Notre Dame prevailed 37–13 under Head Coach Joe Kuharich. In 1966, the teams had two common opponents, Pittsburgh and Navy, both beaten by Duke and ND. Duke won 14–7 versus Pitt, while ND dominated the same opponent 40–0. Duke edged Navy 9–7 while ND eventually romped over the Blue Devils 31–7.

The Blue Devils pre-game column notes included an interesting item. Duke was testing a new sports drink that they named "Green Lizard," described as "an instant salt drink mix with citrus flavor and green coloring that has concentrated lemon juice added to it to help further quench a player's thirst." This was well before Gatorade was invented and tested at the University of Florida.

Notre Dame was installed as a 25-point favorite on this typical November afternoon in South Bend: cloudy, forty-two degrees, and windy. The professional oddsmakers couldn't have been more wrong. In fact, they missed the eventual point spread by a factor of 2.5 times.

Souvenir in Hiding

Junior Jim Canestaro was a pretty fair photographer and had a field pass for the Duke game to take pictures for the Notre Dame yearbook, the *Dome*. While he was on the sidelines snapping away with his 35 mm Nikon, his friend and fellow architecture student, tight end Don Gmitter, signaled him to meet at the tunnel to Notre Dame Stadium as the team was heading into the locker room after warm-ups. Canestaro was wearing a tan London Fog raincoat. Gmitter was sporting one of the special warm-up shells that the team had. In those days, players didn't wear the numbered game jerseys until they emerged from the tunnel to play the game. Perhaps it was to decoy the opposition who might be trying to size up team members through numerical identification.

As Gmitter got to the tunnel, he suddenly whipped off the warm-up jersey and hurriedly handed it to Canestaro with the instruction to hide it under his coat, which he frantically did. It stayed hidden throughout the game and exited with Jim tied around his waist and under the long raincoat. He was certain that his friend would immediately call to claim it. But that never happened. So he started to joke with Don in private. "When do you want that piece of Notre Dame contraband back." Still, Gmitter never asked for the jersey. Eventually it was never mentioned again.

Architect Don Gmitter died suddenly of a heart attack on August 30, 2009. He and Canestaro didn't stay close after graduation. Why Don never claimed his prize will forever be a mystery. It was Gmitter's last home game, something he obviously knew at the time. He had one more year of schooling ahead (architecture is a five-year program) and his bum knee would have probably been unable to sustain the rigors of the NFL anyway. He became a grad assistant working for Parseghian as a coach and scout. Did he want his friend to have a souvenir? Or was he embarrassed on reflection to have lifted a souvenir from the ND locker room?

We'll never know. But Jim Canestaro still has the jersey—in hiding.

Pin Them Down

A few years ago, linebacker Kevin Rassas met a former offensive guard from the '66 Duke team named Carl Gersbach. He was delighted to meet someone who had played on the Notre Dame team and he wanted to share his personal experience with Kevin.

We were really psyched to be playing Notre Dame. We had a light workout in the stadium upon arrival the Friday before the game. We could feel the history of all the great players who had been on this field.

Saturday came and the stadium started to fill while we were warming up and we got really pumped. We returned to the locker room for the final words from our coach. He said not to get distracted by all the history and hype. He said if we win the toss we will defer and kickoff to Notre

Dame. We will pin them down, force then to punt and get great field position. We will go on offense and go right down the field and score, get them in a hole and keep them on their heels.

We kicked off. Then Nick Eddy ran it about eighty yards for a touchdown! After the ensuing kickoff we took the field to run our first offensive play. I had decided that on the first play I was going to hit All-American candidate Pete Duranko with everything I had to let him know that he was in for a tough game. When I got into my stance I saw the two biggest forearms that I had ever seen, on each arm there was a shiver pad with the name "DURANKO" in large letters. On the snap of the ball I was hardly out of my stance when I was hit with the hardest forearm shiver in my life. It was so hard that it spun my helmet around and I was looking through the earhole! I returned to the huddle in a daze. So much for the strategy to pin Notre Dame down and to show Duranko who was boss!

Irish Maul Duke

Out of the gate, Nick Eddy ran for a seventy-seven-yard touchdown on the second play from scrimmage. This began what was to be a 43-point first half for the home team. However, Eddy would re-injure his shoulder pass-blocking just a few plays after scoring, and was removed.

In sustaining this injury, Eddy became a thread in the fabric of the media coverage for the entire following week. Would he play or wouldn't he play at MSU? It would be a tough week of uncertainty for the fifth-year senior from Lafayette, California. "I used to listen to Notre Dame play every week on the radio," he once said. "By the time I was a senior in high school I knew there was no other place I wanted to go to college."

After that first touchdown, the Notre Dame scoring parade continued virtually unchecked. Larry Conjar ran two yards into the end zone behind center George Goeddeke for the 2-point conversion. ND 8–0. A pass by Duke quarterback Larry Davis was intercepted by John Horney. He lateraled it to a trailing Tom O'Leary on the Duke thirty and Tom finished off the fifty-five-yard scoring play with thirty yards of his own. Joe Azzaro converted the PAT. ND 15–0. Bob "Rocky" Bleier ran through a ballet of blocks on the right side of the offensive line for five yards and another TD. Azzaro converted. ND 22–0. Then another Davis pass was intercepted by Jim Smithberger. Irish QB Terry Hanratty found

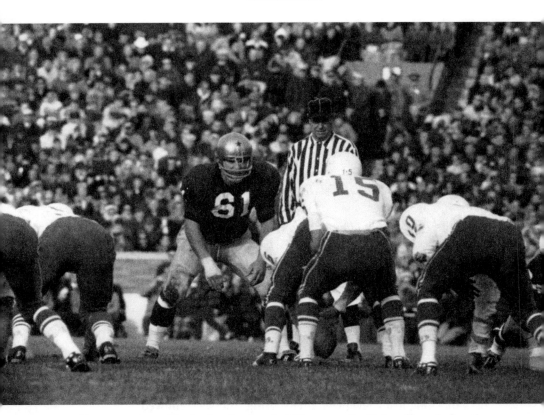

Team captain and linebacker Jim Lynch (61) surveys the Duke offense before the snap. *Source:* University of Notre Dame Archives

Bleier over the middle on the Duke twenty-one and hit him in stride. He completed the forty-five-yard pass play with his second touchdown of the day. Another Azzaro PAT and the Fighting Irish were ahead 29–0.

Trapped deep in Notre Dame territory, Blue Devil Dave Dunaway punted, only to be blocked by Dave Martin on the seven-yard line. Larry Conjar steamrolled over center again for the touchdown, with another Azzaro point added. ND 36–0. Then Jim Lynch intercepted another Davis pass.

The only hiccup in the Irish attack occurred when Hanratty was intercepted going the other way. But Terry soon made amends and found his buddy Jim Seymour (playing in his first game since the injury at Oklahoma) with a ten-yard scoring strike in the end zone. Azzaro trotted out to kick the extra point. The half ended with Notre Dame on top 43–0. The game was in hand, but the coaches were understandably worried with their Heisman candidate Nick Eddy on the bench nursing the injured sore shoulder.

Ara opened the second half using reserves and play-calling designed to run the clock down without embarrassing the Blue Devils. That didn't stop the Irish from scoring, but it did slow things down somewhat. It is impossible to instruct hungry second-teamers not to score, especially in the final home game of the season.

Halfback Dave Haley ran over right tackle for nine yards and a touchdown. Quarterback Coley O'Brien darted three yards around left end for another TD. Halfback Frank Criniti swept around left end again for ten yards and a score. Azzaro added three more points.

In 1966, Hugh O'Malley was the Irish prep team quarterback. When they finally got down to inserting the fourth team on offense, O'Malley didn't quite know what to do. They had been practicing Duke plays all week to prepare the ND defensive units. They never used the Notre Dame playbook. So when those eager prep team guys finally got in the game, they used the Duke plays. Defensive end Tom Rhoads remembers it well, saying, "We were all laughing and cheering from the sidelines."

The headline in Frank Criniti's hometown paper, West Virginia's *Huntington Herald,* read, "Irish Maul Duke, 64–0." The headline was no exaggeration. Duke Head Coach Tom Harp commented, "There isn't a whole lot to say, except that we were blasted and beaten by a great football team."

In the locker room, Duke linebacker Bob Matheson added, "Eddy was everything we had heard about him—strong and fast. I hate to think what a problem he would have posed if he had stayed in the game." Against Duke, Nick only carried the ball twice. But in so doing, he moved up to the number nine position of all-time Notre Dame rushers with 1,570 yards on two hundred eighty carries and a 5.6-yard average (up until this injury in the 1966 season, Nick had a 7.4-yard average). Remember this didn't include any credit for kick returns (which are now counted in NCAA stats).

The defense recorded another shutout by forcing seven turnovers. The leaders in tackles were Jim Lynch (seventeen), Ron Jeziorski (ten), Pete Duranko (eight), Kevin Hardy (seven), and John Horney (seven). Duranko and Alan Page each had two tackles for a loss, and Allen Sack added another.

This game did post some stat sheet anomalies, especially given the final score. ND had seventeen first downs, Duke fifteen. Times carried were even at forty-six. ND had sixteen passes thrown, Duke twenty-eight, and as for offensive plays, ND had sixty-two, Duke seventy-four.

Perhaps the most ironic statistic of all, the 64 points scored by the Irish, was exactly the same number of individual Notre Dame players who got to see action in the final home game. On this rare Saturday afternoon everyone wearing a gold helmet played.

24

TRUE CONFESSIONS

Plainville, Connecticut, November 14, *Associated Press*:

The priests at Our Lady of Mercy Roman Catholic Church asked a favor of the parishioners.

"We're sure you'll understand," the four priests said in a letter read at Mass Sunday, requesting that the parishioners come to confession a half hour later Saturday.

They explained that the regular 4 p.m. confessions time would be right in the closing minutes of the Notre Dame–Michigan State football game.

The request came from Fathers Gerald Corrigan, James O'Connell and John O'Mara, – whose Irish origins are evident from their names—and Father Franklin, who says, "Put me down as mostly Irish."

On that very same Sunday morning, the Notre Dame coaching staff had already convened in their cramped offices on the first floor of the Rockne Memorial Building. The task at hand was to prepare for Michigan State. The film of their Duke game wasn't really of significant help. Film from MSU would be essential. That, and the scouting report by assistant coach John Murphy who was in Bloomington, Indiana, for the MSU–Indiana game on Saturday, which the Spartans handily won 37–19. Sunday would be the last quiet day the Notre Dame coaches would have to prepare. By Monday the media feeding frenzy had exploded.

Thus began the most intense week in Ara Parseghian's coaching tenure. Parseghian recalls:

> It was like going to a bowl game, only worse. I'd never been to a bowl game as a coach. And at Notre Dame we didn't start going to bowls until 1969. So I had no inkling of what to expect before the Michigan State game. But the game was for the National Championship. Everyone understood that. So the press onslaught was like nothing I've ever experienced. It made it much harder to prepare for the game.

Iowa

Undoubtedly, at some point in the season leading up to the Michigan State game, Ara had a private conversation with Athletic Director Moose Krause pondering what the season would have looked like had they been playing Iowa. In 1960, that's how the Notre Dame schedule read: November 19, 1966, at Iowa. But the Iowa athletic administration opted out of their contract with the Irish in December 1960. Instead, they eventually scheduled a game in Miami against the Hurricanes on the same date. The reasons for the change are unclear and the participants have long since gone to glory.

Perhaps the Hawkeyes were still smarting from the shenanigans in 1953 when they played to a 7–7 tie in South Bend, a game they should have won except for Frank Varrichione's questionable injury time-out that forever labeled the undefeated team as "the fainting Irish." In 1963, well after the schedule change was decided, the visiting ND Football team was called back home on Friday, November 22—Fr. Hesburgh's unilateral decision in response to the shock of the Kennedy assassination. The decision to cancel the game was ultimately followed by many major college programs with games on the next day—but it wasn't followed by all. The home contest in Iowa City was probably a significant lost revenue opportunity for the University of Iowa because the game was never rescheduled. It has always been assumed that the 2–7 Irish would have certainly lost.

Looking to fill the unexpectedly open 1966 date, Krause called his friend Biggie Munn, athletic director at Michigan State. The Spartans also had an open date on November 19, and at the time they were quite satisfied to play just a nine-game schedule. The appeal to State was the opportunity to schedule the game, with all the additional revenue, in East Lansing. So the deal was struck. Notre Dame at Michigan State, November 19. Largely as a result of this scheduling addition and the unhappy fallout from conference teams playing their final home games, the Big Ten Conference instituted rules that essentially prohibited future out-of-conference games so late in the season.

For the record, the Iowa Hawkeyes had a miserable two–eight season in 1966. Michigan State clobbered them 56–7. They lost the game at Miami 44–0. At some point it must have occurred to both Krause and Parseghian that Iowa would have been a much easier opponent than Michigan State in 1966. So a scheduling oddity forever adds to the lore of the "Game of the Century."

Hate State Week

It was hardly a secret on the Notre Dame campus that the scheduled contest at Michigan State was the biggest game of the season—not just for the Notre Dame team, but for all of college football. While the game would be played 150 miles away, it would nonetheless become the greatest distraction from campus normalcy in the history of Notre Dame. Professors who had scheduled midterm exams would later lament that they hadn't fully comprehended the degree of distraction. Many would be forced to throw out test results and reschedule exams later in the semester. The role of football in the psyche of the campus was somewhat better understood and tolerated in the 1960s. No event since then has ever tested this tolerance to the same degree.

On Monday, Tuesday, and Wednesday evenings there were impromptu pep rallies held at selected dorms. Key Irish players would stop by after training table and be asked to speak over bullhorns to excite the student crowds. Enough of the Marching Band would show up informally to provide the musical glue that has bound the Notre Dame population for ages. The crowd would disperse and retire to the highly-agitated state of studying that permeated the typically laconic campus before an away football game. But this wasn't just any away football game. Everyone knew the stakes— the National Championship.

As if the campus needed additional pregame fever, more was provided quite unexpectedly. Midweek, an airplane flew over the campus and dropped thousands of leaflets disparaging the Irish and perhaps echoing on some variant of "Kill, Bubba, Kill." This phrase would appear on virtually everything associated with Michigan fan support in East Lansing. The leaflets were supposed to be a distraction to the players and student fanatics. They had just the opposite effect. The campus focus became sharper and the team's determination became even more intense. If the Notre Dame Alumni Association had paid for this stunt, it couldn't have been more effective. Nothing quite like this had happened before or has happened since.

Thursday was the official pep rally in the old Fieldhouse, complete with Ara and the team. Recollections of this event still give chills to those who were there, players and students alike. Except for a hoard of press people wandering around campus, the event was strictly a family affair. The Fieldhouse was filled to capacity at 4,500 (this is the only capacity figure that has survived Fieldhouse legends). Accounts of the event followed the script for a typical pep rally with the crazed excitement that would be expected. Ara was quoted as saying, "We respect the Spartans, but we are not going to Lansing to lose." The usually quiet and understated Alan Page added, "I think our defense is better than theirs."

One newspaperman writes of Ara "stabbing" a roll of toilet paper out of the air with his left hand (Ara is ambidextrous, but favors his left hand). No detail was too small for the voracious press, which at one point was generously estimated as numbering 700 on the Notre Dame campus prior to the game. The final speaker at the Thursday pep rally was football captain Jim Lynch. "Speaking on behalf of the number one football team of the nation," he said, "Notre Dame will beat Michigan State."

Betting Line

Early in the week, Notre Dame was installed as 4-point favorites by those that make their living making predictions of this sort. A *Detroit Free Press* article on November 17 quoted a friendly bookie as saying,

"In twenty-five years of business, I've never seen so much action on any proposition. Most of the big money is on Notre Dame. Nationally some $30-50 million will be wagered on the game." He added, "This does not include the 'creeps' who bet among each other rather than with bookies."

The mathematical rationale for the spread is hard to reconcile, even forty-five years later. Professional oddsmakers try to balance the anticipated action on both sides of a bet—making their money as the middle man. This would mean that the organized betting on Michigan State to beat the Irish was also quite heavy, but not heavy enough to offset the generally irrational behavior of Notre Dame Subway Alumni. In the minds of most people—especially among the "creeps"—the game was a toss-up.

Apart from the so-called professionals, predictions about the game appeared from every corner. Even Notre Dame Athletic Director Moose Krause proffered, "The winner will score at least four touchdowns."

Looking back, only one prediction could be found that correctly put the final score into accurate perspective. Dennis Kraft of the *Elkhart Truth* wrote on November 17:

> Now football fans have their eyes focused on Nov. 19, 1966. Saturday's clash brings together again two unbeatens and the "possibility" exists of a stalemate. "It could turn out to be a dull game for the fans, unless they like solid defensive play," Irish Coach Ara Parseghian said.
>
> The Spartans downed the Irish a year ago, 12–3 with "perfect" defense." "In all my years of coaching, I have never seen a more perfect defense than the one State used against us last season," Ara unsmilingly remarked.

In a *Chicago Sun-Times* article the Wednesday before the game, State Head Coach Duffy Daugherty was also thoughtfully attempting to diffuse the media hype. "This won't be a wide-open scoring battle. A break could decide the game. And it could all come down to a field goal. I think the honest feeling of both myself and Parseghian is that there is greatness on both teams involved."

Friday

The Notre Dame team had a final practice early on a chilly Friday morning in South Bend. With just enough time to pack gear and have a hasty lunch, the team boarded the regularly scheduled Grand Trunk train from South Bend's Union Station at noon. It would be the next-to-last train that a Notre Dame Football team would ever board.

Apart from the game itself, this train trip would be a memorable experience for the team members. All of them were in good spirits. The trip was a throwback in time. At crossings and station stops along the way, especially before the train crossed the state line into Michigan, the team was greeted by crowds with handheld signs of encouragement. At one stop, nuns with their uniformed grammar school classes waved and cheered wildly for the Irish. It was something out of the Rockne Era, the 1920s.

Arriving in Lansing, the cheers quickly turned to jeers and the signs were distinctly less friendly. For the duration of the visitors' stay at the Jack Tar Hotel, there was a white Cadillac parked outside with "KILL, BUBBA, KILL" painted on it in black letters. That phrase became the predominant MSU chant of the weekend. The Notre Dame players diffused the effect of the message once it was determined that the slogan lacked proper sentence construction—it lacked either a subject or an object. They started to make fun of it after that.

The biggest sports story of the day unexpectedly occurred at the Lansing train station. Future All-American halfback Nick Eddy had been carefully nursing an aching shoulder all week, but it was feeling much better. He was expected to play on Saturday. As Nick tells the story, he had a new pair of wing-tip dress shoes that he wore on the trip. The Notre Dame tradition of professionally-dressed travel squads (jackets and ties) was enforced by Parseghian. The new leather soles weren't scuffed up, so they were quite slippery. As Nick stepped down the expanded metal steps from the railroad car to the station siding, his footing slipped. He instinctively grabbed the metal handrail and in so doing wrenched his already tender shoulder. On the step just below him was the diminutive Sports Information Director Roger Valisseri who narrowly escaped injury himself from the tumbling Eddy. This instantaneous action by Eddy exacerbated the shoulder injury. Constant overnight therapy would prove fruitless. A disappointed Eddy would be confined to the sideline the following day, the biggest game of the season, and perhaps the biggest game of the twentieth century.

Freshman Game

In the absence of the breaking story about Nick Eddy's misstep off the train, the biggest story out of Lansing could have been the freshman football game on Friday evening between the Irish and the Spartans. This contest was concocted by both schools to give their freshman teams a taste of college action. Other than the fact that both teams dressed in Spartan Stadium, the whole affair was more like an extension of high school. The teams were bused to the Lansing East High School field that, unlike the on-campus stadium at the time, had lights. On this frosty cold evening in November, the stands were filled to overflowing with an estimated 8,000 people in attendance. No doubt, about 500 of them were there to cover the big game the next day for media outlets.

This game had intrigue of its own, beyond the obvious preview of the major event on Saturday. Each team had a marquee player that would be showcasing his talents for the first time in school colors, both defensive linemen. For Notre Dame, eyes were on Mike McCoy, the six-foot-five, 270-pound defensive tackle from Cathedral Prep in Erie, Pennsylvania. On the State sideline was 270-pound Tody Smith, the little brother of MSU All-American Bubba Smith. McCoy would go on to have an outstanding college career followed by a distinguished ten-year career in the pros. The younger Smith was a good player, but he wasn't a carbon copy of his brother. Players like Bubba Smith come around once in a generation. There was another person on the field for MSU who would attain athletic notoriety, defensive back Steve Garvey, who relinquished playing college football for playing professional baseball and became an All-Star first baseman for the Los Angeles Dodgers.

Other than the extreme cold and the high-school atmosphere, those people in attendance have two distinct memories about this exhibition game. First, both head coaches, Duffy and Ara, were in attendance and were practically elbow to elbow in the confines of the smallish high-school press box. Second, Notre Dame eventually won the game 30–27, but the manner of the victory is what is still remembered.

Linebacker Mike McGill was injured in the Oklahoma game and out for the remainder of the 1966 season. On November 19, he gave his two tickets to the Notre Dame – Michigan State game to his parents. He and his younger brother watched the game on television from a Lansing, Michigan motel room. *Source:* Collection of Mike McGill

The Irish frosh ended the first half up 14–0 on two touchdown passes from quarterback Tom Gores to receiver Dan Furlong. After huddling around their bus during the freezing intermission, Notre Dame went out to a 21–0 lead early in the third quarter after Larry Schumacher ("the only Negro on Notre Dame's freshman team") took the opening kickoff eighty-eight yards into the end zone. But Michigan State came back with a fantastic rally, aided by two successful on-side kicks. With 8:08 left in the game, the Spartans went out ahead 27–21. Notre Dame backs Ed Ziegler and Jeff Zimmerman pounded the ball and evened the score at 27 with 2:28 on the clock. That sent some fans toward the exits, expecting a successful PAT and an Irish 1-point victory. The kick was wide.

More fans drifted toward the exits, now expecting a tie. The Irish held on downs and got the ball back with under two minutes on the clock. They were able to advance the ball to the MSU nineteen-yard line. With fourth down and only 1:15 remaining, the Irish had only one option to win the game—attempt a field goal. There were no distance place kickers on the freshman squad, so they improvised. Fullback Ed Ziegler hit a thirty-two-yarder (with distance to spare) and sealed the victory for the ND freshmen. It was the first and the last field goal attempted by Ziegler over the entirety of his football career.

Fifty Thousand Letters

The biggest off-the-field controversy the week before the game surrounded who would actually be able to watch it on television. In the new contract between the NCAA and ABC, it was stipulated that no single team could be on a national broadcast more than once every two years or on a regional broadcast more than twice in any two-year period. Notre Dame had already been on a national broadcast in 1966, the home opener against Purdue. The NCAA was responding to the fears of many member schools that paid attendance at college games would decline if there were a key national game on the tube every single week.

The math was rigged so that Notre Dame and many of the powerhouse football schools couldn't be on television more that three times in any two-year period. It made preseason game selection by ABC quite difficult because some of the important games weren't even evidently important until the season unfolded—like Notre Dame at Michigan State. Traditional rivalries were considered safe choices: Harvard–Yale, Army–Navy, Michigan–Ohio State. But even those games couldn't be broadcast for two consecutive years under the guidelines, except to regional audiences. It was a mathematical mess, created by college-educated people who should have known better.

The rule didn't last long. The Notre Dame–Michigan State contest was the first to put the NCAA on the ropes. Allegedly, over 50,000 letters were sent to ABC network headquarters in New York demanding to see the game. The veracity of this claim is suspicious because ABC was itself seeking relief to broadcast what had emerged as the biggest college game in many years.

So by midweek, a compromise had been worked out, a bending of the rules. The game would go on before the regularly scheduled national game between traditional rivals UCLA and Southern California. The game would be shown to almost the entire nation, thus effectively creating the first college football doubleheader. But a small sliver of geography would be held out so a regional game in the South could be broadcast. Thus, the big game was technically a regional telecast— to about ninety-five percent of the nation. According to ABC publicist Beano Cook, "We're putting out enough material to make *Gone with the Wind* look like a short story.

The *Wall Street Journal* even put a preview article about the big game on the front page of its Friday edition—something it rarely did for a sporting event.

The ABC play-by-play announcer for the game, Chris Shenkel, related two stories about the game.

> *I was the spokesman for the Lincoln Mercury Sports Panel and a friend of Lee Iacocca at Ford. He said, "Come on by and you can drive a Shelby Ford GT-40 street version to East Lansing." There was a four-lane highway, and I got it up to 140 miles per hour with ease. That very car is now in a British museum.*
>
> *I remember taking the ramp up to the press box instead of the elevator because I wanted to get a feel for the game. I thought, "Holy mackerel, what is happening here today?" because the fans were really with it. I knew it was really big when I saw that even Jimmy Cannon [sportswriter] showed up, because he had always kind of pooh-poohed college football.*

Nonplussed

The Notre Dame team followed the normal pregame schedule for an away contest. They walked to nine a.m. Mass at the nearby St. Mary's Cathedral and returned to a nine forty-five pregame meal and meeting at the hotel. Leaving at eleven thirty a.m., the team was bused to the stadium with a police escort. Except for the extra tension, the morning before the one thirty kick-off went normally.

Pregame warm ups by special teams take place before the entire team takes the field for calisthenics. It's a time for a handful of players and specialty coaches to have the full range of the playing field to practice kickoffs, punts, and field goals. As place kicker Joe Azzaro was warming up, a scruffy, white-haired older gentleman in Spartan green approached him and started a casual conversation about kicking. The man was very personable, and Azzaro initially took him for a groundskeeper. It was only when the fellow walked away that the light went on. The man was Duffy Daugherty, the Spartans' head coach. Why was he on the field? Perhaps to get into the head of Azzaro—a preview of the role kicking would eventually play in the game. Perhaps it was just to assess field conditions, which were adverse for kicking; it was windy, cold, and the field was frozen hard. Azzaro was nonplussed. It was his twenty-first birthday.

Ticket Holders

The 10,000 tickets in the hands of Notre Dame fans created enough vocal presence to be heard on the field. But the folks from South Bend had mixed color loyalties. Some wore the traditional blue and gold. Others were decked out in kelly green, and they got lost in the crowd that was already filled with Spartan green. Popular buttons read "ARA'S ARMY" and "ARA'S LYNCH MOB," both accessories printed with white letters on a green background.

The State crowd was in a frenzy. There was a scarecrow-like figure of a Notre Dame football player hung in effigy from the smokestack of the MSU power plant. Other than the ubiquitous "KILL, BUBBA, KILL," there were other messages on banners in the stadium designed to irritate the Catholics from South Bend: "HAIL MARY FULL OF GRACE, NOTRE DAME'S IN SECOND PLACE," and "BUBBA FOR POPE."

Among of the crowd filing into the stadium were linebacker Mike McGill's parents, as they had the two tickets designated for each Notre Dame player. Mike was on crutches and in a cast from his ankle to his upper thigh, having had surgery after the Oklahoma game where he memorably hopped off the field. He didn't go to the game to watch his teammates. There were only two tickets and he wanted his parents to go. He stayed with his little brother in a Lansing motel room and watched the game on TV, just like everyone else in the nation who wasn't at Spartan Stadium.

Guy with the Cigar

The face value of a ticket to the ND–MSU game was five dollars. They were a precious commodity. Scalpers were easily getting one hundred dollars per ticket before the game. If you were from Notre Dame and had a ticket, it couldn't be had at any price. The ticket allotment to the visitors was limited under contract to one-seventh the capacity of the stadium, rounded up to 10,000 tickets. This included members of the team who made the trip but didn't dress, players' families (two tickets each), favored alumni, season ticket holders, and the official University traveling party. The Notre Dame Marching Band did not make the trip. A student lottery was held on campus for the remainder of the allocation, exactly 500 tickets.

Today, Coach Parseghian has one indelible memory from before the game. Just before kickoff, the teams were on their respective sidelines. Standing next to Ara was a gentleman with a topcoat, fedora, and a lit cigar. This wasn't a face familiar to the head coach, so Ara challenged him. "What are you doing here?" The man responded, "Watching the game, same as you." The fellow was ushered away by security. Ara still claims that Duffy packed the stadium with his friends and found ways to get everyone in, even if it meant crowding the Visitors' Bench. The guy standing with the team on the sideline was a clear reminder to Parseghian that his coaching counterpart would pull out all the stops to win the game. Before the opening kickoff, the Irish head coach was already fit to be tied.

25

ARA DOESN'T DO
DUMB THINGS

One year ago Michigan State beat us. I remember their defense
screaming at us from the sidelines – they looked like kamikazes.
Crazed madness. They forearmed illegally to the face, they hit and
swarmed and piled after the whistle. When we looked at film, we
were amazed that so few State players were knocked off their feet.
We were "out-bluffed!" They showed aggressiveness – yelling and
screaming – one thing burned my ears and stuck with me – their
linebacker Thornhill said, "you don't want it!"

Together we have to stand so united, so strong, so ferocious,
that we'll not only block and tackle them – we'll wage personal
wars. The worst thing you can do to them is beat them.

—*The Phantom*

The Notre Dame–Michigan State game, as it was played
on November 19, 1966, may be accurately summarized
with just five simple sentences. The hitting was ferocious. There was no winner. Nobody played to tie. Those
involved in the game left the stadium unsatisfied. Players and coaches
are still remembered for, if not haunted by, the experience.

After all that has been written about this contest—and that has been
considerable, perhaps more than any other college football game in
history—it is worth the time and effort to seek truth by relying only

on primary sources. The most accurate source are: 1) the official game record, play by play, as recorded by official scorers, 2) video tape of the game that remains from the ABC-TV broadcast, and 3) the first-hand accounts of the players and coaches. Everything else, especially third-party accounts, is unfortunately replete with misinformation, prejudice, and baseless opinion.

The need for primary sources was hammered home early in the process of researching the subject. Notre Dame assistant coach Brian Boulac was consulted. He had his memories of this game and was generous in helping the cause of building an accurate record so many years after the fact. Then he was shown the video tape of the game. Frequently he would shake his head and comment, "I just don't remember it that way." The tape was reviewed multiple times; in fact it was left at his home so he could review it in private. One frequent television image is that of Ara Parseghian on the sideline, Brian standing right next to him. While the box—Ara's filming contraption—was banned, Brian nonetheless had one of the best seats in the house. And Brian's memory is very sharp. So he *will* be considered a primary source. But the conclusion is that other observers not directly involved with the game just aren't that reliable. After forty-five years, they remember what they think they saw, or more dangerously, what they wished had happened.

For the record, Michigan State didn't lose their bid for the National Championship on November 19. Yes, they could have been permanently installed at number one if they had beaten Notre Dame. But that didn't happen. Given the perspective of history, they actually lost their claim for a portion of the number one ranking at Columbus, Ohio, on October 15, when they barely eked out an 11–8 victory against a mediocre Buckeye team. In the course of a ten-game season, the Spartans only played three teams with winning records—against Purdue, Michigan, and Notre Dame. In what is historically considered a weak schedule, including conference games, Michigan State allowed 99 points.

Also, for the record, Notre Dame didn't retain their number one ranking on November 19. The two major polls were divided between the two teams after the game. The Irish didn't even win the game on points, as many people have tried to suggest over the years as if this were a boxing match. The two teams played to a tie. The Irish only regained undisputed claim to the number one spot on the following week. The

National Championship was awarded for a "body of work" over the course of the entire season—where Notre Dame clearly had the superior record. That is undisputed.

But comparisons of this game to a heavyweight title fight have merit. Everybody who was there at Spartan Stadium is in one hundred percent agreement on this singular point. It *was* a brutal game.

227

First Quarter

> Notre Dame won the toss and chose to receive. Michigan State will kick and defend the south goal.
>
> Kenney kicked-off to Conjar at 12, downed by Waters after a 15 yard return.

That's how the game began, as officially recorded in the press box. The first series for Notre Dame included one first down after runs by Conjar, Bleier, and Hanratty. Then Larry Conjar had two more runs for positive yardage before Bleier was downed for a loss on a draw play. This forced a punt. Defensive lineman Kevin Hardy would be called on to punt, his first punt in a college football game. By the end of the game he would be experienced at it.

Michigan State was obviously tense when they started their first possession on their own eleven-yard line. John Horney stopped MSU quarterback Jimmie Raye for a two-yard loss. On the next play, Raye fumbled and Regis Cavender recovered for another loss of five yards. The third play, a six-yard run by Raye, was short of a first down and forced a punt from the MSU eight-yard line. Dick Kenney blasted a fifty-four yard kick that set-up the Irish on their own thirty-eight. Looking back, this impressive defensive stand by the Irish could be viewed as a lost scoring opportunity should they have recovered the fumble or blocked the punt from the end zone. It would be a day of defensive dominance and strange luck—good and bad—that affected both teams.

The next Notre Dame series was central to the outcome of the game and unfolded as follows:

1-10	ND 38	Hanratty's pass for Bleier incomplete.
2-10	38	Hanratty's pass for Bleier incomplete.
3-10	38	Hanratty's pass to Gladieux complete, downed by Phillips after twenty-six yards.
1-10	MSU 36	Gladieux, downed by Thornhill, gained one.
2-9	36	Hanratty rolled out right and was stopped by Smith and Thornhill after two.
3-7	33	Hanratty pass for Bleier incomplete, broken up by Phillips.
4-7	33	Hardy, back to punt, got a bad pass from center and passed incomplete.

Even though MSU only got the ball on their own thirty-three-yard line after that disappointing sequence, significant damage had been done to the fortunes of the Irish. The rollout by Hanratty was actually a QB draw-play brought in from the sideline. It was called as a halfback draw, but miscommunicated in the huddle. The tackle, a grab by Charlie Thornhill and a finish by Bubba Smith, was fierce. Smith landed on Terry Hanratty as he was falling—Terry insists even today that it was clean. The fall separated Hanratty's shoulder, but he didn't immediately know the extent of the injury. On the next play, Hanratty threw a weak and errant pass toward Rocky Bleier as his shoulder screamed in pain. Grabbing his arm and trotting off the field, he would be done for the day and for the remainder of the season. That day at Michigan State, Hanratty only attempted four passes and had a single completion.

Just as unfortunate as Hanratty's turn of events was the punt play. The punter, Kevin Hardy, tried to recover from a bad snap. Unable to get the kick off, he spotted his outside contain man George Goeddeke, wide open. The athletic Hardy instinctively threw a pass. Goeddeke was normally the offensive center, except on long snaps. He was inserted for Jim Seymour who was held out of punt coverage to preserve his sore ankle from open field shots. Not hearing the ball kicked, Goeddeke turned just in time to see the ball in the air headed his way. He lunged but missed it and MSU defender Jess Phillips leveled Goeddeke as he came down. His ankle would be severely sprained and he was forced to leave the game for good. With no score in the first quarter, Notre Dame lost their starting quarterback and starting center within seconds. Three future All-Americans were now on the bench (Eddy, Hanratty, and Goeddeke) and they were still in the first quarter. That was a punch to the gut on the sidelines. Sophomores Coley O'Brien at quarterback and Tim Monty at center would be thrown into the melee for the remainder of the afternoon.

The Spartans would be frustrated on offense. Running, especially up the middle against the Notre Dame front four, was virtually impossible. Their bruising backfield of Dwight Lee, Clinton Jones, and

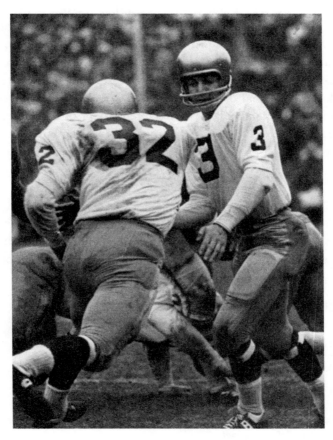

Replacement quarterback Coley O'Brien (3) hands off to fullback Larry Conjar (32) in the second half of the Notre Dame – Michigan State game. *Source:* University of Notre Dame Archives

Regis Cavender would only have sixty-three net yards all afternoon. So Duffy Daugherty started to call plays for his quarterback to roll to one side or the other with the option of passing. No matter the call, Raye always rolled right, away from Alan Page. Jimmie Raye would have twenty-one running attempts and seventy-five net yards. He also attempted twenty passes, completing only seven, with three interceptions. The QB option would be the Spartan's stock-in-trade play for the remainder of the game.

The two teams traded hard-hitting possessions. Just before the end of the first quarter, MSU got the ball back on their twenty-seven-yard line after another Irish punt. The very next snap was one of the defining plays of the game. Raye hit talented receiver Gene Washington for a forty-two-yard passing gain. It would be the longest pass completion of the afternoon. This gave the Spartans the ball on the Notre Dame thirty-one. The play would trigger a successful drive for State's only touchdown. After that drive, the Spartans would enjoy their best field position for an offensive series for the remainder of the game. It was followed by nine consecutive running plays featuring Jones, Cavender, and Raye.

Second Quarter

The Irish starting defense was scored on for the first time since the Purdue game. The final sequence that began the second quarter officially reads:

1-goal 9   Cavender downed by Smithberger after five-yard gain.

2-goal 4   Jones downed by Horney and Lynch, made no gain.

3-goal 4   Cavender over right tackle for a touchdown.

Ten plays went seventy-three yards at 1:40 (started in previous quarter).
Kenney kicked the extra point.
Michigan State 7–Notre Dame 0

On their next possession, the Irish got one first down and were forced to punt again. In the minds of many, the next sequence is the most memorable of the game.

1-10	MSU 19	Jones at left guard, downed by Horney, no gain.
2-10	19	Jimmy Raye ran right end behind a Clint Jones block and went thirty yards before Smithberger caught him.
1-10	49	Lee broke over right tackle and O'Leary tripped him after fourteen yards.
1-10	ND 37	Cavender downed by Rhoads, gained one.
2-9	36	Lynch intercepted Raye's pass and Jones tackled, Lynch fumbled and Jones recovered the fumble for one and ten on thirty-six.
1-10	36	Lee downed by Duranko, lost two.
2-12	38	MS penalized five yards for delay of game.
2-17	43	Raye passed complete to Washington who was pushed out of bounds by O'Leary after seventeen yards.
1-10	26	Cavender downed by Horney and Duranko after one.
2-9	25	MS penalized five yards for illegal motion.
2-14	30	Washington missed Raye's pass incomplete.
3-14	30	Raye's pass to Cavender incomplete.
4-14	30	Kenney kicked a forty-seven-yard field goal (ball on thirty-seven).

Ten plays; drive started on the MS nineteen.
Michigan State 10–Notre Dame 0.

This would be the last time Michigan State would score. They would not get beyond the Notre Dame forty-six-yard line for the remainder of the contest. But it is clear from the video and from the record that State started this drive with momentum. Notre Dame gave up some large chunks of real estate before the Jim Lynch interception-fumble.

That play by the ND captain was a momentum-changer for the Irish. The interception was one of those that a linebacker dreams about. The tackle of Lynch on the play is one football fans will talk about for as long as football is played between the two schools. Lynch had his feet taken out from under him as he was unsuccessfully attempting to jump the tackler. He flipped in midair, landing directly on his head. A photo of the moment of impact appeared in *Sports Illustrated*. It should have been on the cover. Jim's high school sweetheart, Gloria Quatman (today Mrs. Jim Lynch) from Lima, Ohio, was sitting in the stands with Jim's parents. She grabbed Jim's mother's arm and said, "I think he's broken his neck." Miraculously, Lynch bounded back up and remained in the game.

Notre Dame was on the edge. The team couldn't tolerate losing another future All-American. That play by Lynch further toughened up the defense. Holding the Spartans to a field goal was a victory of sorts. Probably no other college team in America at the time could attempt a forty-seven-yard field goal and believe they could make it, even with a twenty-miles-per-hour wind behind them. The barefoot Hawaiian kicker, Dick Kenney, was that good. The kick established the line in the sand for the Irish defense. Any MSU field position inside the Notre Dame thirty-five would likely mean points for them. They never got that far again.

1-10	ND 46	O'Brien's pass to Seymour incomplete.
2-10	46	O'Brien passed to Gladieux, downed by Summers on the ND forty-three. Gain of eleven.
1-10	MSU 4	O'Brien passed to Bleier complete, knocked out of bounds byPhillips after nine.
2-1	34	O'Brien passed to Gladieux complete, who caught the ball on thegoal line and stepped in for the TD.

Four plays carried fifty-four yards at 10:30.
Azzaro kicked extra point.
Michigan State 10–Notre Dame 7.

The game turned to favor the Irish after that.

Kenney kicked off to Quinn on the eight and he returned thirty-eight yards, downed by Chatlos.

There was still 10:30 to be played in the first half. Michigan State would have the ball twice and Notre Dame once. Both teams failed to make a first down for the remainder of the half. The collisions on the lines were extraordinary. They could be heard in the stadium's upper deck. The first half statistics were quite equal, as would be expected.

Premonition

The last sequence of the first half merits serious scrutiny, something very few observers have deigned to do. After a Notre Dame punt by Kevin Hardy, the ball was downed by Jim Seymour at the MSU one-yard line. Seymour was now back in the game to replace George Goeddeke, who was injured while replacing him on punt coverage earlier in the game.

1-10	MSU 1	Raye sneaked for two, Lynch made the tackle.
2-8	3	Raye ran right end for a three-yard gain.
3-6	5	Raye sneaked at left guard and made three, Lynch tackled.
4-3	8	(End of Quarter)

Backed up deep in his own territory, Head Coach Duffy Daugherty called three safe running plays, all to his quarterback Jimmie Ray. He didn't dare call a pass play that could have been intercepted for a possible Notre Dame run back and score. He knew that punting the ball might create a miscue that could result in a Notre Dame score. So he elected to run out the clock as best he could. He did what every experienced coach would do in the same situation. It was the right thing to do under the circumstances. In effect, he played to keep the scoreboard frozen at

10–7. No one has ever criticized him for doing it. Keep that in mind as the final plays of the second half unfold.

There are a couple of oddities to this sequence. The timekeeper on the sidelines allowed the time to run out when the clock should have been stopped. The refs didn't catch this as they ran into the locker room. There was no television camera synchronized between the clock and the field action, and also no provision for review. If there had been any of these safeguards in place, it would have given ND a few additional seconds to run a couple of plays before the end of the first half. More curious is Notre Dame's decision to refuse to call time-outs and to try to get the ball back with decent field position. It is simply never mentioned.

Third Quarter

The quarter started with fireworks that, ultimately, didn't factor into the game.

Azzaro kicked off to Waters who carried the ball from the ten- to the thirty-yard line. Pergine tackled.

1-10	MS 30	Raye fumbled and Horney recovered for ND on the thirty-one.
1-10	MS 31	O'Brien's pass for Bleier intercepted by Phillips on the two and tackled there by Bleier.

Looking back, as unfair as it may be, that interception may have ended one of Notre Dame's two best shots at winning the game. After that play, each team had the ball twice before the final quarter.

Notre Dame's second drive started at their twenty-yard line. O'Brien had completions to Rocky Bleier, Larry Conjar, Bob Gladieux, and Dave Haley. That was followed by runs by Haley, Bleier, and Conjar.

Another Irish halfback was forced out of the game in this sequence, Bob Gladieux. In 1991 he recounted it this way: "I was going out for a pass against the grain and MSU's Jess Phillips was going with the grain. He hit me when I was midair. It was a clean hit. My quadriceps [were] splattered. In fact, my thigh pad was shattered. That leg still bothers me a little when one of my kids sits on my lap."

As the quarter ended, O'Brien went back to pass, found no one open, and then ran for no gain. The ball rested on the MSU ten-yard line.

Michigan State 10–Notre Dame 7.

Fourth Quarter

Opening the quarter, with fourth down and three yards to go, Joe Azzaro kicked a twenty-eight-yard field goal into the wind. Thus ended Notre Dame's second opportunity to take the lead in the game. The tie was tallied.

Michigan State 10–Notre Dame 10.

Each team had the ball five times in the final stanza. There were only three first downs, two by the Spartans, and one by the Irish. A desperate fight was underway. It had everything to do with winning and nothing to do with not losing. The defensive units played with abandon. For most of the season, neither team had used first-stringers this late into a game. They were at the brink of exhaustion. Fortunately, Notre Dame defensive back Tom Schoen intercepted two of Jimmie Raye's passes. Michigan State never got closer than the ND forty-six-yard line. After the second Schoen interception, the score sheet read as follows:

Notre Dame

1-10	MS 18	Conjar downed by Thornhill and Richardson, gained two.
2-8	16	Haley downed by Hoag and Smith for an eight-yard loss.
3-16	24	O'Brien passed incomplete to Bleier.
4-16	24	Azzaro's kick for a field goal was long enough but wide to the right and no good.

(continued on next page)

(table continued)

Michigan State

1-10	MS20	Jones downed by Duranko for six-yard loss.
2-16	14	Raye's pass for Washington incomplete.
3-16	14	Cavendar up the middle, downed by Pergine after getting fifteen-inches short of one down.
4-1	29	Raye sneaked for the first down with inches to spare.
1-10	30	Jones met Lynch and Horney trying left end for a two-yard loss.
2-12	28	Brenner caught Raye's pass for an eight-yard gain. Schoen tackled.
3-4	36	Raye's pass to Brenner incomplete.
4-4	36	Schoen called for fair catch but fumbled and recovered on the ND thirty.

Notre Dame

1-10	ND30	O'Brien downed by Thornhill after four yards.
2-6	34	Bleier downed by Webster and Hoag on the draw after a three-yard gain.
3-3	37	Conjar downed by Thornhill. Made two yards but was still short of one down.
4-13	9	O'Brien sneaked for first down with a two-yard gain.
1-10	41	Smith downed O'Brien going back to pass for a seven-yard loss.
2-17	34	O'Brien sneaked for five yards as the game ended.

Michigan State 10–Notre Dame 10.

It all sounds pretty straightforward when you read it forty-five years later. But interesting details need to be inserted. First, the Azzaro field goal attempt was into the stiff and swirling twenty-miles-per-hour wind, making it a long forty-one yards, a tough kick for the steady ND placekicker. Azzaro says, "The ball came off my foot cleanly and I thought it was going to be good. Then the wind took it." Witnesses claim the kick was wide by about a foot. That's how close Notre Dame came to winning the game—twelve inches or thereabouts.

When State got the ball back after three plays, they were confronted with a fourth and one. They went for it. This was heralded by the ABC announcing team, composed of Chris Shenkel and Bud Wilkenson, as a courageous and daring move by MSU coach Duffy Daugherty. After three more plays against the Irish defense, the Spartans were forced to punt.

This was where Notre Dame came close to losing the ball—and the game. The pigskin fluttered in the variable wind and Tom Schoen fumbled a fair catch on his own thirty—well within the range of Kenney, especially with the wind mostly blowing behind him. Fortunately Schoen recovered his own fumble. It was controversial at the time, as State was scrounging for the loose ball. Years later, Ara identifies this recovery as one of the best plays of the game.

The sequence of six Notre Dame plays with only 1:36 on the clock will probably be debated for the remainder of time. If you recall Alan Page's observation from the very first team meeting with Ara, the coach's moves all make perfect sense. Think position and possession. Parseghian was not about to give the Spartans another chance on offense, especially within Kenny's kicking range. The first order of business: maintain possession.

The only way for the Irish to score from its field position was to maneuver for a field goal. They had to get to at least the MSU twenty-five-yard line to do this. The Spartan coaching staff had this distance figured out as well. State positioned seven defenders back in a "prevent" configuration through the entire sequence, in effect creating a picket fence with a theoretical goal line at the twenty-five. Ara's challenge became how to achieve position and keep possession.

Coley O'Brien was on 0–6 passing up until that point in the fourth quarter. Ara suspected something was wrong. Brian Boulac remembers Tom Schoen (the backup QB in 1965) being instructed to warm up on the sideline, which he did. The only sensible option to maintain possession in that position was to run and to hope for a weak seam in the four-man front.

With fourth down and one, Ara made the most courageous call of the entire game. He decided to go for it. Practically nobody remembers this, especially Spartan fans. If they made it, Notre Dame would retain possession. If they didn't, MSU would probably win the game. The broadcast announcers weren't nearly as gushing about the courage of Parseghian's decision as they were only moments earlier when Duffy did essentially the same thing. This singular call is generally forgotten in the debate, and yet it permanently defines Ara's credentials as a winner. Quarterback Coley O'Brien rushed for two yards to the right behind guard Dick Swatland and tackle Bob Kuechenberg and made the first down.

On the second to last play of the game, Ara called for a rollout option pass, hoping to get close enough for another play or two and a field goal attempt. He had judiciously saved his time-outs. Again, this call is generally forgotten—some people have mistakenly called it a run. O'Brien was dropped for a seven-yard loss by a charging Bubba Smith, who grabbed him from behind. This changed the position and put the ball back in Kenney's field-goal range yet again. Today, Ara believes that another key play of the game was Coley O'Brien's holding onto the ball after Bubba Smith's savage blind-side tackle.

If the game had ended on this play, it's likely the (un)fortunate play-for-tie controversy would never have begun. With a second down and seventeen to go and only six seconds remaining on the clock, the game was effectively over. O'Brien didn't have the arm strength for one last Hail Mary pass. So Ara called a quarterback sneak. Take away that play or have O'Brien throw the ball into the tenth row of seats; either way, the historical controversy is moot. One play, a quarterback sneak on second and seventeen, no less, turned all the hype about the "Game of the Century" into a reality.

One persistent question is still raised. Why did Duffy Daugherty elect to punt on the second Michigan State fourth down when he had to know his team probably wouldn't have the ball again on offense. He was obviously trading possession for position, a logical strategy that relied on the strength of Kenney's leg. He was hoping for a mistake, and it almost happened on the fumbled punt.

Defensive lineman Tom Rhoads aptly summed up the MSU strategy and the Notre Dame response in their final possession. "Michigan State wanted Ara to do something dumb. Ara doesn't do dumb things."

Statistics

The statistic that jumps off the pages forty-five years later is that there were sixteen punts in the game, eight by each team. That correctly speaks to a defensive struggle. The tackle leaders for Notre Dame were Jim Lynch (thirteen), John Pergine (twelve), John Horney (eleven), Tom O'Leary (nine), and Kevin Hardy (seven). Alan Page had zero tackles in the game, primarily because State was afraid to run to his side of the field. The tackle leaders for MSU were Charlie Thornhill (sixteen), Jeff Richardson (thirteen), and George Webster (ten). Bubba Smith had only two solo tackles and was in on four more, although all of them seemed to come at important times in the game.

Lost in the fog of forty-five years is the fact that Notre Dame attempted more passes than Michigan State. ND attempted twenty-four passes (twenty by backup O'Brien) while MSU's Jimmie Raye went for only twenty. It was a dicey weather day for passing. There were only fifteen completions; Notre Dame had eight and MSU had seven. Michigan State had more first downs overall, thirteen to ND's ten, and they led in net rushing yards by one hundred forty-two to ninety-one.

There were no complaints about the officiating after the game. There were just six penalties called, only one against Notre Dame for five yards.

Of the fifty-player Notre Dame travel squad to Michigan State, thirty-two saw game action. Ten were sophomores. The official game record reads:

Left End: Seymour, Rhoads
Left Tackle: Sieler, Duranko
Left Guard: Regner, Hardy
Center: Goeddeke, Monty, Kelly, Page
Right Guard: Swatland, Pergine
Right Tackle: Kuechenberg, Lynch
Right End: Gmitter, Stenger, Horney
Quarterback: Hanratty, O'Brien, Martin, Azzaro
Left Halfback: Gladieux, O'Leary, Burgener, Criniti
Right Halfback: Bleier, Smithberger, Quinn, Haley
Fullback: Conjar, Schoen, Dushney

Reflections

An examination of Notre Dame's scoring at Michigan State provides an interesting insight into the makeup and character of the team. On the only touchdown, Tim Monty hiked the ball to Coley O'Brien. Monty was just a sophomore and was part of the Oldsmobile travel squad, not the regular travel squad, to Northwestern only seven weeks earlier. At about 215 pounds, he was supposed to snap the ball and then block the guy lined up over his helmet, 275-pound Bubba Smith. O'Brien, another sophomore called in to replace starter Terry Hanratty, was playing in his third week after returning from hospitalization. He had a personal physician on the sideline. Coley threw the ball over the middle to sophomore Bob Gladieux, who was slotted into Nick Eddy's vacant position at the last minute. Gladieux would score 6 points. Later in the game he would be hit so hard that his swollen thigh would remove him from the game and also finish his season.

On the tying field goal, the key players who had to step up were long-snapper Jim Kelly, holder O'Brien, and Joe Azzaro. The boy who was told he'd never play football again, the boy who practiced over the family grape arbor, the boy who drove the Oldsmobile squad to Evanston, would score 4 critical points that day. And in the absence of a strong but unpredictable wind, he would have won the game.

Summary

The Notre Dame–Michigan State game, as it was played on November 19, 1966, may be accurately summarized with just five simple sentences. The hitting was ferocious. There was no winner. Nobody played to tie. Those involved left the stadium unsatisfied. Players and coaches are still remembered for, if not haunted by, the experience.

26

APPLESAUCE AND SOUR GRAPES

When the game finally ended, there was a momentary eerie silence in the stadium. This is how the experience has been described by multiple players, coaches, and fans who were there. Eerie. "That is how I remember it playing out. I was there. Forty-yard line behind Notre Dame bench just fifteen rows up. And yes, it was 'eerie' afterwards. We just sat there staring at the scoreboard. I think the fans were exhausted by what they saw and heard on the field, something that could not come through on television."

As time elapsed at Spartan Stadium on November 19, 1966 the score was tied and an eerie silence fell over the crowd. *Source:* University of Notre Dame Archives

242

This is how Mike Collins (Notre Dame '67) remembers it. He knew and lived with many of the players and was a sports director for the student radio station WSND. As of this writing, he is entering his thirtieth year as the public address announcer at Notre Dame Stadium.

Everyone in the confines of Spartan Stadium knew the game was finally over and that it had been brutal. Later, much later for some, they would reflect that they had witnessed something historically significant. Ticket stubs and programs would become highly collectible.

MICHIGAN STATE Spartans
NOTRE DAME Fighting Irish

Souvenir Program

This program cover for the Michigan State – Notre Dame Game has become highly collectible, as have ticket stubs to the game using the same graphic art. 10,000 tickets were made available to Notre Dame under contract, while nearly 80,000 were packed into every corner of Spartan Stadium on November 19, 1966. *Source:* University of Notre Dame Archives

But at the time it was hard to absorb the result. Everyone was exhausted. And everyone wearing green and white was especially frustrated because their season was now over. That frustration started to leak out once the eerie silence was broken.

Forty-four years after the fact, Ara clearly recalls exiting the Spartan Stadium field on November 19, 1966. He was running toward the locker room through the crowd of players, coaches, and bystanders when he started to hear the taunts: "You chickens." "Hey coach, why did you play for a tie?"

There were many variations on these insults, most of them unprintable. The person often identified on the MSU side as a prime instigator of the verbal assault was Assistant Coach Hank Bullough (who later, as a pro assistant coach, would be credited with developing the now-popular three–four defense). After what Bullough had witnessed first hand, he should have known better.

But frustration is a powerful force. Walking off the field, Michigan State insiders instinctively knew that they had not landed the knock-out punch. In fact, MSU had a rather weak showing in the second half, especially on offense. In the absence of "Ara doing something stupid," they were now probably out of the running for any stand-alone claim on the National Championship, especially if Notre Dame were to beat Southern Cal. Even if Notre Dame lost in California, a shared award, probably with Alabama, would be the best they could have done.

Ara wasn't immune from the catcalling as he tried to jog off the field. He was fuming when he finally got to the visitors' locker room. As he tells it, "When I got inside the coaches' room I saw an apple on the table. I took that apple and threw it as hard as I could into the shower room, smashing it against the wall." Does he mind that story being retold? "Hell no, I was damn mad. The kids on the field, on both sides, had played their hearts out. They all deserved credit for what they had done. Nobody played for any tie, I can tell you that." It's a real shame that Ara wasn't able to get this simple message out as his final word on the matter.

The head coach collected himself and addressed the team in the locker room before the press was allowed in. He recalls telling them how proud he was of their effort, their comeback against adversity. Then he explained that they still had a chance to be National Champions if they went to Southern California and won convincingly. The coach had already assessed the situation and turned the page to the challenge for the coming week.

Injuries

As testament to the brutality of the game, there were big challenges for the Notre Dame medical team and trainers as the team showered and collected their equipment. The crowded locker room was filled with carnivorous reporters. Attending to the casualties became difficult at best.

Rocky Bleier unexpectedly needed immediate attention after he urinated blood in the locker room. The considered decision was that he was well enough to make the trip back home. He would be immediately hospitalized when he returned to South Bend, leading to the diagnosis of a lacerated kidney—a serious injury. He would still be in the hospital a week later. Terry Hanratty had his arm in sling. It was excruciating to move any part of his upper body. The painkillers didn't help much. Getting out of his football pads and pants required delicate help. Bob Gladieux's thigh had ballooned-up and was packed with ice. None of these players, Bleier, Hanratty, or Gladieux, would play another down of football in 1966. Jim Seymour passed out in the locker room, exhausted. George Goeddeke was hobbling around with crutches taking weight off his severely-sprained ankle. For all practical purposes he was also finished for the season, although he would hobble to play one "charity down" the following week. Coley O'Brien was going through the motions to act normally, still drinking orange juice as protection against diabetic shock. He would remember virtually nothing right after the game and to this day his friends all claim he was "out of it." Nick Eddy quietly changed into street clothes. His sore shoulder was still throbbing, but he was hopeful of playing the next week back in California, his home state. The guys with simple cuts, scratches, and bruises—and there were many—had to fend for themselves.

Mike Collins further remembers, "We waited outside the locker room. Even players I knew as classmates were not talking afterwards, it was if they had spent everything they had and many were hurting. At that point I don't think a one of them had it figured out that a win the next week would give them the Championship. I always have thought that Jim Lynch got a concussion on that hit he took after the interception. He seemed like a zombie outside the locker room and stared at me like he did not know who I was, which he did."

The overwhelming sentiment was to get everyone home as soon as possible. There was a private train waiting for them on a siding within view of the stadium. Getting to it became the immediate goal.

Beatty

While that train from Michigan State's campus to South Bend rumbled south, some folks in America were actually seeing the game on TV for the first time via delayed broadcast. To parts of the country, the

Kentucky–Tennessee game was broadcast live with a delay of the game from East Lansing. It is because the entire ND-MSU game was taped in color for rebroadcast that there even exists a record of the game as it was seen by millions on television.

One of the more interesting recollections about the 1966 MSU–ND game comes from an unlikely source. Jim Beatty was one of America's premier distance runners. He was the first person in the world to run the mile indoors in a time under four minutes (3:58.9 on February 10, 1962 in Los Angeles), and the 1962 Sullivan Award winner.

Surprisingly, Beatty has been a life-long Notre Dame Football fan. In fact, it was only at the last minute that he decided to attend the University of North Carolina over ND, because of coaching and weather. It is a decision that he jokingly claims his mother never forgave him for (his middle name is Tully, after his mother's side).

In 1966 he was keenly interested in the "Game of the Century." Only weeks before, the Irish had manhandled the Tarheels in South Bend, so Beatty's loyalties were no longer split. As he tells it, there was a wonderful "Cheers-like" bar in Charlotte called the Rathskeller. The football game was on tape delay in North Carolina, the result of that arcane rule that no team could be on national TV more than once during a season—not live, anyway. While most of the country saw the game in real time, in selected places it was blacked out and played after the game was in the record books. The regulars at the Rathskeller wanted to enjoy the game as it was unfolding, so everyone that entered the bar was instructed not to tell anyone the final score, even if they knew it.

Before one fellow could be given the appropriate warning, he walked in and, seeing the game, made some comment like, "Some game, ending in a tie." The patrons were annoyed, at first. But knowing the outcome had the effect of making the game have increased meaning; understanding the key plays and turning points were of even more importance. Beatty's mind is crystal clear about this day and where he was. He still follows the Irish religiously.

Aftershocks

The immediate reaction of the press, at least by those who actually witnessed the game in person, was relatively balanced. If you were there and then checked the stat sheets, it was obvious that you had witnessed one heck of a college football game. After that, partisanship would spin the stories to appease the home-market readership. One remarkable exception was written by Joe Falls, Sports Editor for the *Detroit Free Press*, in his article "There Is a Time to Gamble."

Bless me, Father for I have sinned . . .

I rooted for Michigan State.

But now I would like to repent. The winner, and it hurts me to say it, was Notre Dame.

On Monday morning the vote will go out to the Associated Press in New York: 1 – Notre Dame, 2 – Michigan State, etc., etc.

And let's not hear any of that tripe from Birmingham that Alabama is the best team in the nation. Bear Bryant's boys snuck in the back door when AP held that ridiculous poll last January.

Make no mistake about it—the two best teams in the land were on display here Saturday and our grudging admiration goes to the Fighting Irish.

They were up against everything and still managed to pull off a tie in the most nerve-wracking football game that could possibly be played. It was a classic in the truest sense of the word.

The Irish lost their quarterback, Terry Hanratty, early in the game. Their best runner, and maybe the best runner in the country, Nick Eddy, never got onto the field.

George Goeddeke, their first string center, also went out early in the action.

And here they were, with only half a backfield in the bull ring that rivaled anything [that] Madrid or Mexico City could offer, with a 10–0 score against them . . . and they came back and got a 10–10 standoff and barely missed winning it with five minutes to go on Joe Azzaro's field goal try from 41 yards out.

A lesser team could have collapsed when Nick [sic] Kenney put that 47-yard field goal through the bars midway in the second half . . . because here Michigan State had all the momentum, all the drive and almost all the fans behind it.

In the moment that they waited for the kickoff after Kenney's field goal, my heart was pounding at the prospect of a rout, which would have made this the sweetest day of the season, and the feeling came on strong that Michigan State might even have shut out this team that was running up those ridiculous 64–0 scores against people like Duke.

From then on you had to give your admiration to these Notre Dame players. Quit? Why, they came back and played their best ball of the day through those final 40 minutes.

And as the pressure mounted, until it became almost unbearable to sit still in your seat, the Irish made all the big plays.

It was magnificent the way this little Coley O'Brien immediately rallied the Irish for their touchdown, because simply ask yourself this question—who is Coley O'Brien?

He looks like a tumbleweed being blown across the flat prairie lands, no bigger than the quarterback at North Farmington High. And certainly, no cover boy.

The people at Time probably never heard of him.

But he fused the spark in his team and before you could utter the magic words, "We're No. 1," the Irish were on the scoreboard and back in the game.

He led them 54 yards in three quick strikes and you just can't be any more authoritative than the way he hit the streaking Bob Gladieux on the goal line for the touchdown.

Right then, I started getting scared.

You can stack up the statistics and arrange them in any order that you want but the Irish won this one and even if it might put the Spartans on top, I hope Notre Dame closes out with a victory over Southern Cal. They deserve the No. 1 ranking.

This is not an attempt to demean Michigan State, to get off the hook for all the needling I've given the Irish fans in the last few weeks. But it would be less than fair to be prejudiced at a time like this. You've got to give them their due.

It was regrettable that the game ended in a chorus of boos from the highly partisan crowd as Ara Parseghian chose to settle for the tie instead of trying for a bolt of lightning in the last minute.

It would have been far better to see the Irish making an all-out effort to break the tie. But there is a time to gamble, and there isn't a time to gamble.

This wasn't the time.

It was impressive the way Michigan State kept calling time out with the seconds ticking away. But to ridicule the Irish for killing the clock . . . Well, it's just sour grapes.

Seldom— in fact never—has a game affected me the way this one did. You can believe this or not, but I awoke with a knot in my stomach Saturday morning.

I wanted Michigan State to win so badly, it hurt. If the Spartans lost, I had my lines rehearsed . . .

"AAARGH," I would say, "humble pie tastes awful" . . . and don't bother writing your nasty letters. Duffy and I were taking a vacation in the upper Peninsula to see who could make the biggest splash from the middle of Mackinac Bridge.

Well, Daugherty doesn't have to apologize for anything, or explain anything. He showed more guts in this one afternoon than many coaches do in an entire career.

Fourth and one on his 30 . . . three minutes left . . . go for it and risk the chance of blowing the game and the whole season and leave yourself wide open to be second-guessed the rest of your natural life?

Or punt?

Duffy didn't hesitate. He sent in a play, a keeper by Jimmie Raye, and whether it worked or not, and it did, it was the boldest move any coach could make.

And then, unwilling to settle for the tie, Daugherty kept ordering those time outs in the fading moments, hoping somehow his boys would wrest the ball loose from the Irish.

They took the coach-of-the-year honors away from Daugherty when the Spartans lost to UCLA in the Rose Bowl last January. But if there's any justice left in the land, they should give it to him this time around.

You see, Michigan State played a helluva ball game too. The Spartans are a superb team.

In fact, they're the No. 2 team in the land.

This is an honest account from a writer who admits his bias and had every reason to slant the story to provide solace to Michigan State loyalists. Of course, he couldn't help himself in praise of Duffy Daugherty. The MSU coach was very well liked by sportswriters, almost as if he were one of their drinking buddies. In truth, Daugherty wasn't slighted for coach-of-the-year honors in 1965; he was so honored by the Football Writers of America. But losing in the 1965 Rose Bowl certainly didn't improve his resume. Consideration of Duffy for this award again in 1966 would be logical (the award went to Army's Tom Cahill). But there was at least one superior candidate, Ara Parseghian. The Notre Dame head coach was highly respected, liked by many, but not adored by the press. Recall that Ara had also made "the boldest move any coach could make," going for the first down with the game on the line. The irony is that he has never been properly credited for this. To the contrary, the second wave of media coverage that started on the Monday after the game was highly critical of Ara, unfairly so, and borderline vitriolic to a large extent.

The pinnacle of negativity was achieved in the *Sports Illustrated* cover story (November 28). The prosaic cover photograph of tangled players in the final play of the game was done by another emerging young photographer, Neil Leifer. The heading was, "Notre Dame Runs Out the Clock against Michigan State." The bold banner insert in orange read, "Furor over No. 1."

The accompanying article was formatted next to a full-page color photograph of Jim Lynch landing precariously on his head in what may have been the turning point of the game. Notice that the trite title was designed to compliment this amazing photo.

AN UPSIDE DOWN GAME

College football awaited an epic that was supposed to decide the national championship. But it all fell apart when Michigan State faltered after a fast start, and Notre Dame took the easy way out.

By Dan Jenkins

Old Notre Dame will tie over all. Sing it out, guys. That is not exactly what the march says, of course, but that is how the big game ends every time you replay it. And that is how millions of cranky college football fans will remember it. For 59 minutes in absolutely overwrought East Lansing last week, the brutes of Michigan State and Notre Dame pounded each other into enough mistakes to fill Bubba

Smith's uniform—enough to settle a dozen games between lesser teams—but the 10–10 tie that destiny seemed to be demanding had a strange, noble quality to it. And then it did not have that anymore. For the people who saw it under the cold dreary clouds or on national television, suddenly all it had was this enormous emptiness for which the Irish will be forever blamed

Put the No. 1 team, Notre Dame, on its own 30-yard line with time for at least four passing plays to break the tie. A No. 1 team will try something, won't it, to stay that way?

Notre Dame did not. It just let the air out of the ball. For reasons that it will rationalize as being more valid than they perhaps were under the immense circumstances, the Irish rode out the clock (see cover). Even as the Michigan State defenders taunted them and called time outs that the Irish should have been calling, Notre Dame ran into the line, the place where the big game was hopelessly played all afternoon. No one really expected a verdict in that last desperate moment. But they wanted someone to try. When the Irish ran into the line, the Spartans considered it a minor surrender.

Later in the article, Jenkins continued:

Notre Dame Coach Ara Parseghian made the decision to end the so-called "game of the century" that way. The players only followed instructions, some of them perhaps reluctantly. "We'd fought hard to come back and tie it up," Ara argued. "After all that, I didn't want to risk giving it to them cheap. They get reckless and I could have cost them the game. I wasn't going to do a jackass thing like that at this point."

With this singular article, the news cycle for the 1966 Notre Dame–Michigan game was extended from one week to . . . well, *forever.* The writer deserves no literary credit for this. The article may have been a stylistic success, creating controversy and selling magazines, but it was also a factual fantasy that didn't match up with the action that millions of people had witnessed for themselves. It was almost as if Jenkins watched the game on TV from a barroom in East Lansing, asked the regulars what they thought throughout the afternoon, and made his notes between pool shots.

LIFE Magazine reporter Joe Bride puts the prevailing attitude behind the article into perspective forty-five years later.

I knew Jenkins fairly well. I suppose more as a courtier than a friend. The SI people drank in the same watering hole the LIFE people did. It was a small little white table cloth semi-dive on 49th Street between 5th and 6th Avenues. Jenkins was a center-of-attention guy, very much the raconteur, always telling stories, many of them about his relationships with famous and carousing athletes, the great majority of them Texans.

251

I remember interviewing Bobby Layne and telling him a couple of stories and activities that Jenkins had attributed to Layne. Layne said, "That Fort Worth boy is still full of bull shit like he was back in Texas. But he sure can tell a story and talk up a storm. He never had that accent until he came up east."

Andre Laguerre, the early SI Managing Editor, firmly believed the magazine needed a new breed of famous and semi-famous writers to succeed, or famous literary figures (read in no articles from famous sports columnists), but a lot of articles from folks like Jenkins, John Underwood, Frank Deford, and William Faulkner.

Considering Jenkins to be of the same literary caliber of William Faulkner is absurd. In fact, even in his home state of Texas, Jenkins wasn't always considered a fan favorite. In the very same issue of *Sports Illustrated* that carried the ND–MSU story was the following letter to the editor:

Sirs:

Dan Jenkins' article insults A&M as an educational institution and it casts a reflection on many distinguished graduates. The Aggies may have crawled out of the woodwork to go to College Station to see their football team soundly trounced by a fine Arkansas squad, but that night Dan Jenkins was the only termite in Kyle Field.

Jack Roeder, Houston

Samsonian Defensive Strength

In his end of season wrap-up on college football, the respected Allison Danzig wrote the following, printed December 25, 1966:

Notre Dame and Michigan State, mighty teams of Samsonian defensive strength, met in 1966 in one of the memorable games of intercollegiate football, and the largest television audience to view a regularly scheduled college contest (33,000,000) and a record crowd of 80,011 at East Lansing, Mich., saw the top-ranked goliaths fight to a 10–10 tie.

The Fighting Irish continued to hold top place in the national poll of sports writers and broadcasters. But in the coaches' ranking they were ousted by Michigan State, probably because, after wiping out the Spartans' 10–0 lead, they virtually froze the ball on running plays in the last minute and a half to protect the tie, rather than gamble with passes to win.

A week later, Notre Dame annihilated Southern California, 51–0. With this final demonstration of its scoring power, which Michigan State had no chance to match because its season had ended, it went back to the top in the coaches' ranking. The National Football Foundation differed with the two polls and awarded the MacArthur Bowl to both teams as joint champions.

Ranked after the Fighting Irish and the Spartans, both of whom had spotless records except for their tie, was Alabama. The Crimson Tide was the only major team undefeated and untied.

The Notre Dame players and coaches had no idea that this was how their season would ultimately conclude as they began practice for the Southern California game. The polls had been announced on Tuesday morning. The AP had Notre Dame as number one, but UPI had Michigan State as number one, probably a tip of the cap to Duffy by his fellow coaches, most of whom hadn't witnessed a single play from the game (there was no video tape of the game to be distributed). This was unexpected. Looking at the depth chart as they began practice on Monday afternoon, the Irish had many reasons to be concerned, most notably the loss of so many key players. With a short week of practices and a cross-country trip ahead of them, Notre Dame's task at hand was daunting.

27

OVERTIME

The Pebble

The 1966 Notre Dame–Michigan State game is the pebble in Ara Parseghian's shoe that just won't be dislodged. The last play the coach called against Michigan State was a quarterback sneak. The play-for-a-tie branding of the game has been impossible to shake ever since. Even readers of this book, absorbing every effort to explain and illuminate the truth and desiring to expunge Ara's pebble, won't be able to erase this branding. It is permanent.

But an unexpected transition has been unfolding over time. Because of this branding, the game has gone down in history as the most memorable college football contest of the last half of the twentieth century. We have only Ara Parseghian to thank for that, as well as his incredible grace under pressure for nearly half a century. Katie Parseghian, the first lady of Notre Dame Football, also deserves recognition for being the shock absorber all these years.

The controversy just doesn't die. After the 1966 season ended, Ara was attacked mercilessly. The truth became irrelevant. Some of the coach's comments just fueled the fires. The more he said, the worse it got.

I'm not a conservative coach. I think my 17-year record speaks for itself in that respect. But I couldn't be coaxed into playing Russian roulette, where you put one bullet into a six-shooter and rev the cylinder and then put the pistol to your head and pull the trigger hoping the bullet is not in that chamber.

I don't drive cars 90 miles per hour through dense fog hoping that nobody's in my path. I just don't take a calculated risk. And putting the ball in the air against Michigan State was a calculated risk. We hang onto the ball, we can't lose. We put it into the air, we can lose. It's as simple as that.

Well, if we tie Michigan State, they're through. It's their last game. They're done. But we still have Southern Cal. So we stand off the Spartans and we get our overtime or extra innings against the Trojans.

People hear what they want to hear and believe what they want to believe. There are more than enough people who dislike Notre Dame to keep the fires of discontent burning. Prejudice or jealousy, it really doesn't matter why. It is inconvenient to be reminded that the entire controversy of the 1966 tie has spun around a single play called by Ara— to hold the ball with six seconds left and virtually no way to throw into the wind for a seventy-yard pass completion, with seven defensive backs lurking to run back an interception. Ara doesn't do dumb things. It's just not in his nature.

Rules

Surprisingly, after the game, an outcry to create collegiate rules that would settle ties didn't really materialize. The pros had begun adding an extra fifteen-minute period to break ties back in 1955. The 1958 Championship between the New York Giants and the Baltimore Colts is the game most recognized for the first use of overtime. Since 1974, the NFL has used a variation on the theme: sudden death. The impetus for the change at the professional level probably had a lot to do with gambling and with wanting to make the Sunday games a TV draw.

College football viewed itself as a purer version of the sport, beyond the reach of gamblers, and sidestepped any rule change until

1996—again, probably with the forces of network television and Las Vegas cheering in the background. While the tie-breaker rule has made for more excitement on *Sports Center*, it may not be fair to the players. After sixty minutes of equal scoring, the character of an entire exhausted football squad shouldn't turn on a coin toss or a single play. But now there is no going back.

Deep in the crevices of the argument, the 1966 ND–MSU game is sometimes mentioned as the impetus for the rule change. It shouldn't be. Consider the facts. Michigan State didn't advance the ball beyond the Notre Dame forty-six-yard line throughout the entire second half of the game. Only once during the entire game did they advance inside the thirty (on their only TD scoring drive). Under current NCAA overtime rules, State would have been awarded field position on the twenty-five-yard line, a position on the field that it hadn't earned for over forty minutes of play during the contest. Fair? You be the judge. But don't ask the '66 Notre Dame defense to answer this hypothetical question.

A more interesting debate resulted from number one playing number two: Why couldn't a surrogate playoff for the National Championship happen every year. The scheduling of top teams playing late in the season is random at best, the result of scheduling agreed to years in advance. To address this, the Bowl Championship Series was contrived for the purpose of matching the two best teams at the end of each season. The first BCS title game was in 1998. Even with its cadre of regular detractors at the end of each season, the system has worked surprisingly well.

It is interesting to speculate whether or not Notre Dame and Michigan State would have been selected for a rematch had this system been in place in 1966. It is doubtful. The folks in Alabama certainly would have cried foul, and with good reason. Again, invoking the 1966 tie as part of the justification behind establishing the BCS doesn't fit the facts. Michigan State would probably have been odd man out in 1966, and would be even more frustrated today.

It is a tribute to the integrity of college football history that neither Notre Dame nor Michigan State is considered a loser for their efforts that resulted in the 1966 tie game. The players can all hold their heads high. The National Football Foundation and Hall of Fame recognized both teams as co-National Champions—the only legitimate body to do so. Therefore, the 1966 Michigan State players sport National Championship rings, green stones with a diamond (as Duffy Daugherty promised), which are quite the conversation piece on football Saturdays in East Lansing.

Fame and Fortunes

The 1966 National Championship placed the capstone on a return-to-glory story at Notre Dame that would endure throughout Ara's coaching tenure. The financial fortunes of the chronically hand-to-mouth University of Notre Dame were forever elevated after 1966. Notre Dame enjoys one of the highest endowments of any university in America, and for a time it surpassed the collective endowments of all Catholic colleges. Coeducation and world-class facilities are the visual evidence of Notre Dame's success. Football, and the 1966 boys of autumn, specifically, may be thanked for a large contribution to this evolution.

Everybody recalls the historic role of radio in building Notre Dame Football awareness. Largely due to the success of Ara's early teams, starting in 1968 a one-hour syndicated TV highlight show hosted by Lindsey Nelson and Paul Hornung was broadcast on Sunday mornings. That singular show was so popular that it disrupted Mass attendance for many ND loyalists. Ask any Catholic family from that era about the words "now to further action later in the quarter." They are a permanent part of the Notre Dame lexicon, at least as familiar as prayers in Latin used to be. They were a precursor to something more significant. Today, Notre Dame remains the only college with an exclusive network television contract. The revenue goes to the general scholarship fund.

The personal fortunes of players who were in the now-famous game are incomparable in the history of college football. Forty-three players from the two teams would eventually be drafted by the pros. That has to be some kind of record. Thirty-five players from the two squads would log playing time for National Football League teams, twenty-four from Notre Dame and eleven from Michigan State. It is more amazing when you consider that four more Irish players could have gone professional. Allen Sack, who was drafted, elected to go to grad school for a PhD. John Horney became a medical doctor. Don Gmitter returned to Notre Dame to finish his fifth year of architectural studies. Coley O'Brien elected to attend the Notre Dame Law School (but third string QB Bob Belden was drafted by and played for the Cowboys).

Just as remarkable is the fact that four of the first eight players drafted in 1967 were from Michigan State: Bubba Smith (first), Clint Jones (second), George Webster (fifth) and Gene Washington (eighth)—all African-Americans.

257

The first Notre Dame player drafted in 1967 was Paul Siler (twelfth), followed by Alan Page (fifteenth) and Tom Regner (twenty-third). Notre Dame would have other first round picks in later drafts: Kevin Hardy (1968), and George Kunz and Jim Seymour (1969). The complete list is presented below as a tribute to these players.

• NOTRE DAME

Name	Drafted by (round)	Played for
1966 (Supplementary Draft)		
Nick Eddy*	Detroit (second), Denver (first)	Detroit
Pete Duranko	Cleveland (fouth), Denver (second)	Cleveland, Denver
1967		
Paul SilerOakland	New York Jets (first)	New York Jets, Oakland
Alan Page	Minnesota (first)	Minnesota, Chicago
Tom Regner	Houston (first)	Houston
Larry Conjar	Cleveland (second)	Cleveland, Philadelphia, Baltimore
Jim Lynch	Kansas City (second)	Kansas City
George Goeddeke	Denver (third)	Denver
Tom Rhoads	Buffalo (third)	Buffalo, Cincinnati
Allen Sack	Los Angeles (sixteenth)	

* Injured and did not play in MSU game

(continued on next page)

Name	Drafted by (round)	Played for

1968

Name	Drafted by (round)	Played for
Kevin Hardy	New Orleans (first)	San Francisco, Geen Bay, San Diego
Mike McGill*	Minnesota (third)	
Jim Smithberger	Boston (fifth)	
Dave Martin	Philadelphia (sixth)	Kansas City, Chicago
Dick Swatland	New Orleans (eighth)	Houston
Tom Schoen	Cleveland (eighth)	Cleveland
John Pergine	Los Angeles (eleventh)	Los Angeles, Washington
Rockey Bleier	Pittsbutgh (sixteenth)	Pittsburgh
Steve Quinn	undrafted	Houston
Brian Stenger	undrafted	Pittsburgh, Boston

1969

Name	Drafted by (round)	Played for
George Kunz *	Atlanta (first)	Atlanta
Jim Seymour	Los Angeles (first)	Chicago
Terry Hanratty	Pittsburgh (second)	Pittsburgh
Bob Kuechenberg	Philadelphia (fourth)	Miami
Jim Winegarder	Chicago (fifth)	
Ed Tuck	Miami (sixth)	
Bob Gladieux	Boston (eighth)	Boston, Buffalo
Eric Norri	Washington (eleventh)	
Bob Belden	Dallas (twelfth)	Dallas
John Lavin	Kansas City (twelfth)	
Tom Quinn	Chicago (thirteenth)	
Kevin Rassas	undrafted	Atlanta

* Injured and did not play in MSU game

• MICHIGAN STATE

Name	Drafted by (round)	Played for	259

1967

Name	Drafted by (round)	Played for
Bubba Smith	Baltimore (first)	Baltimore, Oakland, Houston
Clint Jones	Minnesota (first)	Minnesota, SanDiego,
George Webster	Houston (first)	Houston, Pittsburgh, Boston
Gene Washington	Minnesota (first)	Minnesota, Denver
Jeff Richardson	New York Jets (sixth)	New York Jets, Miami
Charlie Thornhill	Boston (ninth)	
Jim Summers	Denver (ninth)	Denver
Dick Kenney	Philadelphia (fourteenth)	

1968

Name	Drafted by (round)	Played for
Jesse Phillips	Cincinnati (fourth)	Cincinnati, New Orleans, Oakland, Boston
Drake Garrett	Denver (fourth)	Denver
Dwight Lee	San Francisco (fifth)	San Francisco, Atlanta
Bob Apisa	Green Bay (ninth)	
Jimmy Raye	Los Angeles (sixteenth)	Philadelphia

1969

Name	Drafted by (round)	Played for
Allen Brenner1968	New York Giants (seventh)	New York Giants

The "Game of the Century"

Fred Rothenberg, AP sports writer, did a five-part series of articles in 1979 under the title *The Game of the Century*. Here's his assessment written thirteen years after the tied battle:

> *It was 1966 and for one glorious year, an undefeated football team helped Notre Dame avoid the student stridency and Vietnam War passions that were turning other schools into battlegrounds.*
>
> *That year, the battleground at Notre Dame was the football field. In South Bend, Ind., Saturday was as much a religious day as Sunday and the pursuit of the national championship was a crusade for the entire student body. With no separate athletic dorms, students and athletes shared their lives, ideas, good times and the dream of a final No. 1 ranking.*
>
> *But that team is not best remembered for the national title of the nine games it won, nor for the army of players it sent to the pros. That team went down in history for the one game it didn't win—a 10–10 tie with Michigan State, a standoff that has as much right to call itself "the game of the decade" as any other.*

Forty-five years later, the moniker "Game of the Century" still applies. The 1966 Notre Dame–Michigan State game, as it was played on the field, has as much claim to the title as any other. But in some important off-the-field ways, it stands alone.

It is generally agreed upon which post-war-period college football games were the best: Notre Dame–Army (1946), Notre Dame–MSU (1966), Texas–Arkansas (1969), Notre Dame–Alabama (Sugar Bowl, 1973), and Nebraska–Oklahoma (1971). Only one other game from this list finished in a tie: Notre Dame 0–Army 0. That game was also hard hitting and is remembered today for one signature play, Johnny Lujack's shoestring tackle of Doc Blanchard, which prevented a touchdown. This game, played in Yankee Stadium, is also historically unique because four players who were dressed that day went on to win the Heisman Trophy—Lujack, Blanchard, Glenn Davis, and Leon Hart.

Any of the five games above could make a convincing claim to the title "Game of the Century." Take your pick. But ask yourself this: Do you even know the winners of the other games, or the final scores? There is something elegant about ties. Nobody wins, and everybody wins. They *are* memorable.

It is undisputed that the Notre Dame–Michigan State game in 1966 was the most important college football game in half a century. There is no other single football game that was at the vortex of so much change in American society.

The game claimed the largest television audience ever to watch a football game (33 million households). At that point in time and for years thereafter, even the audience that tuned in to watched Super Bowls was smaller. The largest single audience for *American Idol*, perennially the top show in recent years, was 29 million homes. Collegiate athletics was becoming an electronic media phenomenon, and this singular ND–MSU game catapulted this evolution forward. It was also the first game of the very first college football doubleheader on television (the second game was USC–UCLA). After November 19, 1966, Saturdays would forever be the exclusive purview of college football during the regular season.

The impact of the game on opportunities for minority athletes is undoubtedly the most enduring legacy. Michigan State had a number of exceptional black football players in 1966: Regis Cavendar, Clint Jones, Dwight Lee, Jimmie Raye, Bubba Smith, Gene Washington, and George Webster. Notre Dame had only one. Alan Page remembers, "The school was not very integrated. There were maybe two other minority ballplayers. As people, we were living in our own little football world without much of a social conscience. The fact that I was in a school that had 25–30 minority students had an impact on my memories. That's why they're not as fond as some others. I really didn't have much of a social life."

Michigan State can rightfully claim a leadership role in accepting and integrating minority football players into its program. It wasn't easy. One Chicago newspaper speculated that Duffy would never have trouble recruiting as long as he didn't run out of bananas. Prejudice was that blatant. There was great talent playing in high schools throughout the South. But Southern colleges, and especially large state universities, were slow to integrate. In fact, coaches at Southern schools actively promoted ballplayers to their Northern counterparts, lest the athlete show up in a game against their team. To his enduring credit, Duffy Daugherty welcomed these players with open arms. Duffy was color blind.

261

According to MSU's George Webster, "Duffy was my man. When I was inducted into the Michigan Sports Hall of Fame, I said, 'If it wasn't for Duffy, the integration of college football would not have happened as quickly.' I grew up 17 miles from Clemson, but in 1963 I would not have been able to go there if I wanted to."

The TV videotape of the 1966 game is interesting to watch forty-five years later from a nonpartisan perspective. The game appears to be as fully integrated as any contemporary college game. It was. But in 1966, the sport wasn't, and neither was the nation. That lack of integration changed quickly (though perhaps not quickly enough), in part through exposure to the largest audience ever to watch a football game in America.

If someone were assigned to put a video recording of a single college football game into a twentieth century time capsule, they might have been wise to select the Notre Dame–Michigan State 10–10 tie. Overall, it was *the most important* game of the century.

Myth and Mythology

> Between the idea
> and the reality,
> between the motion and the act,
> falls the shadow.
>
> —T.S. Eliot, "The Hollow Men"

That Ara Parseghian played for a tie against Michigan State in 1966 is a myth, plain and simple.

Being interviewed by Rothenberg years later, Ara said:

I was frankly shocked by the reaction of the press to what had taken place. I was attempting to get into field goal position. The play selection was rather conservative. But who says you have to throw the bomb? What is very difficult for the fan to understand is the knowledge the coach has on the sideline. There's no sense in giving away the game in the last minute of the contest. God, the game ended in a tie. There's nothing in the rules that says you can't win by a field goal. But the press took the position that we had gone for the tie.

But the mythology of the ND–MSU game endures. And now it serves everyone from both teams quite well because the game cannot be forgotten or dismissed.

Michigan's George Webster admits, "I know why Ara went for the tie . . . He still had the USC game and you don't want to lose. Ara's a smart man. But the only way Notre Dame could prove they were better would be by beating us."

Regis Cavender would fantasize about a rematch. "I thought it would be great if the two teams got together at a neutral site, without the press, nobody in the stands, and just our squads in full pads. Bring in the coaches, some referees, doctors and a couple of semis of tape, blow the whistle and just see what happens. Then let everybody know about it afterwards."

State player Tony Conti reflects, "It's taken me 35 years to finally get over the tie. Actually, I'm over it. It's a helluva novelty. It didn't hurt me. The things you don't get over are a death in the family or losing a finger in a meat slicer."

Over time, some of the Spartans have even come to Ara's defense. "Parseghian got a bum rap for that," says Regis Cavender. "It was one decision of thousands that he made in that game. Unless you walk in his cleats, you can't possibly know what is going on in his mind and everything he has to consider."

Charlie Thornhill has also mellowed with time. "Ara made the right call. He knew he had an extra game. Duffy was pretty conservative, too. Trying to win, but without making mistakes. Ara was one of the greatest coaches of all time. People need to stop hounding him."

To the outside world, Duffy Daugherty curried the image of a jovial Mister-Softy coach. The reality was quite the opposite. Opposing coaches would tell you that he was hard-nosed to the point of being ruthless. He never quite got over the disappointment of 1966. He would frequently needle Ara in public and then hide behind an ah-shucks-I-didn't-really-mean-it persona. When the two men were at functions together, Duffy would approach the microphone and say, "Nice tie, Ara." The line was always good for a big audience laugh, with Ara just shaking his head.

Catching Daugherty in an unguarded moment was rare, but it did happen on occasion among his closest friends. One such time was at a card game (gin rummy) at the Rochester, New York, home of his good friend Gerry Zornow, the CEO of Eastman Kodak (sponsor of the Kodak All-American teams). Asked about Ara's decision in front of a few close friends, Duffy was still the master of double-talk. One person at the card table, *LIFE's* Joe Bride, remembers the essence of the response. Duffy said, "I never criticized Ara for that decision." Well, coach, what would you have done in Ara's shoes? "I probably would have done something like have my quarterback go back for a pass and throw the ball up into the seats." We can only wonder if he would have really done that with Bubba Smith crashing over the line trying to dismember *his* quarterback. Probably not.

Notre Dame's offensive tackle Bob Kuechenberg has his summary quote down pat after all these years. "The game ended in a tie. People have been critical of Ara and that's not fair. But that's also the beauty of it all. Who would have thought that after all this time people would still be talking about the game. And, we're still National Champions."

Undisputed.

28

TO HELL WITH UPI

Irish! You are hurting . . . But unbowed and unbeaten. There are no sophomores on our squad. Michigan State made all of you grow up . . . Beyond any point of inexperience.

Southern Cal out there is different from anywhere else in the world.

I remember the "Irish" squad walking the long empty walk from the field to the tunnel. I remember their full-grown bodies —shaking with sobs of dejection. I recall the fantastic turn of events that robbed us of a National Championship.

—*The Phantom*

Ara Parseghian had two years to prepare for walking onto the turf at the Los Angeles Coliseum in 1966. The memories of 1964 had to come flooding back. The coach was returning with another number-one-ranked Notre Dame team. This group of guys was probably even more talented than the team that came within one minute, thirty-three seconds of winning the National Championship. Parseghian thought he was robbed by inept (perhaps biased) officiating in 1964. The filmed visual evidence supported his claim. So the coach was preparing his team for every possible contingency, except one. He knew he couldn't predict how the refs would call the game.

Eighty-eight thousand five hundred twenty people would sit in typical sunny Southern California weather to watch the match-up, including almost all of the 18,623-person USC student body (three times the size of Notre Dame). It would be the largest crowd that year to watch a football game, college or professional. For Notre Dame, would it be another upset by the Trojans, or a National Championship and football immortality? Either way, history was going to be made that afternoon. If you weren't in attendance, the radio was the only way to keep track of the game action. There was no over-the-air television, as ABC had already worn out its welcome at the NCAA when it came to airing Notre Dame games. Southern Cal had also been on a national telecast the week before, so they were at their limit as well.

As Ara looked across the field during warm-ups, he might have spotted Craig Fertig, who joined SC Head Coach John McKay as an assistant in February 1965, one week after graduation. It was quarterback Fertig who threw to Rod Sherman on November 28, 1964 to beat the Irish 20–17. Then there was also that damned white horse, Traveler, who was mounted by a half-naked middle-aged man in a costume pretending to be a Trojan, and who cantered up and down the sidelines every time USC scored. Parseghian hated that horse.

Southern California entered the game ranked number ten. They had just been designated the Pacific Eight Conference representative to the Rose Bowl, a decision that came with some controversy from cross-town rival UCLA. The Bruins (3–1 in conference) had beaten the Trojans (4–1 in conference) the week before by a score of 14–7, also at the Coliseum. So USC was motivated to prove their dubious bowl selection to the local media. A win against traditional rival Notre Dame always added incentive. Being able to knock off the number one team in the land completed their motivational trifecta.

Battered and Bruised

After a morning workout on Thursday and a Thanksgiving lunch spent together in the South Dining Hall, the Irish departed South Bend by a United Airlines charter for California, battered and bruised. They would use Friday for a light workout and to acclimate to the time change.

Terry Hanratty was out for the season with a separated shoulder. He would pace the sidelines in Los Angeles with his arm in a sling. Coley O'Brien would start his first game as quarterback. (As irony would have it, it was also his last game to start at quarterback.) Doctors were still trying to regulate his diabetes medications and his diet to ensure his optimal physical performance. Only recently, after forty-five years, he mentioned that he had a severe cold the entire week before this game and never felt one hundred percent at any of the five pregame practice sessions.

Center George Goeddeke was dressing, but limping and not scheduled to see any game action. Tim Monty, Goeddeke's 215-pound sophomore replacement, would be called upon to fill in again. At least he had survived over forty-five minutes of Bubba Smith's punishments without injury.

Halfback Rocky Bleier was also out for the season, as was his immediate replacement Bob Gladieux. Bleier was back in South Bend in a hospital room, although Gladieux, on crutches, was able to make the trip. Bleier's roommate, second unit defensive back Dan Harshman, was getting his first start at offensive halfback. He was converted to this position at that week's Monday practice, and had spent the four intervening days learning the offensive playbook.

At the other halfback position, Nick Eddy was still nursing a sore shoulder, but he was expected to see action. He was determined to play in his last Notre Dame Football game and he wanted to score at least once more in front of his California family and friends (he had scored in the Cal game in 1965, played in Berkley).

Jim Seymour had been diagnosed with mononucleosis the Monday before the game and wasn't at one hundred percent strength, but felt good enough to play. The weakest team Notre Dame had suited-up all season was being called upon to win the now-biggest game of the season, and for the national title, nonetheless. Everyone believed they could and would do it. All they had to do was look into Ara's eyes. He would find a way. The banner draped over the back of the Notre Dame bench said it all: "To HELL WITH UPI, WE'RE NO. 1."

Digging Deep

On their first possession, Notre Dame drove to the two-yard line on sixteen plays. This was a down and distance situation that Larry Conjar had consistently made all season and convincingly did again, scoring the first touchdown. The USC team was keying on Conjar as the player they were most determined to stop. There was considerable jaw-boning in the first series of plays. After Larry's consistent success, it stopped. With a Joe Azzaro PAT, the Irish were off to a good start 7–0.

With Southern California moving the ball after the kickoff, Tom Schoen intercepted a Troy Winslow pass on the SC forty and ran it in for the second touchdown. Another Azzaro conversion made it 14–0. The next first-quarter Notre Dame points were also scored by Azzaro on a thirty-eight-yard field goal (ND 17–USC 0).

With the defense now holding the USC offense to small gains and no points, the Notre Dame offense became a little more adventuresome. Quarterback Coley O'Brien connected with sophomore classmate Jim Seymour for thirteen yards and a touchdown (ND 24–USC 0).

On the next drive, O'Brien hit a stretched-out Seymour again, this time in the end zone, for thirty-nine yards and another touchdown. Seymour was to say forty-five years later, "I could beat my defenders all afternoon long." Add Azzaro's perfect record at kicking extra points and the halftime score was Notre Dame 31–USC 0. The Irish were halfway home. So far the officiating hadn't been a factor.

For motivation, not much needed to be said in the locker room at halftime. On the blackboard were the words, "We relaxed in 1964" (when they finished the first half ahead 17–0 and didn't score at all in the second half). The 20 additional points scored by the Irish in the second half weren't a matter of running up the score, as it was later accused. It was a long-overdue tribute to their head coach, proving that they wouldn't let up, and providing the team an insurance policy.

On the first drive of the second half, Coley O'Brien found the newly converted halfback Dan Harshman with a twenty-three-yard scoring pass. When Notre Dame got the ball back the next time, Nick Eddy fulfilled his dream, scoring his last touchdown for Notre Dame in California for his family—especially his mother—to see. He did it on a nine-yard run, gift-wrapped by the entire Notre Dame offensive line

This photo captures the touchdown pass thrown by Coley O'Brien (3) to Jim Seymour (85) in the end zone of the Los Angeles Coliseum. Blocking are Dick Swatland (59) and Larry Conjar (32). This first half touchdown with PAT made the score Notre Dame 24, Southern California 0 – effectively putting the game out of reach for the Trojans and guaranteeing a National Championship for the Irish. *Source:* University of Notre Dame Archives

(center Tim Monty, guards Tom Regner and Dick Swatland, tackles Paul Siler and Bob Kuechenberg, and tight end Don Gmitter).

When Southern Cal next got the ball back, they became impatient (or more like desperate) for a score. Linebacker Dave Martin stepped in front of a receiver and ran the interception back for a thirty-three-yard score (ND 51–USC 0). The second teams were inserted into the game midway in the fourth quarter. With two pass interceptions having been run back for touchdowns in the game, the claim that Notre Dame ran up the score is ludicrous.

There was a singular moment of sportsmanship that had nearly been forgotten over the years until recalled by the man involved, George Goeddeke. Very late in the game, the injured center was inserted at tight end, just so he would have a memory of playing his last game at such a momentous time. Noticing that the hobbling Goeddeke was going in, from across the field on the USC sideline Head Coach John McKay gestured to his defensive team not to hit him. It was a classy move by a legendary coach. Goeddeke was unaware of the gesture until informed about it after the game. If only he'd known. This is the same guy who was called upon to play two weeks after an appendectomy in the final game of the 1965 season against Miami. The irrepressible center chased his would-be blocker across the line of scrimmage trying (unsuccessfully) to make a block and re-injuring a swollen ankle in the process. Let the record show that George played in his final college game.

At the end of the game, the Notre Dame team carried Ara Parseghian off the field on their shoulders. A UPI telephoto captured the moment and, on Sunday morning, appeared on sports pages across the nation.

Locker Rooms

The highly-quotable Coach John McKay is often cited with saying to his team after the game, "Go take your showers, those of you that need them." While the legend always gets a chuckle, nobody steps forward to confirm it. Making jokes after the defeat didn't really fit the situation or the character of the man. It's mentioned here because you'll likely read it elsewhere and may want to know the truth.

The truth is that a deeply-disappointed Coach McKay had a good coach's sense of the moment.

I guess I've never seen a better team than Notre Dame was today . . . Let me tell you one thing about Notre Dame—that the coaching is tremendous. I know Ara had to piece together a new offensive lineup. But on that first drive, the team put together 17 consecutive plays to score on an 80-yard march. Why, 17 plays without a mistake is terrific—even if there's no opposition. Let's face it, Notre Dame is a better football team than us. If we played them a hundred times we'd have trouble winning one or two.

Eleven months later, Southern Cal would beat Notre Dame 24–7 in South Bend.

Disappointed linebacker Adrian Young captured the game dynamics as follows: "Their execution was excellent. But they weren't that good. We just didn't play well."

Tackle Gary Magner reinforced the theme. "It's the best team I've faced. They were gunning for the national championship and they got it. But nobody should run up a 51–0 score on the Trojan football team. Not even the Green Bay Packers."

The mood in the visitors' locker room was obviously joyous, reinforced by an undercurrent of nervous relief. An emotional Ara Parseghian addressed the team. "Thank you. Thank you for today's victory, for the whole season, and for the past three years. And thank you especially for this." "This" was the game ball. Today it resides prominently in Parseghian's home office.

In front of the press, Coach Parseghian waxed, "This is by far the best football team I've ever coached. Not only that, it is the best-balanced college football team, offensively and defensively, I've ever seen in my life. They just gave me the ball and tossed me in the shower. I enjoyed it."

Also sensing the historical nature of the coaching moment, Ara went further to say, "I want to pay tribute to the team for the determination it displayed, I want to pay tribute to our little 165-pound quarterback [Coley O'Brien] and I want to pay tribute to our medical team that got him ready." This comment exposed the silent fear that Ara had hidden since coming out of East Lansing. His backup QB was medically challenged and the fortunes of his team depended on a one hundred percent effort from their number three quarterback—which they got.

O'Brien had played beyond everyone's expectations. The feisty quarterback was twenty-one of thirty-one for 255 yards and three touchdowns. He had more completions in this game than Terry Hanratty had in any of his previous nine starts, or any other Notre Dame quarterback had ever had in a single game. The twenty-one completions would stand as a Notre Dame record until 1970, when it was broken by Joe Theismann.

Jim Seymour (with antibiotic assistance) had eleven receptions for 150 yards and two scores. In his final game, Larry Conjar carried nineteen times for sixty-two yards, a 3.26-per-carry average. In front of his family, Nick Eddy had eleven rushes for fifty-five yards, a 5.0-per-carry average, and a coveted final TD in California—with his mother in the crowd. By necessity, backups saw plenty of rushing action—Ron Dushney carried four times for thirty yards, and Dan Harshman had eight carries for twenty.

Other statistics further highlighted the separation between the two teams. ND had thirty-one first downs, SC thirteen. As for total plays, ND had eighty-two for 461 yards, SC had sixty-nine for 188 yards.

A secondary story of the game that received little attention was that the Notre Dame defense registered its sixth shutout, on the road, in front of the largest football crowd of the year against the number ten team in the nation. The strength of Notre Dame defense was underplayed by the media throughout the season, overwhelmed in print by offensive stats that were much easier to tally. But looking back, you can't be anything but overwhelmed by Notre Dame's consistent record of success. No other team in modern football history has allowed an average of 2.4 points per game over an entire season. Not one.

After Math

John Hall of the *Los Angeles Times* captured the aftermath as follows: "It was the end of the war. Name a war. Any war. Notre Dame won it. Notre Dame demanded unconditional surrender."

Comments after the game reflected the contrast between the two teams, who were obviously more equally matched than the final score indicated. Building on Southern Cal mistakes that kept compounding, Notre Dame had emerged a convincing winner. It was Ara Parseghian's one hundredth win as a college coach, making it doubly memorable. But it was also the worst defeat of a Southern California football team in history. And it still is, forty-five years later.

Natural Rivals

As such a tremendous defeat, this game would become the perennial bulletin-board fodder for every remaining confrontation between Parseghian and USC Head Coach John McKay. McKay is often quoted as saying that "he'd never let Notre Dame and Ara beat him again," something he persistently denied saying until his death in 2001. In one of his final interviews, McKay clarified the comment. "I said that Notre Dame would never beat us *51–0* again." What was actually said is immaterial.

Both coaches always started their seasons knowing that winning the ND–USC game would be crucial to their success. Since the intersectional rivalry began in 1926, this fact had often been the case. During the Parseghian–McKay years, the National Championship in college football was determined in some fashion (directly or indirectly) as a consequence of this rivalry. But McKay's alleged vow got some traction, because none of Ara's teams beat the Trojans again until 1973, the next time Notre Dame was named National Champion. After 1966, John McKay's record against the Irish was 6–1–2.

McKay left college coaching to become the head coach of the expansion Tampa Bay Buccaneers in the NFL, although he eventually returned to USC. After his passing, Coach McKay's ashes were spread over the turf at the Los Angeles Coliseum.

The following year in 1967, the Trojans would travel to South Bend and beat the Irish 24–7. For this game, McKay and the team brought reinforcements, their marching band (the USC band has performed at every ND game, home and away, since 1966) and a junior college transfer at tailback with unstoppable moves and speed. This junior had a career day—160 yards on thirty-eight carries and all three SC touchdowns. The kid with the killer smile would go on to win the Heisman Trophy in 1968—O.J. Simpson. Southern California would be crowned National Champions.

Notre Dame extracted some revenge in 1968 with a 21–21 tie over the number-one-ranked Trojans in Los Angeles. Simpson was held to fifty-five yards, his lowest output for the season. That game was the first to capture a larger television audience than the 1966 Notre Dame–Michigan

State contest. That tie, late in the season, contributed to the final rankings. When Ohio State beat USC in the Rose Bowl, they were named standalone National Champion. The debt to Woody Hayes and the Buckeyes for slowing down Michigan State in 1966 was repaid.

Celebrations

Rocky Bleier was confined to a hospital room in South Bend, still recovering from his lacerated kidney. His recollection of the ND–SC game has never been told.

> I listened to the game on the radio in my hospital room. That was the only way to get the immediate play-by-play. The game wasn't on TV, at least not in way that I could see it from the hospital. I remember how great it was to score all those points in the first half. And when the team scored some more after halftime, I started to relax a bit— knowing that we were going to win. When the game ended, I was still all alone. After a few minutes a couple guys I knew from South Bend came to visit me. They had been watching the game in a lounge somewhere. They had been playing a game where each would have a shot and a beer every time Notre Dame scored a touchdown. By the time they got to my room they were feeling no pain. That's when my celebration really began.

It was widely circulated, somewhat in jest, that if the Irish were to beat the Trojans, they wouldn't have to buy drinks anywhere in Los Angeles on Saturday night. The fans from UCLA were still smarting from being shafted from a Rose Bowl invitation by a conference committee after beating the Trojans the week before. By all rights, they should have been going to the Rose Bowl (again) to play Michigan State (again), a team slighted by the irrational rules of the Big Ten Conference. That would have been quite a rematch. A number of Irish players (those of legal age, of course) remember heading out on Saturday night to test the theory. By all accounts, UCLA fans made good on their promises.

A good portion of the team (including most of those not of legal age) went to a party held at the Los Angeles home of Don Gmitter's friend from Notre Dame, Doug Simon, whose father was a local judge.

It was here that Hollywood got into the mix. Actor-singer-comedian Jimmy Durante showed up and, from the piano, entertained the boisterous group. Then he posed for pictures. One that was taken, which all the participants would love a copy of today, had Terry Hanratty, Frank Criniti, and Ron Jeziorski, all guys with distinctive noses, posing side by side in profile with "the Schnozzola." Also at the party was actor Scott Brady who was a familiar character in many B-grade westerns. A year earlier he had passed on the opportunity to be in the initial cast of a low-budget TV show about space travel—*Star Trek*. Grad assistant Brian Boulac remembers being at this party, probably the only "official" to attend. The players thought of him more as a friend—one of their own.

The sophomore roommate threesome of Terry Hanratty, Ron Dushney, and Bob Gladieux decided to leave the party early to test the generosity of the UCLA faithful. But Gladieux, still on crutches, slowed the exploration down. The other two boys put him in a cab with instructions to drop Harpo off at the Ambassador Hotel, where the team was staying. The cabbie must have taken the instructions literally, because when Hanratty and Dushney eventually returned early on Sunday morning, they found Gladieux asleep, with his crutches, lying in the bushes next to the hotel entrance.

By comparison, quarterback Coley O'Brien spent a rather subdued evening having dinner with his dad (a Navy admiral who had flown in to see the game) and extended family members, saying, "You know, we still didn't really know what the polls would do after that game. But we knew we had done all we could do."

Ara took the coaching staff out to dinner and made an early evening of it. He didn't want to horn in on the celebrations that his players were having. Moreover, because he knew the no-alcohol team rule was unenforceable—and certainly being violated—he really didn't want to know where the players were.

An official team trip to Disneyland was scheduled for Sunday afternoon. Almost all of the players had grown up watching the *Mickey Mouse Club* on television, perhaps wondering why girls like Mouseketeer Annette Funicello weren't in their grammar school classes. Some of the players still have photos taken with Mickey Mouse. A photograph of Coley O'Brien and Jim Seymour on a fire truck in a parade at Disneyland made the newspapers.

Less sentimental players bypassed the Disneyland trip and continued testing the promise of free UCLA libations. On Monday morning, seniors Allen Sack and Tom Rhoades were still feeling the effects of a late Sunday night and almost missed the charter flight back home. It's funny now.

Three players had no time to celebrate with the team at all. Together, they departed for LAX right after the game. Jim Lynch, Tom Regner, and Nick Eddy were already scheduled on a Saturday evening flight to New York for a guest appearance on the Sunday evening *Ed Sullivan Show* with other members of the Associated Press Kodak All-American Team. They spent time with Michigan State All-Americans Clinton Jones, George Webster, and Bubba Smith. Eddy, who was able to bring his wife Tiny with him, remembers, "Those were good guys, and we had a lot of respect for each other. We got along well and we all had a good time in New York City." It was only eight days after the "Game of the Century."

Monday

An editorial appearing on Monday in *The Oregonian* addressed the contentious point of the Irish running up the score.

> *The Notre Dame football team, last week criticized for being overly conservative in the last minutes of its 10–10 tie game with Michigan State, this week is being pilloried for "pouring it on" in a 51–0 slaughter of the University of Southern California. Apparently the Fighting Irish can't win in their battle with the sports columnists, no matter how they play the game.*

The United Airlines chartered flight from Los Angeles to South Bend, with all the Notre Dame team on board, was diverted to Chicago's Midway Airport due to a snowstorm. Notre Dame students returning from the four-day Thanksgiving break confronted the same travel difficulties getting to campus for their first day of classes. The team was put on chartered buses that carefully made their way across the Indiana Toll Road and eventually turned up Notre Dame Avenue at about six p.m. It was dark. There were no crowds lining the slick avenue amidst the gusting wind and blowing snow. The team thought that the campus might still be deserted because of the storm. But then the buses pulled up right next to the old Fieldhouse. The place was filled to bursting. The 1966 Notre Dame Football team was finally home, undefeated.

Behind the scenes, Joe Doyle had been pressing his contacts at the Associated Press for an early release of the final football rankings

277

Head Coach Ara Parseghian admiring the MacArthur Bowl, flanked by Fr. Edmund Joyce and Moose Krause. The MacArthur Bowl, named after General Douglas MacArthur, is the solid sterling silver trophy awarded by the National Football Foundation and Hall of Fame to its selection as National Champions. Notre Dame was awarded the trophy in 1964, shared it with Michigan State in 1966, and reclaimed it in 1973 – all under Coach Parseghian. *Source:* Notre Dame Sports Information Collection (normally released late Monday evening for print on Tuesday mornings). He finally got the word by telephone. It was officially announced to this Notre Dame family reunion, "Number one, Notre Dame." UPI would agree. Undisputed.

If December 3, 1949 is the pinnacle of Notre Dame Football history, then November 26, 1966 is the second-highest peak. Mark the day. That was when Notre Dame Football returned to glory after seventeen years. The Notre Dame table was rock solid.

29

COMING OFF THE MAGIC CARPET RIDE

What happens after Notre Dame and after football? It's a question that has a multitude of answers. But one thing is for sure, things are never quite the same after you leave Notre Dame. At the time of the 1966 team's twenty-fifth reunion in 1991, a sportswriter asked center George Goeddeke about it. His replied, "The hardest adjustment I had was coming off the magic carpet ride. Where do you go from winning the national championship and then playing pro football? Believe me, I enjoy what I'm doing. I'm not despondent. But I've never found total satisfaction, and I'm afraid I never will."

Misconceptions

People tend to have preconceptions, or more accurately, misconceptions, about college football players. They are categorized as dumb jocks who couldn't get into a reputable school without size, speed, and the ability to bench press their body weights. If you want to know how unfair this stereotype is, just consider Notre Dame backup quarterback Bob Belden who reportedly had a perfect 1600 on his SATs.

That's just for starters. The off-the-field records of the 1966 Fighting Irish completely shatter all the misconceptions that even the biggest cynics might have.

Football has always been a difficult ticket for getting into Notre Dame, and getting a ticket out, graduating, had ceased being a presumed conclusion many generations before the 1966 players ever left the womb or heard "The Fight Song" for the first time. By 1966, under the watchful eye of Father Theodore Hesburgh since 1952, Notre Dame was well on its way to becoming one of the nation's top twenty major universities for academics (as measured by the *US News and World Report*)—a position it continues to enjoy today.

In 1981, the College Football Association established the Academic Achievement Award to honor the Division I college with the highest graduation rate among members of its football team. With the demise of the CFA, the American Football Coaches Association has continued this prestigious award. Notre Dame has won the top prize (highest graduation rate in the nation) eight times and finished as honorable mention (among the next four highest graduation rates) twenty times. Therefore, in the twenty-nine years of the award, the Fighting Irish have received recognition twenty-eight times. It takes a graduation rate high in the ninetieth percentile to be so honored. Obviously, there was no award in 1966. But it is interesting to note that the graduation rate in 1966 of ninety-eight percent, hand-tabulated by academic advisor Mike DeCicco, would have certainly placed Notre Dame football-scholars at or near the top of a list of this sort.

After graduation, the team's academic trajectory continued. Over fifty percent of the guys who dressed for practices in 1966—varsity players, backups, preppers, and freshmen—went on to achieve advanced degrees. Not too shabby. Among them are lawyers, doctors, accountants, entrepreneurs, authors, managers, college professors, a university athletic director, an architect, and many leaders in the nonprofit sector. Offensive tackle George Kunz was the latest to earn a law degree in 2010 at the age of sixty-three. Prep team lineman John "Jay" Jordan is a trustee at Notre Dame, and his family's name graces a new science building on campus. The most notable success story may be of Alan Page, who became a Supreme Court Justice in Minnesota. He was also the first defensive player to be named MVP in the NFL. And recently, a member of the '66 freshman squad, Mike Kelly from Erie,

Pennsylvania, became the oldest freshman member of the United States Congress, elected in 2010. This is altogether remarkable, given that the total number of young men on the team in 1966 was about 150.

281

Context is important. Add to the above statistics the fact that at least twenty-eight Notre Dame players from the 1966 squad began their post-graduation working careers in professional football, an unprecedented number from a single team. Even more members probably could have played on Sundays if they had been willing to defer medical school, law school, or graduate school.

Lineman John Lium is an interesting case in point. He personally interviewed with owner Wellington Mara for a chance to try out with the New York Giants after graduation. Mara asked an obvious question. "Why do you think you can play for the Giants when you didn't even start at Notre Dame?" John's answer was, "Because some guys play against the best football team in the country once or twice in their careers. But I played against the best every single day in practice." Mara was sufficiently impressed with that answer and did two things: gave Lium a tryout with the team, and gave him some career advice. "Go to law school," he said. "You obviously have an aptitude for making a convincing argument." Lium played for three years on the Giant's taxi squad, never dressing on Sundays. He also used the time to go to law school. Today, he practices law in New York.

Many other players from the 1966 squad had professional tryouts. After graduation, Joe Azzaro was invited to tryout with the San Francisco 49ers. "When I got there I was one of six kickers they were considering. One of the other guys was Dick Kenney, the barefoot Hawaiian who kicked for Michigan State in 1966. We became good friends. And we both got cut!"

Viewed retrospectively in its entirety, the record of success by individuals on the 1966 National Championship team is staggering by every measure. Tom Reynolds, the walk-on who recently retired as Professor Emeritus from the University of Texas System, has a management theory about this. In his opinion, the underlying formula for this success all goes back to Ara Parseghian and his fundamental philosophy. "I learned two cornerstone principles from Coach Parseghian; namely, focus on your goals every day and have the discipline every day to execute against those goals." He respectfully lectures to his former coach, a little tongue in cheek, at informal team gatherings,

What we learned from you, Coach, was to focus every day on a specific goal, which was then operationalized into a clear plan, in minute detail, for each component within your system [team]. Then all components [positions] within the team simply had to go out and fulfill their specific missions, bit by bit, until we got closer to the overall team goal. You know, Coach, it works great in the real world too—in fact, this is the formula to success in life.

Coaches, especially the great ones, live for moments like that.

Where Are They Now?

Keeping track of the whereabouts of the entire team is a daunting task, now the responsibility of halfback-turned-accountant, Frank Criniti. E-mail helps him tremendously. The guys from the team are in constant communication with each other. Many are retired, or are starting to think about it. As of 2011, the master list for this remarkable football family was as follows:

Harry Alexander, Wilmington, DE	Nick Eddy, Modesto, CA
Joe Azzaro, Pittsburgh, PA	Tom Feske, Kennesaw, GA
Michael Bars, Clarkston, MI	Ray Fischer, Bowling Green, OH
Bill Bartholomew, Portland, ME	Larry Forness, Granger, IN
Bob Belden, Canton, OH	Lou Fournier, Walker, MN
Rocky Bleier, Pittsburgh, PA	Roger Fox
Brian Boulac, South Bend, IN	Mike Franger, Elkhart, IN
Mike Burgener, Bonsall, CA	Joe Freebery, Newark, DE
Jack Butler, Blacklick, OH	Tom Furlong, Middletown, OH
Leo Collins, Plymouth, MN	Bill Giles, Lexington, KY
Larry Conjar, Evanston, IL	Bob Gladieux, South Bend, IN
Frank Criniti, Granger, IN	George Goeddeke, White Lake, MI
William Dainton	Tim Gorman, Barrington, RI
Daniel Dickman, Wexford, PA	Dave Haley, Gilford, NH
Ronald Dinardo	Terry Hanratty, New Canaan, CT
Jack Donahue, Las Vegas, NV	Kevin Hardy, Toluca Lake, CA
Ron Dushney, Peckville, PA	Dan Harshman, South Bend, IN
Mike Earley, Bayonne, NJ	Mike Heaton, Wilmette, IL

Curt Hennegan, Kirkland, WA
Mike Holtzapfel, Florence, KY
John Horney, Atlanta, GA
Bill Hurd, Germantown, TN
Ron Jeziorski, Belmont, CA
John Jordan, Chicago, IL
Al Karam, San Antonio, TX
Gerry Kelly, Costa Mesa, CA
Jim Kelly, Cranford, NJ
Denny Kiliany, Youngstown, OH
Rudy Konieczny, Greenfield, MA
Al Kramer, Grafton, WI
Bob Kuechenberg, Fort Lauderdale, FL
George Kunz, Las Vegas, NV
Mike Kuzmicz, Oceanside, CA
Pete Lamantia, Toronto, Ontario,
    Canada
Chuck Landolfi, Ellwood City, PA
Chick Lauck, Greenwood, IN
John Lavin, Scottsdale, AZ
Jim Leahy, Golden, CO
John Lium, Rye, NY
Jim Lynch, Kansas City, MO
Joe Marsico, Chicago, IL
Dave Martin, Greenwood Village, CO
Joel Maturi, Minneapolis, MN
Paul May, Martinsville, VA
Jim McCarthy, Rockville, MD
Mike McGill, St. John, IN
Terry McSweeney, Tampa, FL
Jack Meyer, Cadillac, MI
Tim Monty, Wellington, CO
Wally Moore, South Bend, IN
Kevin Moran, Huntington, NY
Len Moretti, South Bend, IN
Dennis Murphy, Rochester Hills, MI
Eric Norri, Virginia, MN
Coley O'Brien, Falls Church, VA

Dan O'Connor, Columbus, NE
Jim O'Donnell, Granger, IN
Tom O'Leary, Bloomfield Hills, MI
Hugh O'Malley, Speedway, IN
Alan Page, Minneapolis, MN
Ara Parseghian, Granger, IN
Vic Paternostro, Newtown, NJ
John Pergine, Plymouth Meeting, PA
Jim Purcell, Ridgefield, CT
Steve Quinn, Mount Sterling, IL
Tom Quinn, Lake Forest, IL
Kevin Rassas, Villanova, PA
Tom Regner, Reno, NV
Tom Reynolds, Wilson, WY
Tom Rhoads, Raleigh, NC
Mike Russo, Bloomfield Hills, MI
Bill Russo, Charlotte, NC
Jim Ryan, Burlington, NC
Allen Sack, New Haven, CT
Angelo Schiralli, Hobe Sound, FL
Fred Schnurr, Astoria, NY
Tom Schoen, Euclid, OH
George Sefcik, Cortez, FL
Paul Shoults, Mishawaka, IN
Bill Skoglund, Orland Park, IL
Tom Slettvet, Eatonville, WA
Jim Smithberger, Dade City, FL
Joe Smyth, Blue Bell, PA
Paul Snow, St. Charles, MO
Brian Stenger, Mentor, OH
John Sullivan, Lexington, KY
Pete Sullivan, South Bend, IN
Dick Swatland, Stamford, CT
Tim Swearingen, Gainesville, FL
Ed Tuck, Miami Springs, FL
Roger Valdiserri, South Bend, IN
Alan VanHuffel, South Bend, IN
Ed Vuillemin, Akron, OH

Jerry Wampfler

Tim Wengierski, Jupiter, FL

Gerry Wisne, Naples, FL

Dave Zell, Houston, TX

Jay Zenner, Durham, NC

Bob Zubek

Dave Zurowski, Woodbridge, VA

FRESHMAN TEAM

Jim de Arrieta

Nick Furlong

John Gasser

Tome Gores, Bellevue, WA

Randy Harkins

Bob Jockisch

Mike Kelly

Charles Kennedy

Steve Lambert

Tom Lawson

Brian Lewellen

Bob McConn

Mike McCoy, Jefferson, GA

Jim Merletti

Tom Nash

Bob Olson

Mike Oriard

Dewey Poskon

Vito Racanelli

Don Reid

Jim Rugicka

Jay Standring

Larry Vuillemin

Phil Wittliff, Brookfield, WI

Ed Ziegler, Denver, CO

Jeff Zimmerman

Jay Ziznewski

Devotions

One of the surprises from the process of contacting individuals from the 1966 team was the detour each person wanted to take in the conversation to reveal the things they view as important today, and how those things reflect back to '66. There is enormous devotion toward the Catholic faith, although not surprisingly there is some ambivalence and skepticism toward the institutional Church. Every man is a dedicated father, and quite proud of that vocation. Then, inside each man, there is still this irrational love burning for the University of Notre Dame. This happens to everyone who has ever lived on campus and attended classes, and it lasts forever. Be assured, it has nothing to do with the weather in South Bend. This love manifests itself in a variety of ways, some not always in keeping with the "thinking du jour" of the Notre Dame Administration. But it is a deep, enduring love nonetheless.

The dominant theme that permeates every conversation with the '66 team is the hard core of interest, concern, respect, and deep affection the guys have for each other. The 1966 National Champions started as boys but have now aged into very fine men, Notre Dame Men in the best definition of the term. And forty-five years later, they are still very much a team.

Backup defensive lineman Harry Alexander had a personal tragedy of unimaginable proportions. In February 1979, eight of his immediate family members, including his mother and father, were lost in a tragic house fire in Wilmington, Delaware. The aftermath of the event almost consumed him as well. He credits three factors for his ability to finally make peace with it all. The first was his personal devotion to the Blessed Virgin, the second was his family, and the third was the steady stream of support he received from his 1966 teammates. He is unabashedly grateful for the strength he received from all three sources.

If you want to find George Goeddeke on a Friday night during Lent, you'll be out of luck if you look anywhere but the fish fry at Saint Patrick's Parish in Whitelake, Michigan. George was considered a wild child when he was a student at Notre Dame. What else could you call a guy who rode a motorcycle down the hallways of O'Shaughnessy Hall, a feat that almost got him expelled? Working at his church may not be the total satisfaction he was seeking twenty years ago, but it comes close. Although George has mellowed a lot, the fish don't have a chance with him on the grill.

There is another unexpected, quirky item of interest. A number of the players on the team, at least four, wanted it known that they had named a son Coley. Coleman is a great Irish name to be sure. But their motivation was a profound respect for their gutsy backup quarterback. There may be no trophies for a recognition like this, but Coley O'Brien should embrace with great pride his teammates' simple gesture of name immortality.

Farewell to No. 85

During the fall of 2010, Jim Seymour was just beginning the fight of his life. He'd been diagnosed with an inoperable brain tumor. Between treatments, Jim was able to make it back for a couple of the Notre Dame home games. The 1966 team has a pregame ritual of getting together at The Training Room, a clubhouse with a distant view of the Stadium and the Golden Dome. If you weren't clued in to this address, you would think it was just another tailgate party held in somebody's garage. But the memorabilia on the walls tell quite a different story. The guys who hang out there look nothing like their framed photographs in PR action poses taken forty-five years ago. But they all wear National Champion-ship rings. (Originally, they were given Longines watches that many members of the team still have.) It was here that Jim Seymour wanted to be, maybe needed to be, to face his toughest opponent.

To fully understand desire to be with his teammates, one only has to remember the call to action in Ara's letter to the team from the 1966 Playbook.

Tom Reynolds (left), the "walk on," and Jim Seymour (right), No. 85, at the "Training Room" in October 2010. *Source:* Collection of Mark Hubbard

We will be an inseparable – strong – united force—ready to fight only the good fight—winning if we can, losing only when destiny says we must. Bring on the opponents!

The opponent eventually won. On Sunday, April 3, 2011, the line was long at the funeral home visitation in suburban Chicago. The place was filled with friends and neighbors paying their last respects to Jim Seymour, and offering their condolences to his wife Nancy and the families of their three sons, Jim, Jeff, and Todd. Sprinkled in among the mourners were teammates, again wearing the iconic gold rings with blue stones that marked them as part of a special band of brothers.

Photos of Jim were hung in the reception area. There was an enlargement of the *Time Magazine* cover, along with various awards and memorabilia from a distinguished high school, college, and professional football careers. No. 85 was recognized with All-American honors for all three of his seasons at Notre Dame. Seymour's total of 276 receiving yards in his first game against Purdue is still ranked number two in NCAA football history for most receiving yards—forty-five years later.

Most of the visitors that day knew Jim only as a youth sports coach, father of one of their children's friends from school, a business associate, or a respected member of the local community, the guy next door. The football mystique was something of a surprise, especially seeing a visual record of it all in one place. Jim was like that—humble, genuinely friendly, and never one to take himself too seriously.

The pastor from Jim's family's parish was there to say the customary prayers over the closed casket. The funeral Mass was scheduled for the following morning at Holy Cross Church in Deerfield, Illinois. Various family members spoke extemporaneously to the gathering and with great feeling and heartfelt emotion. For these precious moments, laughing and crying joined hands.

To conclude this private farewell, a group of guys started singing. Over twenty men from Jim's playing days linked arm-in-arm. There was Terry Hanratty, that other guy on the *Time* cover. There was Coley O'Brien, the backup QB who found Jim in the end zone twice in the 51–0 win over Southern Cal, sealing the National Championship. There was Tom Feske, the student trainer who went to Jim's room in Walsh Hall to massage his ankle every night so that he could return to action more quickly and make it through the '66 season.

The song was the Notre Dame alma mater, "Notre Dame, Our Mother": "And our hearts forever, love thee Notre Dame."

The men had a tough time getting through that last line without cracking. The singing wasn't pretty. But it *was* beautiful.

Requiem

"May their souls, and all the souls of the faithful departed, through the mercy of God, rest in peace."

Terry Brennan	Coach John Murphy
Ron Cimala	Coach Tom Pagna
Pete Duranko	Gene Paszkiet, Trainer
Danny Gibbs	Coach John Ray
Don Gmitter	Jim Reilly
Charles Grable	Reverend James Riehle, CSC
Robert Hagerty	Bill Riley
Reverend Edmund Joyce, CSC	Larry Schumacher
Edward "Moose" Krause	Jim Seymour
John Lentz	Paul Seiler
Michael Malone	James Winegardner
Tom McKinley	Coach Joseph Yonto
Robert Merkle	

Legacy

After the 1966 football season, the University of Notre Dame was never quite the same. The solidity of a long-awaited return to football prominence was punctuated by the first undisputed National Championship since 1949 after a seventeen-year dry spell. An emerging post-war alumni base was now in a position to contribute generously to the annual funds and to the endowment. The Frank Leahy generation was sufficiently heartened, so the historically hand-to-mouth University budget received some welcomed breathing room. With Fr. Hesburgh guiding the academic ship, and now with the football program back to where it should have been, Notre Dame was on a roll. It has been rolling steadily ever since. One hates to speculate what would have happened without Ara Parseghian and a National Championship in 1966, but there is no doubt that without those two things, Notre Dame would be a pale shadow of what it has now grown into.

The amount of square footage of buildings on campus is well beyond three times what it was in 1966.

Today Notre Dame enjoys an endowment of $6.4 billion (plus or minus), ranked thirteenth among all institutions of higher learning. ND is ranked third in endowment, only behind Princeton and MIT, for

The University of Notre Dame campus as it appeared in the summer of 1965. The top of the photo is North. The building in the lower left is the Senior Bar, now demolished. In the lower right is the parking lot where construction would for the Athletic and Convocation Center would begin in 1966. *Source:* Notre Dame Sports Information Collection

universities without a medical school. The endowment in 1966 was just $50 million.

The number of undergraduate students at Notre Dame has grown from approximately 6,000 in 1966 to approximately 8,000 in 2011. The all-male bastion, once considered the Catholic West Point, was successfully converted to co-education in 1973. The influx of female Domers did two things. First the campus was normalized as a social place, and this was a vast improvement. Second, the academic standards spiked when the applicant pool more than doubled.

The Fighting Irish have earned three undisputed National Championships since 1966: in 1973, again under Ara, in 1977 under Dan Devine, and in 1988 under Lou Holtz. But there has been a palpable dry spell of consistent national football rankings since the departure of Holtz. The dry spell for a National Championship is now twenty-two years and counting, the longest in the history of Notre Dame, going back to 1913 when the team made history with the forward pass.

Notre Dame Stadium was renovated and enlarged from 59,075 seats to 80,795 seats in 1997, at a cost of $50 million (the amount of the entire endowment in 1966). In 2009, five of the six entrance portals were named to honor coaches who had won National Championships: Knute Rockne, Frank Leahy, Ara Parseghian, Dan Devine, and Lou Holtz. The coach who deserves that last spot will be obvious to everyone . . . when it happens. College football is still "a coaches' game."

The media appeal of Notre Dame Football hasn't wavered much, even through the drought. Most fans still either love or hate the Irish. This visceral reaction has kept Notre Dame as the only university that has ever had a national television contract (with NBC).

As you walk around campus today and marvel at the stature that Notre Dame has achieved in the last half-century, keep in mind that all of it was accomplished by generations of hard workers, each generation standing on the shoulders of giants.

30

HEROES

When you meet the members of the 1966 Irish team today, you are immediately struck by the strong ties that still bind them. They are proud of their accomplishments, as they should be. But nobody is trying to live in the afterglow of the National Championship or even the NFL careers that so many enjoyed. They are totally comfortable walking around campus as virtual unknowns. Many have lived with fame, and they know it is highly overrated as a commodity. They still steadfastly believe in the "team," a refreshing concept when authentically practiced.

As the '66 team gathers together now, usually near campus at The Training Room, the conversations tend to be about how their children are doing and who they have heard from recently. Then the classic question is raised. "Why has Notre Dame struggled for so long to do well on the football field when over twenty Irish players perennially occupy NFL rosters?" You know, the usual stuff—not too different from any other gathering of ND alums.

Then along comes a perceived outsider who wants to write a book about the 1966 season. Like *that* hasn't been done before! Just consider the constant barrage of media exposure that came with playing in a momentous Notre Dame season that spawned the "Game of the

Century." There isn't a pent-up appetite left to tell new stories or retell old ones. Collectively, the 1966 team had already had enough of that.

Quid Pro Quo

A quietly-implied quid pro quo emerges to capture the old players' interests. They'll cooperate in the retelling of their stories if three subjects that deserve attention (but that haven't been part of a normal scribe's agenda) are included in the new book. And they're right in their demands. Compliance with their request is long overdue.

The Finest Coach

Each man is concerned for Ara. They know he got a raw deal in the press for how the last six plays at Michigan State unfolded. And they all know why he has allowed himself to carry the burden of this for forty-five years and counting. He's done it, and continues to do it, to protect the integrity of what they accomplished as a cohesive unit on the field. In sports parlance, he's taking one for the team. Now they want to give something back to him—and the unsuspecting newbie writer has to get it just right. Fortunately, that's not hard to do.

Ara Parseghian may be the finest college football coach—ever. Not just at Notre Dame, but anywhere. This is not just because of what he did on the field, but more importantly because of *how* he did it. The case for this opinion in the confines of Notre Dame history alone is enough to trigger debates in neighborhood bars for another century. Where does Ara fit in the pantheon that includes Knute Rockne, Frank Leahy, Dan Devine, and Lou Holtz? The answer is, at the top. Readers can decide for themselves if there are any ties.

Parseghian's coaching record is incredible. At Notre Dame, he was 95–17–4 with a winning percentage of .819. Factor in two undisputed National Championships in 1966 and 1973 and a third MacArthur Bowl for 1964—all in eleven years at ND. Ara inherited a program in total disarray and made it competitive in his first season, no small accomplishment. Only three times did he lose two games in a row. He wasn't able to pick his opponents or the referees, like Rockne did. And he wasn't able to recruit a college all-star team after World War II, like Leahy did (the exception being in 1953). Ara had to succeed in the modern era within much stricter rules and through a media Cuisinart. Which he did.

There are three behind-the-scenes pieces of convincing evidence that may not enter the barroom debate. They are submitted here for careful consideration.

One: the players unconditionally followed Ara's leadership because they believed he was always the smartest and most well-prepared person in the stadium, no matter where they played. Opponents believed the same thing. Two: Father Theodore Hesburgh holds Ara in the highest regard, and the yardstick he uses doesn't measure wins and losses, it measures character. That fact alone should tip the scales forever. Third: Coach Parseghian never publicly criticized a play or a decision by any of his players or his coaches. You just can't find a single example of that ever happening, even if you read thousands of articles and game accounts. In other words, taking one for the team is a core element of Ara Parseghian's character.

Catholic Central

The second request of the team has proven elusive for almost everyone who has ever written about the 1966 National Championship season. It may be a matter of how the subject of team unity is approached. For outsiders looking in, the season has always been about the plays on Saturdays, the after-game quotations, and occasionally the unusual human interest stories, as if there are still fresh apples to be picked from the tree. That's the best an outsider can do, and many have done quite well.

But insiders see the world of Notre Dame Football quite differently. The members of the team have craved a book written their way, from the inside out. Together, they endured the frigid temperatures of South Bend Februaries. Together, they lived in a social gulag where women could only be idolized because an entire gender was effectively removed from normal daily experiences. An insider would know that football was front and center as the common bond that unified not just the team, but the entire Notre Dame campus. The concept of team unity must be translated through the lens of someone who was actually there. Even then, it is difficult to fully capture.

Talk about unity. The players on the 1966 squad weren't even recruited by the same head coach. Three different personalities with three different agendas were in the mix: Joe Kuharich, Hugh Devore, and Ara Parseghian. But all of the recruits had so much in common that it didn't matter in the end. Over two-thirds of them were from Catholic high schools. Almost all were from blue-collar families. Common backgrounds made the team homogenous from the outset.

There are five different players from four different cities who list their high schools as Central Catholic. One was Alan Page, the only African-American on the team, from Canton's Central Catholic. We may lament that Notre Dame Football wasn't more integrated in 1966, even though ND was among the first major colleges to integrate in the early 1950s. But the net result was that race was never an issue on the football field. That was the way it should have been. Everyone liked and respected Alan, and that was that. The common traits acquired from Catholic secondary education rubbed off and made managing the team easier. The boys were smart, they were disciplined, and they had high school coaches who emphasized the team concept. Most of all, the boys all wanted to play for Notre Dame *because it was Notre Dame*, not some bus stop on the way to the pros and the possibility of obscene wealth. It was a different time, a more innocent time.

The fairness that Ara brought to the enterprise cannot be over-emphasized. Notre Dame Football was a meritocracy. If a player didn't like his lot, he always had Monday scrimmages to prove his case. Ara played favorites all right, every game. He played the guys who wanted it the most. "Pimples for hearts" didn't cut it. He wanted guys with "no breaking points." That three-word phrase became the unofficial motto of the team.

And then there was the aspect of serendipity. How else can the presence of Pete Duranko and Nick Eddy on the 1966 squad be explained. They should have been playing on Sundays, and could have been. But they stayed to play ten more games at Notre Dame. What would the 1966 season have looked like without those two guys?

Not a single player thought of himself as a star—not when he was at Notre Dame, anyway. Because so many of them were so good, there was never a player who would dare swagger around the Notre Dame locker room. That's why the Hanratty–Seymour cover of *Time* was officially discouraged. They played as a team, and the net result was that they became the most honored football team in the history of the University of Notre Dame.

Whispers

At the beginning of this project, when I spoke with the '66 guys in private, they all drifted into an uncomfortable subject, but one that concerned them very much because it was so close to the bone. They whispered when they believed nobody else was listening. It happened repeatedly. One of their own guys, Pete Duranko, was hurting. Their All-American defensive tackle was fighting ALS, Lou Gehrig's Disease. They would have done anything to help Pete. In even softer whispers, they would ask, "Will you please say that in the book?"

Pete Duranko, known as "Diesel," died on July 8, 2011 before the publication of this book. He battled ALS courageously for eleven years. For a person fighting a progressively debilitating affliction with no known cure, eleven years is a long time.

Pete's football credentials were perhaps the best on the team. He started as a fullback in 1963, when single-platoon football was the rule and staying on the field also meant playing linebacker. That position was a closer fit to Pete's size and temperament. With Ara onboard in 1964, he was initially slotted into that position, but was injured at Wisconsin, in the first game of the 1964 season (where he had an interception). This early injury allowed him to have two additional years of eligibility, and thus he became the oldest player on the 1966 squad. He was moved to defensive tackle for his final two seasons in South Bend, achieving consensus All-American honors. Then he was drafted by the Denver Broncos in the second round and played nine seasons in the NFL. He later earned a master's degree and had a career in business management that allowed him to move back to his hometown of Johnstown, Pennsylvania, where his football career was launched at Johnstown Catholic (now Bishop McCort).

People still talk about Pete's size and athleticism. An often-mentioned demonstration of his size was that a quarter could be dropped cleanly through his National Championship ring. He was the strongest man on the '66 team, and a tree climber. His teammates would be reminded of that strength yet again in more profound ways when he was crippled in a wheel chair. His spirit was … there is no adequate word to insert here.

Pete had the natural ability to make his friends laugh. He wasn't the team clown—there were ample worthy contenders for that honor. "Mischievous humor" was the description used in the obituary that appeared in his hometown newspaper. He was more of the sage philosopher-humorist, a Will Rodgers character with a steel girder for a forearm.

At the time of his initial diagnosis, Pete agreed to a second opinion. He traveled to Atlanta and to his former roommate and teammate, Doctor John Horney, who knew an ALS specialist. (At the mailboxes of Dillon Hall on November 19, 1966, Pete was the second person to learn that John had been accepted into medical school.) The deeply-concerned and emotionally-invested physician-friend had to deliver a confirmation of the bad news. He recalls saying something like, "Is there something I can do, Pete, really anything?" Duranko, ever the quick wit, replied, "How about a free prostate exam while I'm here?"

After his illness had advanced, Duranko was asked to speak to the audience at a fund-raiser at New York's Carnegie Hall. It was a full house. When he approached the microphone, he immediately proceeded to sing "Some Enchanted Evening" (from *South Pacific*) a capella. When he was finished, he explained to everyone that he wasn't about to pass up a chance to sing in Carnegie Hall—he might never get another opportunity. That broke the tension and brought the house down.

Back on March 1, 2003, a testimonial dinner for Pete was organized by the Notre Dame Club of Central Pennsylvania. It turned into an impromptu reunion of the 1966 team. As one of the players so eloquently said it, "Do you know how hard it is to get to Johnstown? Six of us rented a Chevy Suburban at the Pittsburgh airport and it took us a case of beer to get there." But get there they did, over sixty people strong from across the country, from the biggest stars to the guys on the prep team to managers and to coaches. The '66 guys are and always have been one team. What they remember best were the stories Pete told late into the night, and their hoping that those stories would never end.

After the Johnstown event, linebacker Kevin Rassas (Nick's younger brother) wrote Pete a letter. In it he said, "The strength of your character and the positive attitude touched not only us, but everyone who participated. I think the turnout of players was a real testament to the impact that you have had on so many people." He went on to write, "On a personal note, I was always moved by how kind you were to me when we were together at Notre Dame. You did a lot of little things that were very much appreciated, the odd handball game together, taking time to ask how I was doing and offering words of encouragement. I truly feel privileged to be among those who were one of your teammates."

Pete Duranko lived his life fully and completed his mission on this earth with the attitude that he had "no breaking point." It was something he learned from Coach Ara Parseghian and practiced daily with his loyal teammates, who then took turns giving strength to him and to each other through Pete's darkest days.

The selection for the cover shot for the Tulsa game program (October 30, 2010) at Notre Dame Stadium was either good planning or total happenstance. The sepia-toned photograph was of the Stadium

Source: University of Notre Dame Athletics

concourse, the bowels of the Stadium where the boys of 1966 began their quest toward immortality on a cold February morning. Today there are impressive oversized banners—at least twenty-feet high—hanging there to commemorate players who achieved All-American honors. On this cover you can make out the images on only two of the giant hanging banners: those of Jim Seymour and Pete Duranko.

So after forty-five years, when you ask the players what it was really like to play on the 1966 Notre Dame National Championship team, when they finally believe you will listen and accurately tell their story, be prepared for them to become glassy eyed, to lean into your ear, and to whisper the thing that means the most. They loved both Jim and Pete and they continue to love each other. There is no breaking point.

We end as we began. At Notre Dame, football isn't a matter of life and death. It is much more important than that.

EPILOGUE

Football is a season at Notre Dame, more important than winter, spring, summer, and fall. It was a thoughtful Fr. Hesburgh that put the 1966 football season into proper perspective, at least as this season made way for others to come.

Scholastic, December 9, 1966

THE FOOTBALL SEASON: FANTASY AND REALITY
By Rev. Theodore M. Hesburgh

Another football season has passed, another great and even fantastic one, thanks to Ara Parseghian, his staff, and his stalwart warriors who practiced hard, played hard against the best, and solidified a proud Notre Dame tradition of doing everything with style, spirit and excellence. All of you helped too, and share the pride of many challenges well met.

A football season is a lot like life, in microcosm. The season begins with warm and sunny days filled with optimism and hope. As the season progresses, the sunshine wanes, the warmth diminishes, and optimistic hope is qualified by the hard lifelike realities of fierce competition, unexpected injuries, and the innate difficulty of sustained human effort. The days grow colder, the rains come, and optimistic vision becomes more realistic. It is always easier to declare the top position in anything than to reach it. While hope perdures, ultimate victory is again a fickle lady, ever to be wooed with all one's might, but never in this life to be securely or forever won. Each week is a new encounter; each season a new challenge. Life is like that too, because it is spent in time, amid all the vicissitudes of personal trials and existential difficulties. Anyone who thinks otherwise lives in a dream world where reality has been entirely replaced by fantasy. But a football season, like life, is authentic and real, as well as somewhat fantastic.

So another football season passes, with all its very real excitement, effort, hope, youthful optimism, and ultimate success, the National Championship. You have lived with it and through it. The cheers all fade away into the dusk. The tissue-draped trees and lawns are cleaned up again for the last time. We return to the real and hard world of books, quizzes, and work yet to be done before the Christmas vacation begins. The stadium, stark and silent, is etched against a gray wintry sky. Nearby, the Library beckons with its myriad lights.

Was it all worthwhile, in this time and in this place? I think so, if we see the deeper meaning of it all. Reality is enriched by fantasy, if fantasy is allowed to illuminate reality, but not engulf it. In another age, as harsh as our own, there were jousts and jesters, tournaments and trials of skill and strength to lighten the harshness and illuminate the lessons of life. A football season has all the same qualities for our day. Life would be dull indeed without these interludes which, in their own mid-Twentieth-Century American way, can explain life to us, make it more deeply understandable and, therefore, livable.

I say all of this in the face of those who in a seemingly superior intellectual fashion depreciate, denigrate, and deplore the football season in our land. Collision on the gridiron is still better, I believe, than violence in the streets. Both have their relationship to equality of opportunity in America, one positive and one negative.

I would hope that in a larger university community in America we might see the football season, with all its appeal to young and old alike, in the perspective of a larger meaning of learning, and education, and life. The football season can, of course, be overdone, wrenched out of all perspective, so that even the fantastic becomes phantasmagoric, as is done by prolonging the season unduly, indulging in an increasing orgy of bowl games, the psychedelic dream makers of collegiate football.

Kept within proper bounds of time, place, and emphasis, I believe strongly that the football season is indeed worthwhile. The noise is ephemeral and does die away. The display, the spectacle, the color, the excitement linger only in memory. But the spirit, the will to excel, and the will to win perdure. These human qualities are larger and much more important than the passing events that occasion them, just as the ebb and flow of all our daily efforts add up to something greater and more enduring if they create within each one of us a person who grows, who understands, who really lives, who does not merely survive, but who prevails for a larger, more meaningful victory in time and, hopefully, in eternity as well.

AFTERWORD

ROGER VALDISERRI

Cheer, cheer . . .

Those of us who love Notre Dame and have been fortunate enough to serve the university in a professional way feel we have been blessed.

In my case, I had the added bonus of being able to tell the rest of the world about the university, its athletic teams and the young men and young women that built their own stories of performance while they were at Notre Dame. And I did this for over thirty-five years. There are many, many stories of individual achievement and courage and many other examples of heart warming and remarkable team success.

To me it is ironic that my first year at Notre Dame as sports information director was 1966, the year the Fighting Irish went on to win the National Championship. What a way to start! Their statistics were overwhelming. Defensively, only 38 points were scored against this team while offensively they piled up 362 points. The team eventually had 22 different players honored as All-America on one team or another. Coach Ara Parseghian and two players, Jim Lynch and Alan Page, have already been named to the College Football Hall of Fame. There are others waiting in the wings.

Behind the team and all the records are countless stories of courage and personal service and success. The captain in 1966, Jim Lynch, spent his summer in Lima, Peru, working for CILA, a service organization serving the underprivileged in remote third-world countries. Several years ago Alan Page was appointed to the Supreme Court in the state of Minnesota. Others have become doctors, lawyers and successful business executives. And there is the well-documented bravery of Rocky Bleier in battle during the Vietnam War. Just another indicator of the character that permeated this special group.

I have always believed that the 1966 team has been a rock-solid example of all that is good in college football and all that is best about Notre Dame. Looking back on the historical record of the 1966 Fighting Irish, I am sure that Notre Dame Nation is still proud of what they accomplished, not only on the playing field, but afterwards in living productive lives.

I wish there were more contemporary stories to be told which highlight the inherent values of college football. But unfortunately, there have been too many instances in which football fans have seemingly become immune to the notion that the players and the coaches should adhere to high standards of behavior, both on the field and off. Indeed, the landscape of intercollegiate athletics is an ever-changing one. It has always been so despite attempts to bring about reform and re-establish some sanity within the framework of the academic experience.

One of the more recent and notable attempts of restoring academic as well as financial integrity into the intercollegiate athletic enterprise, was the Knight Commission. In 1989 Reverend Theodore M. Hesburgh was drafted out of retirement to serve as co-chairman, along with another highly respected educator, William C. Friday, president emeritus of the University of North Carolina. The Commission was a blue-ribbon panel whose aim was restoring the "balance between athletics and academics on our nation's campuses," and to recommend other reform agendas for the conduct of intercollegiate athletics. A number of the Commission's recommendations were implemented by the NCAA.

Since then, however, athletic budgets have been burgeoning, coach's salaries have escalated and the arms race has flourished. Consequently, the elite programs have dashed far ahead of those schools with limited resources. Not a good formula for leveling the playing field. This all serves to point out how the football landscape has indeed changed since the Irish put together one of Notre Dame's finest teams.

In reading this book, one has to be impressed with the diligent research, the time and effort Mark Hubbard invested in interviewing numerous players, administrators and other support personnel and thus was able to give us a vivid story that others who have written about this team were unable to do. And in doing so he again enlivens the personalities, the drama, the essence and the chemistry of a team that refused to lose and one that marched to the drum of a great leader. Notre Dame fans and alumni can proudly salute the 1966 National Champions, today and forevermore.

BIBLIOGRAPHY

Celizic, Mike, *The Biggest Game of Them All*, New York NY, Simon & Schuster, 1992

Dent, Jim, *Resurrection: The Miracle Season That Saved Notre Dame*, New York NY, St. Martins Press, 2009

Hubbard, Donald and Mark, *Forgotten Four: Notre Dame's Greatest Backfield and the Undefeated 1953 Season*, Notre Dame IN, Corby Books, 2009

Maggio, Frank P., *Notre Dame and the Game That Changed Football: How Jesse Harper Made the Forward Pass a Weapon and Knute Rockne a Legend*, Cambridge MA, Da Capo Press, 2007

McGrane, Bill, *All Rise: The Remarkable Journey of Alan Page*, Chicago IL, Triumph Books, 2010

Pagna, Tom and Best, Bob, *Notre Dame's Era of Ara*, Huntsville AL, Strode Publishers, 1978

Pagna, Tom, *The Phantom Letters*, South Bend IN, Hardwood Press, 2005.

Sack, Allen L., *Counterfeit Amateurs*, University Park PA, The Pennsylvania State University Press, 2008

Wallace, Francis, *Notre Dame From Rockne to Parseghian*, New York NY, David McKay Co. Inc., 1966